DÉCOR GALORE

The Essential Guide to Styling Your Home

Laura de Barra

TRANSWORLD IRELAND

TRANSWORLD IRELAND
Penguin Random House Ireland, Morrison Chambers,
32 Nassau Street, Dublin 2, Ireland
www.transworldireland.ie

Transworld Ireland is part of the
Penguin Random House group of companies
whose addresses can be found at
global.penguinrandomhouse.com

First published in the UK and Ireland in 2021
by Transworld Ireland
an imprint of Transworld Publishers

A CIP catalogue record for this book
is available from the British Library.

ISBN 9781848272668

Design by Bobby Birchall, Bobby&Co
Printed and bound in China

The authorized representative in the EEA is
Penguin Random House Ireland, Morrison Chambers,
32 Nassau Street, Dublin D02 YH68.

DÉCOR GALORE

*For Mags, who taught me the true meaning
of making your space a home*

Also by Laura de Barra

*Gaff Goddess: Simple Tips and Tricks
to Help You Run Your Home*

CONTENTS

Leave all your worries at the door. It's time to enter the haus of Décor Galore!

Welcome! You look simply stunning. Vintage? I thought so. Love the shoulders.

We are going to go inside shortly, but let's perch here for a moment. Iced coffee? Fabulous. I want to take some time to tell you about what lies in store. I really think you're going to love it.

We will be taking a wonderful journey through the home, stopping in each room to gain a deeper understanding of her true function, as well as how to get the best out of the space and its contents. My aim is to open up your mind to a new way of thinking about your home and arm you with all the information you need to create a space that is tailored to those who live there. What a stunning state of affairs!

During our time together, I will focus a little on the materials and construction of some décor items, as I hope it will help you source things that not only look great but also last, should you be opting to do any overhauls. High-street purchases can be a low-cost and simple way to add some flavour to a home, but we must be aware that what comes in will someday leave and that it must go somewhere. How long it lasts and if it ends up in landfill is down to us, the gorgeous gatekeepers. Knowing how to buy well is one way to be more responsible. Knowing when not to buy is even better. So, we will, of course, delve into how to update the look of your surroundings and the repairs that will keep what you have with you for longer.

Now (*places glass on saucer*), during this journey we will be covering updates for all budgets and set-ups. So whether you're in the market for making a room in a rental work better or if you're embarking on a full overhaul, there will be tips and tricks to help you along. You will hear me use a few terms that you need to get familiar with.

Zoning: This is the art of sectioning your rooms into areas of use. Zones can be any size, from a dining zone right through to the skincare zone your serums sit in, waiting for you each night. Zones are a glorious way to make sure that you can use your space cleverly and, most importantly, set up your home in a way that works for you. Everyone and every home is different, which is why zoning is so important. It is focused around the user and how they wish to live. As we explore each room, it's a great time to reflect on your current set-up and what zones you need in yours to get more out of the space.

Routes: All rooms have routes. They are the paths most travelled through the space. Main routes are dictated by practical movements – the path from the bed to the en suite, or from the hallway to the couch before one flings oneself down after a long day. These routes may seem unimportant, but they are a vital element when it comes to décor. They will dictate where furniture is best placed, what kind of rug should go down, what will work on the walls, or even what materials are best avoided. As we visit

6   INTRODUCING...

each room, you will have the chance to reflect on the routes you have in your set-up and if they are helping you glide or forcing you to stumble through your space.

Pit stops: Along your routes there will always be pit stops. These are usually surfaces or storage. Ideally a pit stop will house something involved in the route it is on. It could be a hook that holds a dressing gown between the bed and shower, or the top of a dresser between a wardrobe and mirror upon which jewellery is stored. Pit stops, if placed cleverly, can really enhance the use of a room as well as your day, saving time and making life feel a little smoother. If pit stops are not well thought out, they end up becoming pile-ups.

The Min, The Tszuj, The Overhaul: An elegant trio. When it comes to décor, what you can or want to do with your space will differ from person to person. It is important for me that there is a gorgeous seat for everyone at this table. This is why we will always start with the Min.

The Min is about working with what you already have in place. I believe the smallest of changes to the home are as important as the bigger ones. The Min will focus on getting the contents of the space right and making changes that have a high impact with low cost. It may suit renters really well, as a lot of these changes also don't require anything that could go against a standard lease. However, if you are planning a bigger change, I would always encourage you to consider the Min – it will allow you to get the space in order and it could have a positive effect on what you end up doing next.

The Tszuj will take a little more time and consideration but will have deeper updates and more impact. This is the perfect way to create a new vibe in a space or a zone without any major changes or spend. As well as guiding us in terms of any new additions, it also shows us how to rework the things we already have in place and elevate them. Again, this is great for renters or owners.

The Overhaul is more focused towards big changes, with ideas for reinventing the kitchen or bathroom, or making a purchase that needs to be informed. I'm here to arm you with as much information as I can, to make buying and placement a little less daunting.

Now, don't think that *Décor Galore* is just for rooms; she is, in fact, a state of mind! So, we will be making a stop at Christmas and we also have a date with the Dinner Party. Two wonderful events that take place in our homes and I can't wait to help you enhance them.

Right (*straightens skirt, swings keyring from finger*), let's pop inside, shall we? I think the lounge is a great place to start. Follow me . . .

CHAPTER 1

LIVING ROOM

WHO IS SHE?

The living room! What a fabulous place to start. (*Flings open gold-handled double doors, throws hands in the air.*) Lovely, isn't she?

Let's make our way to the couch. I have a story and a *smörgåsbord* for you before we get into her routes, zones and pit stops. You and I love her as our 'living room', but, like many other icons, she has had many names and styles throughout the years.

Early in her career she was the parlour, from the French word *parler*, to speak: a grand room to entertain guests, but only for drinking and talking, never to dine. Then she was the drawing room: less formal but still glam, usually located off a dining room, where you could take closer gal pals for a more intimate hang. The sitting room was another living room, where just the family would sit – no guests here.

The oddest branding of all was her time as the death room. I know what you're thinking, but it has nothing to do with Sunday hangovers lying on the couch. During the 19th century, as people began to live in smaller homes (*leans in, whispers *still massive**), it was where they waked their dead. You see, up until this stage she was always the best-dressed room in the home, as she was the only one seen by guests. This is why she would also be near the front of the home, so guests would not have a chance to see your less favourable quarters. This made her the perfect spot to host a wake and to take posthumous portraits. You know, those eerie staged photographs taken of people after they've died?

I know what you are thinking: how on earth did she take on such a drastic rebrand and go from a death to a living room? As the century came to an end, the death rate was on the decline and the conditions at funeral homes had improved. It was then that an article in the *Ladies Home Journal* suggested that readers reclaim their death room, jazz her up and reinstate her position in our lives as a 'living' room. This idea really took off, as you can imagine, and became quite popular in Europe and the US. People were now able to bring a more relaxed social room to their homes that was not as guest- or death-focused and made for them alone. Rejoice!

To be quite honest, this came at the perfect time, as lifestyles were changing and people were working more. The new interior wave was to have a space in which to do nothing. Radios and TVs were also appearing, so the lounge-style living room was fast becoming the queen of the home.

ROUTES, PIT STOPS, ZONES

This gal's routes will usually be from the door to the couch, but as we mostly now have living areas that are part of multi-use spaces, there will be routes to other zones, such as dining areas, kitchens or our outside space. This is all important to bear in mind for things like rugs and freestanding storage, as these can really affect movement through such a relaxed part of the home. Pit stops here will usually be on top of storage units or the coffee table, so it's good to keep these in mind when buying anything new. You can keep these pit stops as open or as hidden as you like. Zone-wise, the main zone here will be the couch and then smaller zones may be where we read, work out or make a martini on a Thursday evening . . . In short, these zones are all focused around one thing: relaxing.

A space to do nothing

When I think about my living area, I always think of it as the place for leisure time. This is why I prefer to call it a lounge. It conjures up images of lying in a wide-leg cashmere trouser, reading a thick magazine on a slow evening off. The word lounge feels less chaotic and more laid-back than living room. Say it with me: loouuungee.

Whenever I have to set up, decorate or purchase something for a lounge, I always start with one question: 'How do they like to spend their downtime?' It never fails to make a living area work well for the end user. If I make this my starting point and keep it in mind when choosing furniture, colour, artwork, lighting and storage, the lounge zone gradually becomes a sanctuary.

Speaking of purchasing, here are the things that I find essential for a great lounge set-up, a simple 'go to' if you are starting afresh or feel you may be lacking something.

SHOPPING LIST

COUCH
SOMEWHERE TO KICK OFF A HEEL

RUG
PROTECTION AND A GREAT
BAREFOOT EXPERIENCE

TV UNIT
MULTI-PURPOSE FOR BEST USE OF SPACE

LAMPS
A TALL AND
A TABLE TOP

COFFEE TABLE

BIG ENOUGH TO SERVE,
SMALL ENOUGH TO SAVE OUR SHINS

3,500K TO
KEEP US ZEN

LARGE PLANTS
IDEAL FOR ZONE
BOUNDARIES

STORAGE
LOW AND LONG

SOFTS

TO ADD TEXTURE
AND COLOUR

If you are currently looking around your lounge area and feeling like you don't know where to start, but know you need to, the Min is perfect for you. It's all about small changes that will make the space look and feel a lot better. In fact, I would always do the Min regardless.

LIGHTING

If you get lounge lighting right, it can dramatically change the atmosphere and how you feel about the space. You want soft, relaxing light that can really help you to switch off and enjoy your downtime. Here are my three rules for perfect lounge lighting:

Ban the Big Light

Removing the need for the Big Light will make the single biggest difference in the lounge. When we sit with just the Big Light on above us, it can create a feeling of unease – the room feels almost like it's closing in on us, due to the shadows it creates. It is also almost never focusing its light on anything special, just straight down to the centre of the room. Unless you give a spoken word performance each evening, it's a waste. In multi-use rooms, if you ditch the Big Light and just turn on the lounge area, it will literally switch off the other zones and give you the feeling they don't exist. Wonderful.

Perfect pockets

Choosing where to place your lighting is key. I would always have a lamp on at least one side of the couch. It is where you will sit and you need to be able to see what you are doing. From reading and sipping a glass of wine to sewing rhinestones into your tights. Make sure she is tall enough for the spread to light up the seat closest. A perfect, well-lit pocket.

I would also go for a floor lamp with a wide shade in a corner to create one column of light. This will allow the rest of the room to be visible, but not too visible. The joy of having it in a corner will mean, unlike the Big Light, you'll be sending light up as well as down, making the room feel taller.

If you abhor the décor in your lounge and cannot do a lot to change it, lights under shelving or lamps on table tops can help you to bring focus to things you do really like. Perhaps it's a stack of magazines or a nice print – light can draw the eye to it instead of a bad carpet or naff coffee table.

Temperature

Keep the temperature of your lounge lights, measured in kelvins, low. The max you will need is 3,500k for reading, etc. so this will suit the lamps near your couch. All other bulbs will benefit from being 3,000k or under, as they will be so soft and warm that they will only encourage a gorgeous wind-down and never distract.

Candles

Another way to add atmosphere is to use candles. They will have a kelvin of between 1,500k and 1,700k and always invite a relaxing, calm mood to a space. Tall dinner candles are great up high, like on a mantle or dresser, as they give a more elegant touch and allow us to see the flame from all angles. Vessels are great if space is tight, as they are safer to place lower. There seems to be a bit of mystery around candle shopping. Let's take a moment to clear it up.

I am sure you will have noticed that candles can vary greatly in price and quality, so what exactly makes a good candle? Well, it's all right there on the box . . .

Wax

As wax is the main ingredient, what it is made from can really determine its price point and how long it will last, as well as how great its scent throw will be. There are a few options:

Paraffin: Most vessel candles will be made of paraffin wax because not only does it cost a lot less to produce but it can also hold and emit a stronger scent than other waxes. The downside is that it's a by-product (of petroleum), which many dislike due to the toxins it can potentially release.

Soy: This is getting more and more popular, as it is a cleaner burn, comes from a renewable source (soya beans) and has a long burn time. It's more expensive, but you get what you pay for.

Coconut: Coming in hard and fast as a must-have vegetable wax right now. It's said to be the cleanest burn and most eco-friendly. It does burn quite quickly, so is often mixed with paraffin to slow down burn time. Be sure to check the ratios with this one to avoid overpaying for low coconut content.

Beeswax: You will get a long burn time with beeswax and it's said that this wax will actually cleanse the air due to a negative ion release when lit. One thing is for sure: she's not putting anything bad into the air, so she is ideal for allergies, and her clean burning means you're not getting the soot you would with paraffin.

No matter what wax you go for – perhaps it's a blend – you should always be looking for 'ethically made' and 'Fair Trade' on the labels, especially if they are a vegetable wax such as soy or palm. The production of these waxes can be linked to deforestation and we need to make sure we are not behind the demand. Look at the brand and use your goddess judgement to assess whether it is a reach or not.

Scent

Better quality scent doesn't necessarily mean more fragrance, as the highest ratio of wax to fragrance is 9:1 before it becomes a hazard. Scents can be synthetic or natural, with the latter being more expensive. However, most candles use a mix of the two to some degree, as a natural oil will never be as strong as synthetic. If you ever feel like a cheaper candle has stopped smelling after a couple of burns, this is because many candles will only have scent at the top to lure you in when in store. Higher priced candles are whipped the whole way through.

Wick

You ideally want a natural wick. One that is cotton is best, as it won't smoke or mushroom like others. A wick should be thick enough to ensure that it can melt the wax right out to the glass and doesn't stop near the centre. This wastes both wax and scent. This is why you will see higher-end candles with thick or even multiple wicks, as it ensures that a nice even burn is always achieved.

Burn time

The higher the quality, the longer the burn time. The longer the burn time – you guessed it – the higher the price. Candles will almost always have their burn time somewhere on the packaging. The higher it is, the easier it usually is to find.

MAGIC
MEAUXMENT

THE T WHEN IT COMES TO BURNING CANDLES

If you love a candle and burn them a lot, you need to be aware of BSD. This sounds like a fun night in latex underground but actually stands for Black Soot Disposition. When a candle burns, combustion occurs, and so we get that stunning glow. However, when incomplete combustion occurs, we also get soot. This soot floats through the air and settles in smoky patches on the furniture but mainly on your walls. Usually around the picture frames, windows and other fittings. To prevent a build-up of BSD, we need to avoid creating a lot of soot. Here's how . . .

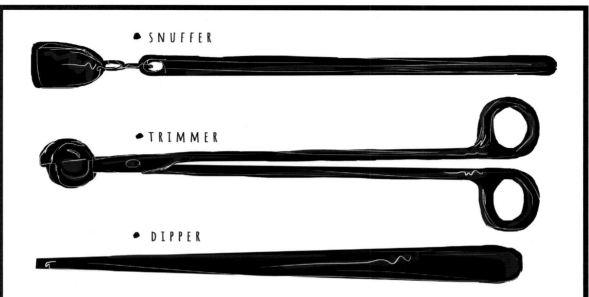

Blending: A great way to avoid soot is to go for a higher priced, well-blended candle. A bad blend will usually lead to a flickering flame, which will cause smoke. Many makers in the amateur candle-making market are not adequately trained in how much of the fragrance should be blended, which can lead to inconsistent burning. Cheaper candles, which are often not blended well due to production costs, suffer the same fate.

Trim: Always trim your wick to a quarter of an inch before lighting. This reduces smoking caused by flickering and also prevents soot marks on the glass. A wick trimmer is a glorious accessory for the avid candle burner, but scissors will do, as long as you don't allow the trimmed parts to fall into the wax.

Stability: A stable flame is key in keeping soot to a minimum. Keep the candle away from draughts that will encourage flickering. Having a candle on a main route, or near a vent or window, should be avoided. Think mountain pose.

Extinguish with excellence: How we put out a candle plays a huge part in how much soot we create. First of all, don't blow. Really! Blowing out a candle can disperse a lot of smoke. Instead, use a wick dipper to dip the wick in the melted wax and stand it back up again. Stunning! An alternative option is a pinch snuffer, which works well for dinner candles. Don't be tempted to use a lid to put out the flame. This will cause a lot of smoke and soot build-up in the glass. Instead, these are for protecting the wax when the candle is not in use and slipped underneath to protect the surface when it is.

TIP

Always allow your candle to melt the wax to the edge before you put it out, especially on the first burn. Wax has memory and so will stop melting at the same point as when it was last burned. If you stop a few centimetres in on the first go, it will always stop here. *Mon dieu!* What waste! It will also prevent you from seeing the flame when she is lit, as she will be hidden.

Candle alternatives

Upon my discovery of BSD and having read further into paraffin, I started to think about my relationship with candles. The process of lighting something to enhance or punctuate my day and add fragrance to the room was not something I wanted to give up, but I did feel like it was something I could do better, something I could tailor to suit me more.

Catalytic lamp

Catalytic lamps, also called perfume lamps or fragrance lamps, were designed by a French pharmacist in the late 19th century to disinfect the air in hospital wards. With the arrival of Spanish flu, people soon wanted these in their own homes as a way of purifying the air and keeping disease at bay. Rather than masking smells, they first work to purify the air and then add fragrance.

If I was moving into a new place, this is what I would use to clear bacteria and odours with a natural rather than synthetic smell or spray. What I love about these is that you can cook a bacon sandwich, pop one on and, provided you follow the recommended burn time per square foot, the odour will be gone in under half an hour. *Bon*, bish.

Wax melts

These have become popular in recent times, but they should be used with caution. Avoid melts made with paraffin and whose scents are made from only synthetic oils. Choose natural or soy wax and a real essential oil.

After lighting, another way to instantly create a new look to your lounge area is to assess your storage.

DISPLAY OR DISGUISE

The things we store in our lounge can have a huge impact on the general vibe in the space. This makes it a great place to start when we want to change things up with little or no spend. Your lounge storage will usually need to cater to three categories:

- Things you like displayed
- Things you like disguised
- Things that cannot go anywhere else

Lounge storage will usually be added to over time without consideration. This can end up making it feel a little haphazard and cluttered, and overall it makes our storage system feel inadequate. This will then lead to the wrong type of storage being added, floor space being lost and no real resolution. To avoid this, and to give a simple but stunning new look to the space, work with what you have first. Divide the contents of your storage into the above categories. The bottom two should be put away first, with the most used to the front or in the easiest-to-reach places.

When it comes to what is left for display, here is my method.

Bottom heavy

All heavier, large items to the bottom. I'm talking magazine stacks, large books, boxes, etc. This way your storage will be weighted properly and it just looks so much better. Your bottom shelves should always be your fullest, as it makes it feel more balanced. If you don't have enough 'big' items, throws rolled and stacked can add some gorgeous texture and also act as an easy filler.

Create a counter

A shelf or surface around elbow height is ideal to turn into a station for items you use often. I use mine for my cheese board accessories and a mini bar, so I have an area outside of the kitchen that I can prep at when I have people over. It's also displaying stuff that looks great. Painting the back of these shelves or adding foil can make it actually feel like a separate station to above and below.

Bellybutton to brows

For the smallest items displayed in a unit, I will dot them around between these areas. Any lower or higher, they get lost. The eye will usually focus on the shelves at this level, so if you don't feel like you have enough display-style bits here, and want to add to it over time, a great temporary measure is glassware. Pull it out of the kitchen, group it and display. It looks calm and chic, and you free up some kitchen storage. You can then swap it out when you buy something meaningful for the spot. I think a ceramic plant pot with a bundle of dinner candles or two rows of coupes are so much more appealing than something picked up on the high street just to fill a spot.

Beret and beyond

Anything higher than eye level should be light and minimal. Vases, jugs, bowls, etc. This should look the least cluttered and have a few bigger but less weighty items. It works from both a visual and a safety point of view.

Adding new storage

Once you've found a place for everything you have sorted, you will be able to clearly see if you are lacking storage and if any additions should be concealed or open, which is vital.

Freestanding units

I prefer freestanding units to be low and long, as most of our time in this room is spent sitting down. The feeling of all our stuff looming over us is one to avoid around the couch area especially, so stretch it under windows and along walls up to couch height, or just under the sill, to give the feeling that the weight is with you rather than over you. When your units are lower, you gain a whole load of surface that is lost when it is up high. Perfect for bigger ornaments, large books and lamps. I would also make sure that any units are on some kind of leg or foot, to give us a peek at some floor beneath. This allows a better flow and a feeling of more space.

It is also so much easier to store the bits you don't want out in long and low units, as they are easier to get to and can be deeper. I like to go for as much drawer space as possible, so I can make full use of the interior, unlike a cupboard.

If you want to add more light to a room, your storage can actually help. Low white units tucked under the sill will drag the light even further into the room and make it feel brighter during the day; when the surface is darker, it will deaden it. Avoid cluttering the walls that get the most natural light on them, as shelving or storage will block it rather than bounce it around the room.

Shelving

Shelving in a lounge should be very well thought out. If you do go for a built-in bookshelf, bring it all the way to the ceiling to make it feel more streamlined. Individual shelves should be shallow to avoid making the room feel smaller. When you have the walls cut by a wide shelf, it can make the room feel as if it is stopping there. Never place an individual shelf above a couch, as this would not encourage relaxation.

When it comes to how to store on shelves, my best advice here is to keep it simple and orderly. If you have shelving behind or around your TV, for example, this should be as clean-looking as possible. It can feel a little hectic watching TV with mess framing it. A lovely touch is to pop all white spines or glassware in these shelves to keep a feeling of calm where your eye is focused most. You don't have to group by colour elsewhere, but keeping anything immediately around the TV neutral will help you focus.

THE TSZUJ

Now you have the room looking more orderly and gloriously lit, you can indulge in a little more styling and a few further changes. These take little time and spend and, most importantly, if you are renting, they can come with you when you move.

SHE'S UP THE WALLS

In a room full of practical and low-lying furniture, the walls are where we can add some flair so easily. Although it is a space for leisure and downtime, this does not mean you cannot put up anything bright or visually exciting; the opposite, in fact. You just need to be clever about which walls the madness goes on – keep your busier wall décor behind the couch and out of your eyeline when sitting, for example.

I prefer large frames hanging here over lots of small ones. If you have small children or boisterous pets, these need to be hung with caution. I would keep the lower part of the frame a safe distance from the back of the couch – above head if smaller, shoulders if longer. It's also good to opt for lightweight frames with no glass. A couple of small frames can get really lost behind a couch, as you would need to stand on it to view them. Large frames or canvases can add some gorgeous drama. My general rule is to keep large hanging above large pieces of furniture to avoid large gaps in between them.

SMALL SOFT SWAP

Swapping out small soft furnishings can really lift a lounge, especially in ones where changes are limited. Even the plainest or dullest of rooms can benefit from the addition of soft accessories. The key here is to go for layers of texture –

knits, slubs, weaves – rather than flat fabrics. If you're unsure what colour to go for, I find that neutrals in different textures add such a chic tone to a space and work well with features already there. Even a magnolia wall will be made to feel up to date. The softs that will make the biggest difference are:

Couch wraps and cushions

Covering a bad couch with a large throw can actually make it even more of an eyesore. Elasticated couch wraps are a brilliant way to disguise imperfections, like peeling leather or worn-out fabric. However, if the condition of the couch is good, you are better working with it. Go for cushions in tones that complement the fabric and enhance it. I prefer cushions in uneven numbers and would never go smaller than 50 x 50cm, unless it is a bolster (oh! I do love a good bolster). Try to keep your cushions to a theme – they could all be completely different patterns and textures but a common feature in all is great and more streamlined.

Curtains

Never underestimate the effect your window dressings can have on your lounge. They are another wall feature that can help to kick the chilled vibe of the room up a few notches. Floor to ceiling curtains, especially on a track, can give some real oomph to a lounge, as they create some much-needed softness above couch level. Lounge curtains needn't be a big spend, as blackout and lining aren't a necessity. Some lightweight linen, for example, can give the perfect frame if you want something light and simple. If you are going for heavier, keep the lounge feeling in mind. I always think about fabrics that I would almost like to wrap myself in. Soft and luxurious in muted tones.

Throws

Throws are great for adding texture and styling to a lounge an a simple way. They are also stunning on a cold winter's evening. I would always keep throws folded and draped over arms, or halved and over the back of a couch if you're not too fond of the pattern. Avoid covering the couch seat and back cushions too much, as it can look a little untidy. Neat bundles of texture and colour can instead draw the eye more calmly.

However, if you are using throws to prevent your couch wearing in or staining over time, layering will look less practical and more stylish. You can use a flatter throw to cover the seat cushions and then layer on top with textures, such as chunky knits or faux fur, that are more draped than tucked.

PLANTS

If you have a room that you are really struggling with, plants can add the most gorgeous solution. They are easy on the eye and add a warmth and richness that can overtake a shoddy wall or crap carpet. When it comes to choosing a plant for a living room, you need to first think if you have the floor space should it grow quite large or wide. It is always a shame when a plant gets too big for the space it has grown fond of and has to be moved. If you have a lot of unit tops for display, ferns can be ideal, as they spread out and create a gorgeous soft texture to the space. If you're looking to use plants to help you zone and create a boundary, go for something that will grow up instead of out. I would be mindful of anything that cannot hack too much warmth, as living rooms tend to be where it get toastiest. If you live in a big city, look for plants that are great at air purifying. Sitting with them each evening will be a stunning addition to your routine.

RUGS

Floor coverings can be tricky to get right in a lounge, as you need them to be durable, easy to care for and, also, not an eyesore. The best way to get your rug right is to think about the practicalities first and then you can go as wild or as muted as you like in peace!

Composition

What your rug is made of will determine how she wears, as well as how she holds colour or pattern.

Cha-ching

First of all, I am going to eliminate silk (*brushes a single tear away with a monogrammed handkerchief*). Silk is STUNNING, but she's wasted in a lounge – or in any room where we wear shoes. She's more of a bedroom gal. She is also so expensive that regular life around her can leave you feeling a bit on edge. Would you casually float across the room with a glass of wine in your hand if the floor covering cost €26,000? If you answered yes, call me. I want to walk barefoot in your lounge.

Bling-bling

Wool can be a fab option, as she is warm and so dense that she is great at soundproofing and keeping out draughts. After silk, she feels the best underfoot and because she is a natural fibre she can be pretty easy to care for. But like all great things, she comes at a cost.

Wool mixes are a cheaper way to achieve the feel and look of wool. It may not last as long, but it also won't shed as much as real wool will. Cotton is super soft, but, again, she won't last as long as wool. As she is really absorbent, she will quickly take on the dye of anything spilled, so stains need to be rapidly dealt with. For the same reason, she will fade quicker than wool or synthetics in sunlight.

Ring-a-ding

Polyester is not as glorious to touch, but she will have a good hand-feel and be considerably cheaper. One key advantage is that she rejects spills and stains, so it is easier to keep her looking great. Many high-street rugs will be made of polypropylene and they're what I would put in most rentals, as I know she can last tenancy after tenancy and still look good without blowing the budget. As she's a manmade fibre, she will dent when, say, a leg of a couch is on her for a while, but it's nothing that cannot be solved easily.

Pile

There is not a hope that you can dip that gorgeous toe of yours into the rug-buying pond and not hear the word pile. Multiple times. So let's get to grips with her.

When it comes to textiles, the raised part is referred to as the pile. This doesn't include the backing or glue layer. The pile measurement is related to how thick the raised part is, how dense the fibres of the rug are. But please, let's not mix up pile with quality. People tend to assume a thicker pile means a better quality rug, but that isn't the case. Think of a Persian rug: she is far thinner than a polypropylene rug but is of a far superior quality.

Pile height can vary, but usually it is one of three categories: low (less than a quarter inch), medium (a quarter to three-quarters) and high (three-quarters plus). If you are buying for a high-traffic area, be conscious that the pile will flatten if walked on a lot and a higher pile doesn't necessarily mean a softer hand (or foot, in this case) feel. What the rug is made from will mainly decide its comfort levels. If your rug is a centrepiece and the natural flow of the room means it avoids foot traffic, then high pile can work well. However, if the rug is placed where feet rest and is covering a main thoroughfare, you will get patches of flattening.

There are also different types of pile and each one gives a different look.

Woven

Flat-weave rugs do not have any pile; instead, they have a 'warp and weft'-like fabric. They are either hand or machine woven (hand is obviously far more expensive), are easy to clean, can be rolled up and stored, can be reversible and so on. They're great for a living room that you sometimes eat in, as crumbs are less likely to hide in them than they would in a thick pile.

Knotted

Unlike most rugs, these will not have a backing, as they are hand knotted on a loom. These are very expensive, as they take so long to create, but are simply gorgeous. This is usually how Persian rugs are made. If you ever see a rug with an outrageous price, flip it over – if it has no backing, it is probably hand-knotted. You can also get machine 'knotted' rugs which will be far less expensive and usually have a backing of some sort.

Looped or hooked

In this style of rug, the yarn is pushed through the backing and comes back in again, leaving a loop behind. These rugs feel lovely and soft underfoot. They are more durable, as it's harder to lose fibres, but if you have pets with claws it can be a nightmare. You can get really tight hooked rugs or over-the-top shaggy loose hooks with a boho style.

Tufted

Looped rugs that have had the tips of their loops cut off are described as tufted. A warning: these girls will shed once you take them home. There will be loose fibres even after a good brushing in the factory.

Mixed loop and cut

Different mixes of piles, lengths and types are used to create patterns. If you don't want the rug to take centre stage colour-wise but still want it to have depth, she's a good way to add texture. She can mask stains and hides wear and tear well.

Random shear

A type of pile where loops are randomly sheared. You know when you see rugs that have a distressed feel, almost like 'Hang on, is she a vintage? Or is she moth-eaten?' They came about to cater to the 'antique on a budget' shopper by offering a rug that looks like it's sailed the seven seas to get to your great-great-grandmother's mansion and she's handed it down through the generations, whereby it now lives with you and your bulldog in a loft-conversion in Shoreditch.

Some high-street manufacturers save on the extra cost of the shearing process and actually weave another colour over patches of the pattern to make it look like the backing is showing. A similar distressed look in fewer steps.

There is another type of random shear rug. Using one colour, the shearing plays with light as it hits different parts of the rug. It gives it a more luxurious appearance, like velvet. This, in my opinion, is a way to buy a cheaper rug that looks expensive. It's also a way to buy a one-colour rug that doesn't look flat, which I love. Ideal if you don't want to commit to too much colour but don't want something too plain. It will serve you a muted, tonal appeal that is elegant and soft.

Size

We have all seen it, a rug the same size as the coffee table on top of her. This is usually down to an error: some rugs can be so expensive, people will assume for her cost she is a lot bigger and when she arrives she looks more like a bathmat. My ideal living-room rug size is longer than the couch and square in shape, which helps me to establish the seating area as its own zone. I like to be able to walk on as much of her as possible.

Square rugs give a feeling of space more than a rectangle. The ideal scenario is to have some of the rug sitting under some or all of the furniture, otherwise consider slipping her a few inches under the couch rather than positioning her in the middle of the room. This means your feet will get the most benefit from her. People will often push her against but not under the couch and this leads to dirt gathering. Pushing her under can also make her look a lot bigger.

Colour

The colours you go for are up to you. My only advice is to avoid lighter colours if you aren't up for the maintenance. Don't go too shaggy if you have high traffic or pets (just imagine trying to clean dog wee out of a shaggy, super-long looped ecru cotton rug). As with all rugs on a non-carpeted floor, please use a non-slip mat underneath and stick down corners where needed. We don't want you tripping as you carry a tray of crystal across the room.

THE OVERHAUL

There will be times when you want to overhaul the space. Unlike the kitchen or bathroom, bigger changes to a lounge will usually involve the walls and larger furniture. They are usually with us the longest, so we do need to put some time into changing them.

WALLS

For me, lounge walls are always great in one solid colour rather than in a busy wallpaper or blocking. There is a lot going on in a lounge as an overall visual, a lot of soft furnishings and open storage, so it works best to keep the walls simple. This doesn't have to be white, but it should be a canvas that shows off the contents instead of fighting for your eyes' attention. I like a matte paint in lounges, as it can look so powdery and velvet-like, but most importantly can be topped up easier than a high-shine paint if scuffed by furniture. Keeping the trims and door in the lounge a similar colour to the walls is also key for a calm, streamlined effect. For example, if you are going dark, do the door too to avoid it sticking out.

Don't worry if the thought of buying paint, and painting itself, is starting to make that wonderful scalloped collar feel tight. I have you covered in chapter 10, Hauskeeping, where we will run through it all.

Panelling

Adding texture through wood panelling can be a really gorgeous way to add interest to a wall without it taking over. It can also make the room feel warmer both visually and physically. Panels are ideal if you really want to kick it up a notch and add to the space long-term. Here are some that really suit a living area:

Height

Full Wall: You don't have to do the whole room. This will suit larger uninterrupted walls like behind a couch rather than one with a lot of fixtures.

Dado: This will need to flow through the whole room and, unlike the hall, you want this for furniture rather than people, so I would go for around a third of the wall, height-wise.

Tongue and groove will give a real boho, beachy, earthy style, whereas something like a Jacobean or Shaker will give a more traditional look. My personal favourite? Ribbing. Chic and there's almost an art-deco quality about this gal.

THE COUCH

Couch or sofa? What exactly is the difference? Most people use the words interchangeably, and it doesn't really matter, but I like a good fact for a dinner party! The word couch is said to derive from the French *coucher*, which means to lie down or to sleep. Originally, these were not pieces of furniture designed for sitting on.

The origins of the word sofa are said to be Turkish and from the Arabic word *suffah*. It was designed to make sitting on the floor more comfortable. A sofa is now often thought of as a more formal piece of furniture than a couch, one that offers a more rigid seated position, suited to meeting the parents for the first time or use in an office waiting room.

It doesn't really matter what you call her. I tend to use couch for all: I guess sofa doesn't flow as naturally in a Cork accent. When shopping for a couch, it can be hard to understand why two that look the same can vary in price. Why are some couches €10,000 and others €500? Why are some so hard-wearing they can be passed down to the next generation and others fall to bits in the first year? Why can you fling an entire mug of chamomile over one sofa with few repercussions, yet a single mascara-laden tear will cause a mark you'll never get out of another?

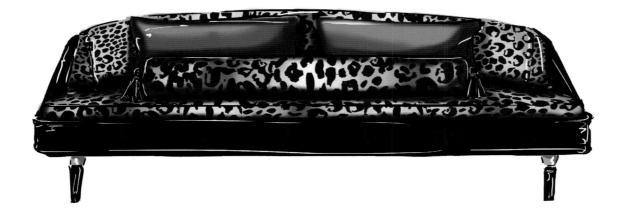

Let's tackle the mystery of couch shopping once and for all, and arm ourselves with the vitals to ensure we find a gal to suit not just the space but also our lifestyle. My aim at the end of this section is to have you up to speed on where your money is going when you purchase a couch and to help you make sure it's on the right things.

Integrity

Couch shopping is so style-focused we tend to overlook the integrity of the piece. The integrity is all about it being able to do its job – it will ensure it will wear well and, most of all, be comfortable. The main elements that make up the integrity of a couch are frame, suspension, cushion filling and fabric.

Frame

She is essentially the skeleton of the couch and hidden from sight when you're shopping, so she can often be overlooked. But she is what will truly determine the lifespan of your couch. Great frames will last a lifetime, and good frames can be easily repaired. Here are the things to look out for to assess her durability and sturdiness.

Hardwood

A frame made of hardwood such as oak or maple is best – kiln-dried hardwood, to be precise. Wood naturally has moisture in it and when it is kiln-dried there is no chance of the wood warping or bending. This process can remove up to 95 per cent of the moisture and will ensure a sturdy and long-lasting frame. In my experience, if a couch frame is made of kiln-dried hardwood, it will be advertised as such. It is a marker of high quality in the sofa world, so brands tend to shout about it!

Softwood

Softwoods are also used in couch frames, but they are not as hard-wearing. To determine if something is a hard or soft wood, you just need to think about it this way: hardwoods are deciduous, softwoods are coniferous. So, pine is a softwood and walnut is a hardwood. Sometimes manufacturers for high-street stores mix hard and soft woods in a couch frame to reduce costs. Always check the description to find out the composition of the frame. If you are spending a lot, be sure to check out the finer details!

Engineered wood

Plywood, particleboard and fibreboard are common in high-street or

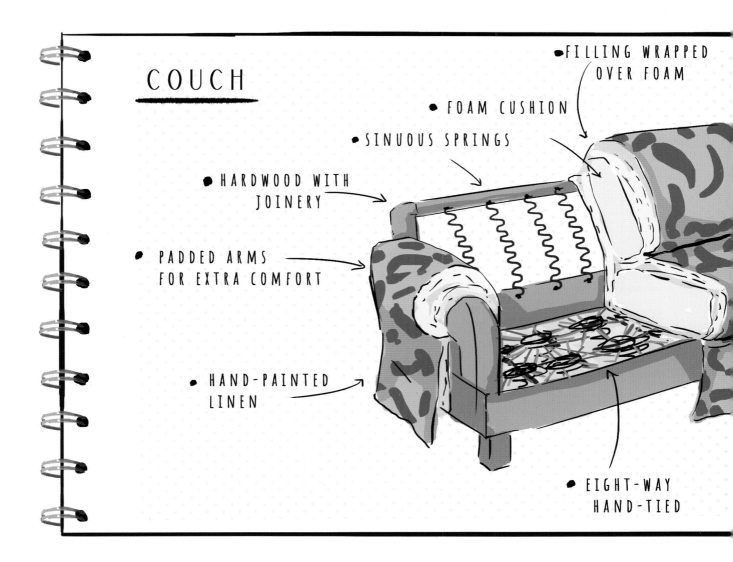

COUCH

- FILLING WRAPPED OVER FOAM
- FOAM CUSHION
- SINUOUS SPRINGS
- HARDWOOD WITH JOINERY
- PADDED ARMS FOR EXTRA COMFORT
- HAND-PAINTED LINEN
- EIGHT-WAY HAND-TIED

flat-pack couches. They are cheaper to use than solid wood and drastically cut the cost of making the couch.

Plywood is the most durable of the three, with some couch makers certain that their plywood frames are as durable as some hardwood frames. Its composition means it can hold fastenings for longer and a good grade of plywood is pretty strong.

Fibreboard is preferable to particleboard, but both deteriorate and crumble over time, and the fastenings can loosen and break. I would avoid a frame with a lot of particleboard or fibreboard if you know the couch will have to endure a lot (children/ house parties/lovers).

Metal

These will be the most robust and hard-wearing but can bend. There are some really stunning exposed metal frame couches. Perfect if you are looking for a more minimal, designer edge. These, of course, will come with a higher price point. You will then have cheaper frames made in all metal but of a lesser quality. Think sofa bed.

You will also often see high-priced couches with a mix of woods, particleboard and some metal elements. Usually this will mean the frame costs were kept low to spend more on fancy finishes, such as velvet tassels. Fur coat and no knickers, couch edition.

The assembly of the frame is also important and there will always be notes in the description. More expensive frames will use joinery and dowels, whereas cheaper frames will have screws and glue. Mid-priced couches will use a mix of both.

TIP

If you've inherited a couch and want to assess the frame, do a lift test. Solid wood is heavy and a solid-wood frame is not easy to lift, so be careful!

MDF is also quite weighty, however, so there's a second test worth trying. Lift one side at the front about 15–20cm (think the height of your phone). If the other leg doesn't lift, you'll know the frame is made from cheaper materials. The frame should be so solid that if you lift the front left to that height, the right should lift too.

Suspension

We cannot talk about the integrity of a couch frame without dipping into her suspension. This is what truly determines the couch's comfort. It provides a platform for cushions to rest upon and ensures the user can move around with ease. You will rarely see anyone remove the seat cushions to feel the suspension when trying out couches in store, but it is well worth doing. The quality of the suspension will often be reflected in the price, so it's important to look at the details in full before making a decision.

Here is what you need to know.

Webbing

Webbing is a series of strips woven to create a grid. It is the cheapest and least effective form of couch suspension. There are two main styles: jute and rubber.

Jute webbing is made from vegetable fibres and is super strong, but it doesn't have any bounce. It's often used with coil springs. Unless it's a handcrafted couch with a good guarantee, the jute could end up wearing out quite quickly.

Rubber webbing, on the other hand, has good bounce and durability. This makes it very popular for couches that are lower to the ground or have a bed underneath with no room for springs. The issue with rubber is that the bounce can wear out and cause sagging or dipping.

Springs

Springs help to give the suspension platform a lovely bounce that moves with you. The response of the springs to your body weight is called a ride and some will give you a better ride than others (*winks and pops olive in mouth*).

Eight-way hand-tied

Not only is she a mouthful, she's the Prada of couch suspension and will give you the best ride of the lot, according to high-end manufacturers. Essentially, each coil is knotted eight times to secure it to the other coils and to the frame, so it can all move gloriously as one to prevent an uneven distribution of weight. As hand-tying is so time-consuming, she comes with a higher price.

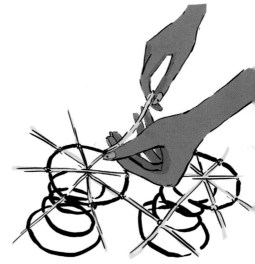

● EIGHT-WAY HAND-TIED

Drop-in springs

These are spring bases that are prepared separately and then dropped into the couch frame. The metal coils are usually connected to metal poles and attached with wire. It can cause a lot of squeaking and creaking over time. They are a good way to achieve the comfort of a spring base on a budget, but, as they are rarely resting on a mesh or fabric bed, they can cause dipping eventually.

Sinuous springs

Sometimes called zigzag or serpentine springs, these are rows of wire that curve like snakes. Stunning. They are usually found when there is no room for springs or when it is a low-rise couch. Many people will argue that sinuous springs are longer lasting and more comfortable than drop-in or eight-way hand-tied springs. Others will say it's a cheap and easy way to cut corners. In fact, it can be both. If the couch of your dreams has sinuous springs, don't be turned off. Look for 'no sag spring' silent wire (wrapped to prevent squeaking) and a high gauge.

Cushion filling

The filling in your couch will determine how long she will last before she needs some work. It's also a huge factor in her comfort level. This is another area that can be overwhelming, so let's get into the finer detail.

Feather

Down (soft underbelly feathers) or feather (any feather) will set you back a lot, which means many with a big budget will opt for it, assuming feather means quality. You'll know something is stuffed with feather or down because it won't bounce. When you pat it, you'll hear a dead sound, but it's super soft and comfortable.

When it comes to choosing feather or down, there are a few things to consider. Feather is expensive, down filling even more so, so if you see a couch described as having down filling at a reasonable price, the percentage of down filling is likely to be very low.

While it is long-lasting, it does need some maintenance. It needs to be fluffed a *lot* to ensure it keeps its shape. This means every time you get up. Feathers can protrude, so always check if there is down-proof ticking fabric to help it hold its shape and prevent them poking out. It also means you can take the cover off without a feather explosion.

Finally, feather fillings are not waterproof, so beware of spills. A key thing to consider if you have pets. Pee is not a friend of this filling.

Fibre

This gives the feel and illusion of feather without the cost. You do need to plump and reshape to keep it lasting longer but not as much as feather. Fibre usually means polyester and it can be a great option if you wish to have that soft sink of feather on a smaller budget, have allergies or don't wish to have any animal products present. Fibre will always thin over time, as there is so much air in it, but you can add more filling to it yourself.

Foam

This is such a popular filling, as it is easier to work with and easier to live with. Foam is seen in the cheapest and some of the more expensive couches, so it can be hard to know why the price differs so much. Best to look at the density and resilience when opting for foam.

Density. Polyurethane is the most common foam found in seat cushions. High-density foam can be both soft and firm: its density refers to its weight per cubic foot. You'll want your foam sofa to have a density of 1.8 upwards. You will see changes in foam over time, but the lower the density the quicker this happens.

Resilience. You'll see 'HR' or 'High Resilience' a lot when it comes to foam fillings. This refers to its bounce back and recovery after you have gotten up from watching *Death Becomes Her* for the 540th time. HR is a great thing to see on a tag.

A final note on filling. You can also get mixes. Quality foam wrapped in feather is a great option, as you get the soft comfort of the feather, and the bounce and resilience of the foam. Again, look for ticking.

Most brands will state in the small print that the cushions on their sofa will lose 23–30 per cent volume in the first few months. If she has arrived and feels a little overstuffed, do not fear. All you need to do is use her regularly and she'll return to her showroom size.

Fabric

While you may think the fabric on your couch is merely there to serve a look, there is a lot more to factor in to make the right decision. It is the first to show obvious signs of wear and tear, and getting it wrong can be costly. My main advice is to get something you can enjoy. Sliding blankets under guests, sleepless nights over spills, or side-eyeing anyone who looks like they are getting too comfortable is not the way you or your couch need to spend your lives. Your couch will be there for the great days, she'll be there for the hours of Netflix, the nights in with friends, the long phone calls and the naps. Let her love you. Choose a fabric that doesn't stress you out, go for twists and flecks that can hide stains and age with grace, pick something low maintenance if you will be using her a lot and, most of all, you know better than crushed velvet.

Before I commit to a fabric for my couch, here is what I ask myself:

What's she in for?

You are getting into a relationship with this couch, so you need to think long-term. If it is pink velvet and you have four children, two dogs and a knack for knocking over drinks, you need to be realistic about what she will look like in the years to come. It makes it easier to make the right decision and avoid feeling disappointed down the line.

How is she cleaned?

Always check what care is needed to keep this fabric looking good. If you see something like 'professional clean only', you're in for a long ride if this is your main couch. See page 242 for a guide to the upholstery cleaning code. These codes will help you see what is high maintz and what will work well.

First, let's take a moment to discuss durability.

Wyzenbeek, Martindale and the Double Rub

I know this sounds like the title of a cheap detective movie involving a dodgy massage parlour, but this is all about the durability of a couch's fabric. Wyzenbeek and Martindale are two tests carried out on fabric to tell us how much friction it can take before it starts to show signs of wear. When you see a figure such as 25,000 after a fabric name, it is one of the most helpful bits of info to establish its durability. But what does it actually mean, and is a higher or lower number better, I hear you ask.

Let's begin with a double rub. A double rub count of 25,000 means a piece of fabric has been rubbed back and forth by a piece of plastic, wire mesh or another piece of fabric 25,000 times before the fabric began to wear through. The higher the rub count, the more durable the fabric.

The Wyzenbeek test is used in North America. She involves a back-and-forth rubbing motion, or a double rub. The Martindale is used in Europe and is said to be a more realistic measure, as it rubs in a figure of eight against the fabric sample. The two are not like for like.

Whichever rub test is used in your region, here is a handy guide to what durability they reflect. Bear in mind 40,000 rubs on a Martindale machine is the equivalent of 30,000 on a Wyzenbeek machine.

NOTE

A note on durability

10,000 or less: This should be a decorative pillow at most. She's more of a 'look, don't touch' kind of gal, so is suited to drapery, throws and things that will not go through any wear and tear.

15,000–20,000: These are fabrics that can only hack some light domestic use and are made from delicate natural yarns such as silk. These girls are for occasional use, so think along the lines of an uncomfortable armchair for an odd perch rather than one for curling up in.

20,000–25,000: This fabric is classed as grand for general domestic use. But be careful: she can withstand some use but not an intense amount. Ideal for bedding or a chair that's not going to be used often.

25,000–30,000: Heavy duty, henny. This is the kind of rating you want on a couch you use a lot. If your filling, suspension and frame are all built to last, your fabric should be too.

30,000 or more: Climb her, roll around on her, adore her. This is the kind of grade of fabric a restaurant chair would have.

Options

Now that you are up to speed on how to spot a fabric that will last, we can talk about the most common fabric options that will be available.

Leather

Don't make that face. I'm talking about real leather, not the 'landlord' sofa that has ruined leather sofas for most of us for life. Leather can be stunning, and she is also durable and keeps the filling in shape. Leather will age and is cold on the skin, but she can be wiped clean and can withstand intense use. She also comes at a price.

Wool and wool mixes

Wool is usually more expensive, as she's a superior fabric and you will get what you pay for. She is comfortable, doesn't wrinkle or fade badly, and won't stain like other fabrics. She is naturally flame retardant and anti-static, which is why she can be good in a home with lots of pet hair. To make her more affordable, you will often see 'wool blend', which means she has been mixed with a synthetic yarn.

Cotton and cotton blends

Cotton dyes well but doesn't hold dye as long as polyester, so she can fade quicker. Because she is super absorbent she tends to stain more than other fabrics too. This is why cotton will often come as a blend in order to make her more durable and suitable for upholstery.

Linen

Ideal if you want a relaxed, boho vibe. Think Pamela Anderson's Malibu home. Linen almost always has a skirt and touches the floor, so looks more like a cover rather than tight, fitted upholstery. She is a low-fuss fabric and a lovely addition if anyone in the home suffers from allergies.

Velvet

The luxurious pop that a velvet couch brings to a room is unmatched. They're usually done in jewel tones which are rich and vibrant, as their depth and intensity also cannot be achieved in other fabrics. The pile and how it holds the light means it can make these rich shades look even more dramatic, and the silhouette and details look even better. Pastel velvets have recently become popular, but for me jewel tones are always what I would go for. Think a bright green velvet couch in a deep navy room. Elegance!

Velvet is not as difficult to care for as you might think. There are two types: natural and synthetic. Natural velvet has a higher quality and price, but she is a lot more work. She's more suited to occasional perching and doesn't do well with spills. Synthetic velvets are usually 100 per cent polyester, can sometimes be washed, can withstand spills and are generally more durable if the couch is in frequent use. Both will need a weekly hoover (with upholstery attachment please!) and can bruise and mark over time, but if you add their weekly care to your cleaning schedule you'll be grand.

Aesthetic

Last stop: we have colour, pattern and texture.

Always go for something with texture. This will make sure that wear and tear is less visible. It will also be more durable. When choosing the colour and style of the fabric, my most valuable advice here is not to go for anything too 'on trend' if you find that your taste changes often. If you go for a more commercial fabric, you'll be able to update her with cushions and throws as the years go by and give her a whole new look.

If you have a very defined style and a look that you always go for, don't be afraid of committing to a bold colour or print that you like. Whatever you add or change about the space in the future will only complement it, so just go for it.

White couches are becoming more and more popular, but if you fear the maintenance, go for a taupe or a flecked neutral that is more forgiving when it comes to stains (with removable covers!). Lighter couches can work really well in smaller rooms, as they don't appear as boulder-like as dark colours.

She's all style

You now have a deeper understanding of what lies beneath, so you can feel far more comfortable when it comes to the more exciting parts. Hurrah!

Size

The first place to start is sizing: do you want two-seater, three-seater, love seat and so on? Like a bed, the biggest isn't necessarily always the best. Take some time to consider what else you will want around the couch, like side tables, lamps and so on, so that you can leave room for these. You may also want two love seats instead of one big couch if you entertain a lot.

Type

Next, you'll need to assess if you're fine with static or need a sleeper or recliner. I would always advise having a sleeper where possible. For me, it means if you have a spare room, you can reclaim it and put it to better use, or if you are in a one-bed, it means your guest sleeping arrangements are a cinch. I would look for a sleeper with storage. It means you can store bedding there and your guest can pop it away each morning with ease. For both a recliner and a sleeper, make sure you have enough room to walk around it once pulled out.

Style

Couch styles can be broken down into three types – traditional, modern or sectional – but it is truly the arms, feet, backs and seats that will shout the loudest in terms of style, so consider these very well. They will also play a huge part in how comfortable the couch is when sitting for long periods.

Arms

These are one feature you cannot change, so be sure they are in keeping with the overall look you are going for, or, if you like to change it up often, are muted enough to barely play a part. Comfort-wise, avid readers will prefer an elbow-height arm upon which to rest an arm. Loungers will like an arm a little over seat height to rest their heads and for feet to fall over. Anyone going for a small couch who loves to curl up will need their arms high. Padded arms for all of these is a must!

Legs

After the arms, the feet are one of the most defining features of a couch in terms of style. If you are trying to make the room feel more spacious, always opt for visible legs. They can be anything from fussy claw and balls to minimal stilettoes. Castors are great if you think you'll move the couch a lot. Turned feet can add a classic feel to a couch, while metal can instantly modernize it. If you plan on having pets, wooden couch feet should be avoided, as they're irresistible to a puppy. Changing the feet can also completely change the look of your current couch and can be a whole lot cheaper than buying a new one.

Expensive, handmade couches will usually have feet that go right up into the frame. These integral feet will be hard to change, should you feel your couch needs a tszuj. Instead you can either opt to reupholster and choose a cover that has a skirt to cover her feet, or you can paint them to give them a whole new lewk. A claw and ball can take on new meaning in hot pink, while a pale wooden platform becomes luxe with a gold rub-on vinyl.

Most modern couches have feet that screw on and off, which is great should you ever want to swap the legs to change the style. Before you shop, check the screw size of the foot by laying the couch on its back and unscrewing one of the feet anticlockwise.

Most feet will have the same size screw but it's best to take a measurement to ensure it matches your chosen replacement. When it comes to height, don't go much higher than the original leg, and never skip the central legs, as it will affect the frame.

Backs and seats

There are three main types of couch backs. Fixed, where there are no cushions and it is padded for comfort. Cushioned, where it will have cushions reflecting the size of the seat cushions. And scatter cushions, where you will have smaller cushions that you can arrange as you wish. Seats will either come fixed or cushioned.

Cushioned backs and seats are the ones to go for if you want a couch that will last a long time. Cushions can be plumped and reset after use and their filling flipped or topped up over time. Fixed backs and seats are harder to salvage. While they will allow you to achieve a more minimal look, the downside is that they show wear and tear sooner and need more of an overhaul to fix.

Couch care

After such an extensive shopping journey to find the right couch for you, it is important to know how to care for it once it comes through the door.

The first thing you want to do is read your warranty and be super aware of what it covers and how long it is for. Then file it in a folder in your emails for easy access should you need it. Couch warranties are always pretty long and rarely used.

Next, you want to make sure you position your couch well.

Positioning

The position of your couch is really important. This isn't about where she faces, it's about how her location in a room can impact the way she is used. It is obvious that a couch should face something that makes sense. The TV, a nice view or a fire are all fab. But there are some locations that are best avoided, if possible.

Placing a couch too close to the door can cause unnecessary rubbing in a home with high traffic (read children) through the main room. A couch near a door will always be more worn on the arm, as people will perch on it a lot. Sectional and corner couches are often popped in a corner, as people think this is their only purpose. In fact, they can be a great way to divide up the zones of the room and their backs are usually a lot lower than other styles, allowing light to flow and adding a sense of space. Move it around and see if it can work outside of the corner.

A thin sideboard or side table against the back of a couch can be gorgeous, whether she is against or away from a wall. It allows for another surface that can be used for display or storage and adds some lovely layering.

I have seen couches pushed up against windows more often than I care to remember.

COUCH STYLES

• Chesterfield

THIS SUITS A MORE UPRIGHT LOUNGER DUE TO ITS FITTED BACK AND ARMS. IT'S A PERFECT CENTREPIECE AND CAN LOOK GREAT IN A BOLD COLOUR.

• Lawson

BIG ON COMFORT. ITS LOW PADDED ARMS AND CUSHIONED BACK ARE PERFECT FOR AN AVID READER OR WATCHING TV.

• Camel Back

A SLIGHTLY MORE COMFORTABLE CABRIOLE, AS ARMS ARE USUALLY PADDED AND ROLLED.
THE QUESTION IS, ONE HUMP OR TWO?

• Tuxedo

AN ELEGANT COUCH. IDEAL USED AS A STYLING POINT. FOR MAXIMUM COMFORT, GO FOR BACK AND SIDE CUSHIONS.

• Modular

THESE USUALLY HAVE LOW OR NO ARMS TO ALLOW THEM TO BE MOVED AROUND TO ACCOMMODATE GUESTS, FOR STYLING OR FOR ADD-ONS. REALLY SUITS MODERN DÉCOR.

• Cabriole

MORE OF A PERCH THAN A COUCH FOR LOUNGING. IDEAL FOR A LARGE HALLWAY OR DRESSING ROOM.

• Mid-Century Modern

HIGH ON STYLE BUT LOW ON COMFORT. PERFECT AS A FOCAL POINT THAT ISN'T USED FOR LONG PERIODS.

• Roll Arm

LIKE A FUSSIER LAWSON WITH LOWER ARMS THAT ROLL AND MORE CURVES. SUITS A MORE TRADITIONAL STYLE OF ROOM.

This is a big *'non, merci'* for me. The condensation that can occur on windows will seep into your gorgeous couch fabric and encourage mould growth at worst and, at best, that horrible damp smell we all hate. If she is positioned in front of a window, pull her out and give her some breathing room.

Light and heat

Just like your stunning visage, you must be careful when exposing your couch to sun and heat.

If you have a very bright and sunny room, your furnishings can become affected. Sun damage can cause bleaching but can also weaken couch fabrics. To reduce the risk, here are some handy tricks. Apply a UV window film and rotate your furniture occasionally to prevent long-term exposure. If she is leather, use a leather oil to keep her supple and avoid cracking. Choose light colours that are less susceptible to bleaching – natural fabrics will fade quicker than something like polyester. Have you ever seen a beach house with dark couches?

As we bid the couch farewell and move to the coffee table, let's take a moment for the chaise lounge. She may be outdated, impractical and take up unnecessary space, but there is not a hope she is not featuring. Just look at her. Glorious.

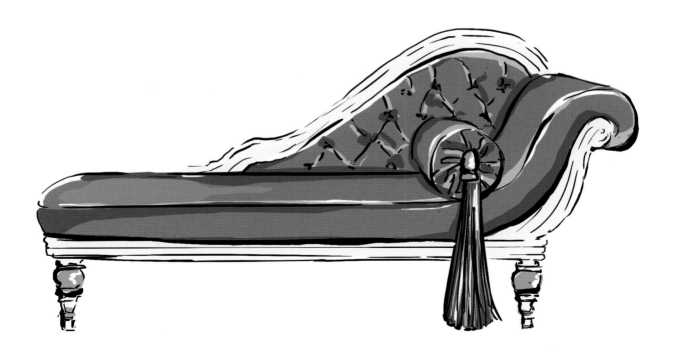

Coffee table

Coffee tables have been a staple in our homes for as long as we've been having guests over for tea or coffee. Now they are more of a styling element and can really elevate your look as well as your comfort levels. If you are in the market for a coffee table, here is what you should be considering.

Style

You want to pair your coffee table to the room. Think of the common accents in a room. For example, I like to always match my floor lamp to my coffee table, or make sure the couch legs match the table legs. It adds a more considered touch rather than being too matchy-matchy. It's like picking up the stitching on a great jacket by wearing a bag the same colour. Divine.

Height

A coffee table that is the same height as the couch is great, as she makes it easier to use. Side tables, for me, should be low but no lower than seat height if being used as a perch, or higher than the arms of the couch if being used for a lamp to avoid bulb glare. Low-rise coffee tables are simply gorgeous but people tend to perch a foot or two on them. Ensure she's either solid wood or metal and not an engineered wood that will chip, strip or bubble under the stress. You want something solid that is not likely to wear, if you are going low.

Shape

If you want to optimize your table top, go for a round table, as you won't have to worry about sharp corners. If you are worried that the table size you want will make the room feel too small, there are some tricks to help you along. Mirrored coffee tables are great at giving a feeling of more space. Ground-floor flats will benefit particularly from these, as they can reflect greenery or the sky from outside into a dark room. You can also opt for all glass or Perspex with zero shelving beneath. This will allow you to see the floor and create a more spacious vibe but still give you the surface you need.

Storage

If you are low on storage, this is a great way to add more. If it's open storage you are lacking, a table with a shelf is ideal. Go for a glass top to really show off what is on display. If it is hidden storage you are after, go for drawers or an ottoman. With storage centrally placed like this, the trick is to go for one that allows you to see some of the floor underneath. Floating tables are ideal, or ones with minimal legs, as they don't cut off the floor entirely.

Materials

Glass will always be a great addition, as it doesn't take over, but it's best avoided if you have children. Instead opt for a soft ottoman in a wipeable fabric that can be touched all day long with sticky hands, bumped into and leaned against – and, of course, still act as a coffee table when needed.

If you want to use the table as a foot rest too, make sure it's fabric and comfortable rather than a metal or wood. You can still use a soft ottoman or pouffe as a coffee table – just place a large tray on top to give you a stable surface.

Side tables and coffee tables need to be able to take hot cups and may encounter spills, so make sure that you use coasters. To ensure that they are used, make them fun, chic or irresistible. Doling out coasters can feel like you're telling guests you don't trust them. If they're gorge, it'll be a different tone.

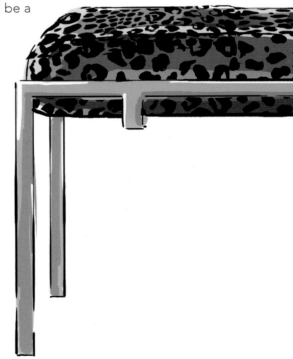

Size

It is said that a coffee table should be two-thirds the length of your couch, but you don't have to stick to that. It's more about how you want to use it and if you'll need to move it often. Whatever you go for, make sure it's one that allows you to use the rest of the room well. Your coffee table should always be a smooth and helpful addition to the room rather than overtake it.

Right (*topping up a red lip*), that was simply glorious! I hope it has given you some good insight into setting up a lounge that works for you. It's so important to ensure the places we relax in are set up as such.

Now, let's grab these empty plates and head to the kitchen. Follow me!

CHAPTER 2

KITCHEN

WHO IS SHE?

Here we are! The room that feeds us. Don't you just LOVE the drama of a kitchen? So complex, so detailed, yet still so inviting. Let's have a ginger juice to give us a kick. (*Slides two coupes across terrazzo counter.*)

When we feel like our kitchen is not working for us, either visually or practically, it can be a little overwhelming. We often assume a complete overhaul is the only answer, and many of us will live with a kitchen we hate for years, counting down the days until we can rip it all out and start again.

This is exactly the opposite of what we should be doing! The kitchen is one room where small changes can have a huge impact. If you don't learn how to make the best use of your kitchen, no marble counter top or American-style fridge is going to truly get you to a place of harmony with her. You first need to establish how you use the room and what you need from her before you help her along visually.

I've been faced with many a dreary kitchen, but budget and time will decide how deep I can go with the changes. No matter what, I begin with the Min.

Clear & clean

Regardless of your ambitions, this stage must be done. Your kitchen may have more cupboards than any other room, but they should be used wisely. Declutter, downsize and give everything a solid clean. As well as gleaming cupboards and surfaces, you also want to brighten grout, thoroughly clean appliances and change the extractor fan filters. Once you have finished a deep clean of a kitchen, you'll know it better, will see what can be repaired and what surfaces get the most punishment. Now you're ready for the next stage.

Assess the zones & flow

Assessing the zones helps you to decide where things should go in cupboards, where your bin should ideally be and where your prep areas should be set up. It is vital to cleverly zone a kitchen. This method is great on moving-in day, the day your new kitchen is finished or if you constantly feel you're working against the space.

The kitchen work triangle

Before we even get down to the look of the kitchen, we first need to work out how she is organized. You may have already heard of the kitchen work triangle – shout out to the home economics hennies! A layout concept developed in the early 20th century, its aim was to speed up the cooking, cleaning and prep processes by reducing the distance between the kitchen's three main work areas: the sink, cooker and fridge. The concept was based around the woman of the home (then deemed the only user) and was first presented at a women's expo. (*Cough.*)

Even though our kitchens and, indeed, their users have changed dramatically since the 1920s, the work triangle has, in a way, stood the test of time. Its core values can be applied to almost any set-up. So let's see how she works.

WORK TRIANGLE

THE TOTAL SUM OF THE SIDES OF THE TRIANGLE MUST BE NO LESS THAN 4.0M AND NO GREATER THAN 7.9M

WITHIN THIS TOTAL SUM, INDIVIDUAL SIDES OF THE TRIANGLE SHOULD NOT BE LESS THAN 1.2M OR GREATER THAN 2.7M

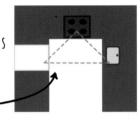

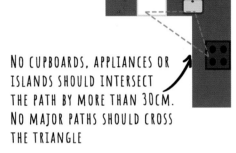

NO CUPBOARDS, APPLIANCES OR ISLANDS SHOULD INTERSECT THE PATH BY MORE THAN 30CM. NO MAJOR PATHS SHOULD CROSS THE TRIANGLE

THIS SET-UP IS A GREAT WAY TO AVOID TRIPS, BUMPS, SPILLS OR YOU CARRYING ANYTHING HOT FOR TOO LONG, SO IF YOU ARE SETTING OUT ON A NEW KITCHEN JOURNEY IT'S GOOD TO CONSIDER THESE RULES WHEN THINKING ABOUT LAYOUT OR AN ADDITION TO THE SPACE.

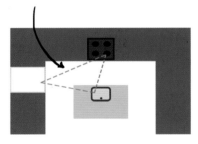

Zones

Once you have decided on a new layout, or have assessed your current set-up, you need to consider the zones of your kitchen. They are as follows:

Core

These are the areas used most. Perhaps your hob, or where you open your food delivery. Wherever gets the most use. Your core areas should have everything you need to hand. Consider this when selecting what gets plugged in where on your counter top and what goes in which cupboard.

Waste

I'm talking sink, bin, recycling, compost, dishwasher. These girls should all be together. Teabag in bin, drain cup, pop in dishwasher. Three tasks that can all be done in a couple of steps. This is the kind of vibe you are looking for.

Prep

My main food-prep area is to the right of my oven. It's next to my bin and sink, but also, as I am left-handed, it makes it easier for me to lean and stir, open doors and set timers within arm's reach of my chopping boards, knives, garlic, prep utensils and so on. This means once I pull out the food I need, I stand in the one spot, podcast on, and prep away. I then like to have a designated counter area for things like hot drinks. So, cups, tea, glass teapots, honey, all in the one space, ideally near the sink, to easily fill the kettle.

To really enhance your zones, consider using the inside of doors above and below. Having a holder for items used often in the zone can free up drawer space and make use of it a breeze. For example, I have films and foil all on the inside of the door below where I prep for the fridge and a chalkboard on the door over my main food storage for shopping lists.

The Min is all about working with what you have and making the most of it. Rethink what is already there and how it makes you feel when you use it, display it or store it. There is no other room in which this has more impact than the kitchen. Clutter on counter tops, boxes on top of wall units and crowded open shelving can all make the area feel overwhelming. Now that you have the more practical side of the Min explored through zoning and the work triangle, let's have a little fun. Why can't our kitchen counter tops be as gorgeous as our dressing tables and as much of a joy to use? We spend as much time at them, after all.

My first rule is to save the bulk of your cupboard storage for items neither nice to look at nor used often. If you are short on cupboard space, layer items in your storage with what you use first at the front. Don't be tempted to keep that rarely used large mixer out just because it's massive. Don't store anything on top of your kitchen cupboards. If people knew the amount of airborne grease this attracts, it would be outlawed.

Chopping boards are a great addition leaning against the walls of your main prep area, as they can add some lovely warmth to the room. The same goes for any larger serving ware that has some charm. It can also hide a bad tile – or protect in the absence of tiles.

Once you have completed the Min, live with it for at least a week. It will change how you see the space and help you envision far more clearly what is actually needed and what could wait. Enjoy using your kitchen with ease and, of course, style.

MAGIC MEAUXMENT

I like to keep items used often on counter tops. But this isn't a supermarket, so get creative in disguising packaging. Don't just go for the obvious and think plastic boxes and sweet jars. Please, no. Dramatic vintage pottery jars can look absolutely wonderful on a counter top and no one needs to know that protein powder bag is inside.

And as I would on my dressing table, I decant! Oils, vinegars, salt and pepper all look great in glassware. As glass is non-porous it will be easy to wash and clean, and it won't absorb whatever is stored inside. It always looks gorgeous having a cluster of interesting glassware on a counter top and it feels even better drizzling oil over a salad with something that could have housed Cleopatra's night cream.

Speaking of glassware, if you're low on space go for glass as much as possible – jugs, vases, teapots, dessert bowls and so on – as they can be displayed without making the space feel cluttered. Glass adds a glossy and chic tone. This is great in a multi-use area, as some of your kitchen storage can spill into the dining or living area and look stunning. Even better, it frees up storage space.

THE TSZUJ

If you are looking to make some minimal changes with maximum impact, the Tszuj is the gal for you. Here we will be making light changes to the key players in the kitchen's overall aesthetic. When you walk into a kitchen your eye will go to the hob, units, tiles and sink, so these are always on my hit list when a space needs a tszuj.

Taps & hob

A sure-fire way to make your kitchen look a little more up to date for little spend is to upgrade the hob and tap. This is one of the first things I do if I cannot make major changes. A tall mixer tap with a pull-out spray nozzle instantly modernizes an old and worn-in sink. Older electric hobs can let down a kitchen and make it feel really shabby and dated. A new hob can cost as little as €150 and make a huge impact both visually and practically.

Units

Kitchens can be easily updated with a lot of consideration and a little She-IY. A good place to start is the cupboards. These are usually the strongest element in the kitchen's overall look and one of the last things to replace. I consider what elements I can change to bring them up to date and style them to my taste. People often begin painting cupboards and realize too late their appliances now stick out or they've enhanced a shoddy wall. Here is how I pare everything back.

Plinths & accents

Some older kitchens will have contrasting plinths (the kickboards at the bottom) or accents that date it. If you're not sure what to do, my favourite trick is to type the description into Pinterest, which yields pages of inspiration on how other people have made your style of kitchen work well. It will also help you see what needs to be painted, removed or reworked to pull off a more modern look.

Handles

Handles can really date the look of a kitchen, yet are so simple to replace. They are an ideal place to start if you are a tenant, as you can switch them back at the end of the lease. Check the screw placement and screw size of the originals before searching for alternatives. You'll need your new ones to match for an easy swap.

Style-wise, handles go through so many trends I find it best to go minimal. Aside from it being a timeless aesthetic, people tend to stand close to counters, so anything bulky can hurt. Also, consider the material. Your hands (and any little hands) will often be oily or sticky in the kitchen, so investing in sisal, leather or canvas could be a disaster if you use your kitchen often.

Lighting

Add lighting under wall units if there is none in place. It is the perfect way to revitalize your units. These needn't be wired in and can be battery-powered and stuck or screwed in place (ideal for rentals). The reason I love these is because you get to avoid the main light always being on, which is so important in creating a considered space. Place them above the main work areas to add task lighting that can also be left on as you dine for some ambience.

Doors off

The fastest way to a new look is to take some doors off your wall units. Filing hinge holes and painting the interior or just the back wall with an accent colour allows you to set up the units as more of a display. Stack your nicest bits inside and you have a whole new look in one afternoon. Cupboards next to a busy hob will get most of the airborne grease, so keep doors on here.

Remove & replace

You can also opt to remove wall units and replace them with shelves. It can be stunning, but if you need lots of storage, shelves may not be enough. However, if you are the proud owner of RFS (really fucking stunning) crockery and glassware, they are a brilliant addition. Again, make sure they are not too close to the hob if you cook a lot. Also, be mindful of depth. Making them around 30cm will discourage too much weight but also give you enough breathing room when using counter tops.

PAINTING CUPBOARDS

I must say, painting cupboards is not for the faint-hearted, which is why it's my last resort, but the look at the end can be worth it. If doing it yourself, it will usually take around three days for an average-sized kitchen, though there is the option to get it professionally sprayed as well.

I will talk about colour a little later in this chapter (see Ch-ch-ch-changing colour, p. 63), but do consider this important point. If you don't have integrated appliances, these could stick out more than the new unit colour. Painting them is an option, but I have rarely seen this pulled off to a great finish. Instead, choose a colour that can complement or blend with your appliances and go for drama on tiles and walls instead.

A note on supplies

Primer – Ensure it is suitable for your surfaces; go for one that is also an undercoat to mute the original colour (if you are painting real wood, you will still need to sand it back and use a suitable primer).

Paint – Eggshell works really well here. Test the colour in multiple places. Assess at night under lighting too as this is usually when you will see the new colour most.

Roller – Rollers are best here as they allow an even coat that won't drip, unlike brush application.

Step 1:

Note the parts you will be painting. Usually it is the front, back and sides of doors/ drawers and the parts of the units that will be seen when the doors are closed. Draw up an order of painting to help you keep track of coats. You will need to check out the drying time on packaging of primer and paint to ensure you give yourself enough time.

Set up an area that allows you to paint and leave all doors/drawers to dry flat. You can use props like tins or boxes.

Step 2:

Remove doors and then handles. It is best to remove the door only. Leave the hinge attached to the unit. Always make sure someone is holding the door and remove lower hinges first.

Clean all the surfaces you will be painting thoroughly; they will be greasy! Then 'key'. This is where you will rough up the surface to make sure it can bond well with the primer. It is essentially sanding down the surface. Use a fine grade sandpaper.

Step 3:

Apply your primer in thin, even coats. If the packaging recommends two coats, go for it! Ensure you allow the advised drying time in full. Ensure that you are not blocking any screw holes with paint.

Apply top-coat paint. I would always do two coats minimum here, with full drying time in between. Pop on the handles first, then screw doors back into place.

Tiles

A tile refresh is a great way to update your space. You can do this alone or as part of a full Tszuj, but it will always help the room if done well.

Tile stickers

Advantages: They can be used in a rental, as they peel off afterwards. They are inexpensive, easy to apply and you can achieve a total transformation. Stickers are also a great way to add some colour or personality to tiles without doing the whole wall. Consider a strip of sticker tiles or using one every few tiles to create a sequence or to cover up one already in place. Don't be afraid to mix colour and pattern here. If you are into bold tiles, go for it!

Disadvantages: You need to carry out the prep well or they will start to peel. They are a cost-effective way to do an update, but you may need an update every few years. If you go for a cheap sticker, they can unpeel and yellow behind the hob, so make sure you are getting ones suitable for heat and moisture! If you love to scrub your kitchen, these can't hack a lot of deep cleans.

Tips

- Always make sure the tiles are cleaned well. If there is any grease present, they won't stick properly and may come off as soon as you cook and generate steam.
- Prep yourself well. Set up a cutting station and clean all counter tops. This needs precision and time, so make sure you have everything before you start.
- Clean your grouting first. A grout pen is also great to freshen it up.
- If the tiles underneath are particularly bold, double up or go for a darker sticker.
- To remove stickers, most packaging recommends a hair dryer to loosen the glue. Then wash down to remove any glue remnants.
- If you are renting, try one tile first, leave it a week, then remove it to make sure you're not going to have problems at the end of your tenancy.
- When cleaning these tiles, remember they are not like regular tiles. Rubbing back and forth a lot will eventually cause them to lift at the edges.

Grout paint

Advantages: A grout tszuj can transform the vibe of a tiled area, especially if the tiles are plain and in perfect condition. A pop of colour like a light pink can add a fun, modern feel. Blue or orange can look fantastic if you like a mid-century lewk. My favourite is a charcoal, as it adds drama to even the dullest tiles.

Disadvantages: If you have a tile that is not glazed, it means it is not sealed and so grout paint will seep through the tile. This doesn't mean you can never paint the grout around each tile; you will just need to source a primer, seal the edges around each tile and then paint. You cannot apply it to damaged grout, as it will make it crumble further.

Tips

- Always clean the grout to an exceptional standard first. A soft bristle toothbrush is great. Grout paint won't sit well on a dirty or greasy surface.
- Opt for a grout paint that can be removed from the tiles with a sponge. This is so much quicker and better than painting on the lines yourself. It works by only bonding with the grout and can be easily wiped off the glazed tile before it sets fully.
- Make sure you sit with the instructions and follow them well. Different paints have different application, setting and care guidelines, so never assume anything based on a tutorial you have seen.

Stick-on tiles

These are thin sheets of faux tiles that can be stuck on over your old tile. They usually come in plastic or vinyl. They can add an instant update to a space – ideal if you are selling your home and want to give the kitchen a lift, or if you plan on changing tiles down the road but want something fresh in the meantime.

Advantages: As these are usually sheets rather than individual tiles, the installation is quick and easy. If you go for an expensive, guaranteed easy-to-remove option, they can be good for a rental, but you need to make sure it's suitable for the locations you have in mind and won't damage your surfaces.

Disadvantages: Because they're made to be easy to remove, the adhesive can actually come away after a lot of exposure to steam. If you leave gaps when applying, this allows moisture to get in but not out – you may have a damp issue down the line. Make sure your sink area is well sealed, if adding tiles in this area. Although usually advertised as suitable for any surface, these will take off paint when removed from non-tile areas.

- Not all brands are of the same quality, so go for a reputable one. I have seen cheap stick-on tiles installed that warped and unpeeled quite quickly.
- Go for sheets that do not have even sides. The best ones look almost like Tetris pieces and slot together like a jigsaw. This will never leave one long edge that will be prone to lifting.
- Use an old loyalty card to smooth them down, so you know all of the sticky side is connecting with the surface below.
- Map out the sections first. Grab a pencil and a level, and mark the grout or wall where each sheet should sit. This will make sure you stay on track and even.
- And, as always, clean the surface well first.

Tile paint

Advantages: Tile paint is a quick and cheap way to update your tiles. You need to prime the surface and then paint over it with a high gloss or chalky matte. In my experience, gloss is more durable, but the matte can give a really gorgeous chalky, modern edge.

Disadvantages: You will have to paint the grout as well as the tile, as it is near impossible to get a good finish doing just the tile. It can scratch, so if you're painting an area that gets a lot of wear and tear either paint a strip up high or choose a colour close to the original tile so that you don't have to constantly top up.

Tips

- Clean and prep well before applying the primer.
- Choose a primer that has great reviews. In my experience, there are some that do a superb job and others that aren't worth using.
- Never use a harsh cleaner or sponge to clean painted tiles.
- Keep the paint and primer for touch-ups.
- All white can be really effective, as you don't notice the painted grout.

Counter tops

Counter tops in a kitchen can really set a tone. If you are unhappy with what you have, there are some She-IY options in place that are pretty easy to do.

Solid wood

A sand and varnish will bring this gal back to life by removing stains and brightening. If you want to change the colour, you can even opt for a stain.

Vinyl

Applying a sheet of vinyl can update your counter tops right away. Just be mindful that this can nick and tear and is not a long-term solution.

Wraps

You can get vinyl wrapping done professionally that will last a lot longer than a DIY vinyl and has a better finish.

Freshen up walls

The kitchen ceiling and walls tend to discolour over time, thanks to grease. This means a fresh coat can make the space feel much better and is such an easy update. Go for something that is designed for kitchens and keep away from mattes. If you are changing colour, there is more on this later.

Window dressing

Kitchens can often have a dated window dressing. Usually a lace or old blind that a thorough wash or replacement can help. In a room with so much airborne grease and odour, consider your window dressing carefully. If privacy is not an issue and you don't have to contend with the sun beating in, consider avoiding it completely.

Should you want to add some interest to a sill or cover a window slightly, go for plants or herbs. If you are going for a window dressing, keep it minimal and chic. Think crisp linens and lightweight fabric that cannot hold moisture or grease in its folds. Always opt for something that can be popped in a hot wash every few months. I would also never apply a full-length dressing. Go for café curtains at most here, if it's ground floor.

Kitchen additions

Many people will add to an existing kitchen to update it. Perhaps it's a new appliance, a dining set or counter seating. To ensure additions enhance the space rather than make it harder to use, check your clearance. You need to make sure whatever you are adding is not stopping doors, drawers and appliances from opening fully and that people can walk around them when open. Doors usually need either 60cm or 90cm (dishwashers).

THE OVERHAUL

If you have the budget to do more intense changes, you may be scratching your head at where to start. There is SO much out there when it comes to kitchens, it's best to start with the most important factor: YOU. To truly have a kitchen that brings joy to your life, you need to keep your life in mind when shopping for it. Here is my guide to the major alternations you can make, which should help you make some decisions.

Island units

It has become quite common to add in an island, but there are some things to be aware of.

Height. Keep the island higher or the same height as the other counter tops (usually 91cm) if you are using it as a work surface or wish to house appliances underneath. If it's more of a 'pop a bottle and arrange a cheese board' space, you can make it a little taller.

Plinth. Don't forget your plinth needs to be indented in those places where you wish to stand close to the counter top. If the sides are completely straight to the floor, you'll have to stand in first position while you prep your vol-au-vents.

Consider the power and plumbing. Sinks, appliances and extractors will all need their supply considered and it usually comes through the floor. Even if you don't want appliances in the island right now, it's good to have that option in the future.

If a hob is going on the island, you will also need an extractor. If you hate the look of an overhead hood, why not opt for one that is built into the hob? Although these, right now, are mainly at the higher end of the market, bear in mind that you're getting two appliances in one, so they can be worth the price tag.

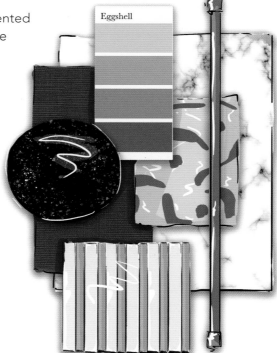

Eggshell

Ch-ch-ch-changing colour

There are so many rules and guides for kitchen colour, it can be hard to navigate. Here is how I decide a colour scheme or update.

- **What are my non-negotiables?** If you are just changing a couple of elements, like the units or walls, and the counter tops, tiles or the appliances are all staying as is, make sure they are considered and complemented by the new colour. If you are going dark, take in pipework, wall edges, windows and other finishes, as it can make any shoddy or uneven finishes and fixtures stand out.
- **Not so obvious:** You don't need to always match to obvious elements. Is there a fleck in your counter or your floor tile that could be gorgeous on a wall or unit? Is the overall tone of the kitchen cool or warm? Considering the less obvious colours at play will help you create a more considered look.
- **Clever colour:** You will always be told to go for light colours, as it will help the space feel bigger. However, you can instead use colour in other ways. If a neat look is key, go for the same tone in everything. Help the units fade into the walls with the same shade, and the same with tiles. Make sure all appliances are integrated, where possible, and that drawers and doors are handle-free. If, like me, you like a kitchen to feel like a cocoon, go for a dark, gothic feel, with deep tones and glossy tiles. If you do spend a lot of time in the kitchen, light and bright is definitely the way to go. It will be better for the mind and focus if you have a neutral vibe. Light neutral colours are also brilliant if you are the kind of gal who loves to change it up every few years. They are easy to paint over, can adapt to your scheme of the moment with just a handle or tile update, and never really take centre stage.

Counter tops

It's said that horizontal surfaces are the ones that have the most visual impact, so quite often a change of counter top can make a huge difference. Counter tops have a terrifying reputation. We've all known someone whose heart is broken by a counter top that requires hours of buffing and treating, or someone who fell out with a friend over a spill. I firmly believe that while your counter top should work aesthetically, it should also be able to take a beating, a spilled glass of wine and a barefoot dance on New Year's Eve. No one should live in fear of their counter top.

You can buy most counter-top materials off the rack, as you would a designer coat, or you can get one made to order, like going to a tailor. The ones you buy off the rack are sold in universal lengths and you cut them to fit your units. The most common sizes are 30mm or 40mm, but you can find them thinner and much thicker. You can also buy natural stone counter tops in the same way, but these are usually a custom fit.

Counter tops for me can usually be broken down into categories by price: cha-ching, bling-bling and ring-a-ding-ding.

Cha-ching

Marble

If you want a really chic and elegant look for your kitchen, then marble is ideal. These counter tops are also known for their high quality and will last a lifetime if cared for well. However, this girl is high maintenance. She is porous, which means she will literally drink up stains, which is why your friend with the marble counter top would rather let you enjoy a glass of malbec while in a headstand on her pink velvet couch than have one sat at her breakfast bar.

Aesthetic

Marble can come in a polished high shine or various levels of matte. You'll often hear people shriek over the 'veins' on a piece of marble. Almost like rivers on a map, these veins determine the marble's overall aesthetic but most importantly can also indicate where it was quarried. This is one of the main factors when it comes to her quality. Similar to diamonds or wine, the minerals present in certain regions can really affect the quality and colour of marble, which will increase demand and, of course, the price point.

Take, for example, Calacatta marble. The reason she is so renowned is that she hails from Carrara in Italy, where the marble veins are still as bold and stunning as they were centuries ago and the marble is strong and long-lasting. In fact, anything Italian will always be of a superior quality due to the minerals present.

Placement

You should pop her in areas where less 'work' is done, as she can get damaged easily by anything acidic, like citrus or vinegars, who will turn the calcium carbonate in the marble to a soluble salt, leaving a white mark and erosion. Dark liquid spills can also stain, as she is so porous. So, for example, your back counters, where you chop and prep, could be a more durable 'marble-effect', while your island, which takes less of a battering, could be true marble. No two pieces are the same, so shop around as much as you can; get to know what kind of characteristics you are looking for in yours. Marble is sold in certain sizes to avoid it breaking, so if you have a larger counter you may have a seam. You will also be limited in your unsupported overhang, so note this for breakfast bars.

Granite

I know, I know, you're screaming at me. You're imagining a black galaxy-fleck granite with red leather barstools and a purple faux crystal light feature. But hear me out. Granite, when done well, looks gorge. She is like the tougher cousin of marble, as she was exposed to even more heat from the Earth's core, which makes her stronger.

Aesthetic

There is such a wide range of granite colours and styles, you are bound to find one that suits you. This is one counter top where colour can affect maintenance. It is said that some dark granites don't need any seal, but always check when purchasing. It has a luxe vibe and if you don't go too into one trend, it will hold its style well over the years. It's also long-wearing, hygienic, can take heat and reflects light beautifully. It is heavy, though, so you'll need sturdy base units.

Placement

You can use granite throughout, but remember to factor in the cost of cutting out sinks and so on. Never skip adding drain grooves. Many people think that these aren't needed, but you can end up with discoloration and dripping onto cupboards.

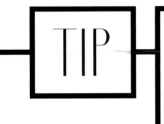

TIP

If you have just moved in and don't know if your granite needs to be sealed, you can do a test. Pour a tablespoon of water onto the granite, then wipe it away after fifteen mins. If the granite darkened where the water was, it means water has got in and it could do with a fresh seal.

Terrazzo

Real terrazzo is a sustainable gal, so a beautiful way to make a mindful purchase. Depending on the process, she can at times be more expensive than marble. Like natural counter tops, after size, the price will be determined by the finish, edge style and thickness.

Aesthetic

As she is a composite, her elements will determine her overall aesthetic. Terrazzo can be marble, glass, granite, shells and so on, mixed with a resin or a concrete, which means a beautiful mix of tones. No two counter tops will ever be the same, which some people go wild for. Great, if you are after something unique.

Placement

Because these gals are usually sold in slabs and have standard sizes, they're better used in one long strip or on an island. They can also look amazing as a splashback.

Quartz

We cannot talk about pricey counter tops without talking about quartz. It has all the glamour, weight and appeal of stone but doesn't need the same upkeep. It is relatively heat- and stain-resistant, so you don't have to panic after a spill.

Aesthetic

Quartz is a more refined version of a composite counter top, as it uses more mineral and less resin, so it looks far more like a stone, especially when pigments are added. You can achieve the look of any natural tile counter top that your heart desires with quartz.

Placement

This is suitable throughout the kitchen, but always ask to see the entire piece. Marble showrooms will always have full slabs on display, but quartz can sometimes be shown in a small section. Seeing the whole piece will give you a better idea of how it will look throughout the kitchen.

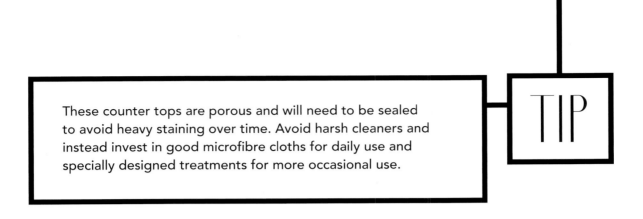

TIP

These counter tops are porous and will need to be sealed to avoid heavy staining over time. Avoid harsh cleaners and instead invest in good microfibre cloths for daily use and specially designed treatments for more occasional use.

Bling–bling

Solid

Solid counter tops are usually made from synthetic materials such as acrylic or resins mixed with a mineral powder. You will see them sometimes referred to as Corian, but this is actually the brand that first started making them. They are super durable, as they are solid the whole way through – no layers to split or weaken. Their level of heat resistance is better than any laminate and, as they are smooth, they are more hygienic than, say, a wood.

Aesthetic

They are mainly made to look like the previous counter tops: she's a low-maintenance version for less cost. The easiest way to tell is to touch her – stone will be cold, whereas faux won't.

Placement

As these are literally made to be counters, they are suitable for all parts of the kitchen. They will always have minimal seaming and be able to achieve bends and curves that many other materials can't.

Stainless steel

The marmite of worktops. You'll either adore or abhor her, but there is a reason why she is the preferred counter top in professional kitchens. She is hygienic, durable, heat-resistant, and easy to maintain and clean. She's also not going to cost a fortune. Fun fact: she was the chosen counter top of one of the *Real Housewives of Beverly Hills*, a woman who owns many restaurants and probably knows how good her properties really are.

Aesthetic

You don't have to go for the professional kitchen look, with a thick counter. If you look up thin stainless steel counter tops you will see how stunning these can be on top of dark wood or painted cupboards. Stainless steel goes from a bulky professional kitchen to a sleek and minimal affair.

Placement

She's grand placed pretty much anywhere but will work particularly well in a kitchen with other stainless steel details, like a fridge, or behind the hob.

Brass

OMG, I dai. I just love the look of a brass counter top. They add a pop of luxe that works really well in smaller kitchens, as it reflects light so well. If you have a newer property that you want to inject some older charm in to, it is also perfect.

Aesthetic

I adore that a patina will develop over time and change her appearance. For this reason, if you like everything bright and uniform, she's not for you, but she is ideal if you want high glamour. You can seal her to avoid colour change, but this can affect how antibacterial she is. Mix with dark wood cupboards in a minimal style, with deep green glass subway tiles. Divine.

Placement

You might want a strip of something else near the hob, as leaving a hot pan on these counter tops can cause warping. Although trivets are popular, as they give us a surface to pop a hot pan onto, I prefer something like a large block of a heat-resistant material that adds to the warmer aesthetic.

Ring–a–ding–ding

Laminate

Laminates are the cheapest way to get a natural counter imitation. You can also install them yourself. She is essentially layers of paper soaked in resin which are then heated to bond them into a sheet. This is then wrapped over a base of engineered wood. The higher the price, the better the materials used and the more layers. Laminate has come a long way in recent years, with many looking great and lasting well. As well as the quality of the imitation, look for things like her resistance to water, heat and scratches, and anti-fingerprint finishes for anything high shine. She's not the greenest choice, so if you are choosing laminate don't buy one that will need to be replaced in the near future.

Aesthetic

Laminate is usually imitating a marble, stone, terrazzo or quartz, just as a laminate flooring imitates wood. You can also find solid-colour laminates. They are usually bought in breakfast bar (2,000mm) or worktop (3,000mm) lengths and then you cut them down to your required size. When it comes to thickness, if the laminate is emulating a stone, go for thinner to make it more realistic.

Placement

These can work throughout the kitchen, but you will need to have a draining board in place, as it gets damaged by too much moisture.

Wood

You can get some wooden worktops for the same price as laminate, but this will be for beech or something similar. Oak will last much longer, but she needs to be looked after. No heat on this girl and very little exposure to water. Ensure your wood worktop is from a sustainable source. This will be in the description.

Aesthetic

I adore that over time these age and take on a new tone – to me, it makes an older one appear even more priceless. They are also timeless as an aesthetic and don't date. You can change up everything else in the kitchen, style them differently many times over and they will adapt easily.

Placement

Once sealed well, these work anywhere in the kitchen. Don't make the mistake of thinking she's like one big chopping board. You will damage her, and also wood is not a hygienic worktop to cut on. She needs to be seriously scrubbed to remove bacteria and you don't want to put your counter through this. Some woods have a higher oil content and will work better around a sink, so bear this in mind if you are going for wood throughout.

Wall tiles

Tiles can really add to or take away from a kitchen's aesthetic, but never underestimate the practicality of these gems and the work they do. Behind the hob and sink are the main areas that need tiling or a splashback, for obvious reasons. However, I would always advise tiling right around the counter tops for a more finished look.

Height

The height your tiles run to will usually depend on what is above.

Units: Your tiles should cover all walls between the counter top and the bottom of the wall units (usually 45cm). They will most likely need to run a little higher behind the hob to meet the bottom of the extractor. I would never tile above wall cabinets, as it would be difficult to keep them clean; you'll also never see them all and so it can be a waste of money.

Shelves: For areas with shelves above counters, the most popular option is to tile to the first shelf only. You can, of course, stop a little lower or leave a scalloped edge 10cm or so below. I would essentially treat the first shelf as though it is the bottom of a unit.

Nada: Where a counter area has no wall cupboards above, around the sink for example, raise the height of the tiles in this area to match the height behind the hob for consistency. If there is no cooker hood, simply have the tiles in the open area a line or two higher than the height of the tiling beneath the upper cupboards. If there are no units or shelves at all, as a guide go around 60cm. You can also opt to tile to the ceiling, but I would make sure it's a classic tile and can run completely uninterrupted.

Tile alternatives

You don't have to go for tile; you can go for a marble look, stainless steel, glossy or matte splashback panels, or even mirror – one of my favourites.

I absolutely love mirrored splashbacks in a smaller space, as they reflect the task lightning so well and make a room look much bigger. They also allow you to see the room behind you as you cook and prepare, which I always find more relaxing. If you choose mirror, make sure it is suitable for behind a hob; you cannot use a regular mirror. Toughened mirrored splashbacks are ideal, as they absorb heat and you can opt for one with a tint, like bronze, if you wish to add more warmth to the space.

Another look I adore is matching the splashback and counter, especially if it is a light marble or marble effect. It can look luxurious and timeless. As long as the material is wipeable, heat-resistant, waterproof and can protect your walls, you can go for whatever you love. You also don't have to stick to just one style. If you adore a tile that cannot sit behind a hob but is suitable everywhere else, you can pop something else behind there. Mixing panel splashbacks and tiles can be really effective.

Timeless tiles

I get chills when I think of the subway tile. It is a classic, fail-safe design that has been around a long time and has a stunning history. It was born, like all good things, out of necessity and this is why I believe its practical edge is what keeps it so popular even today. As the name hints, subway tiles were first designed to be used underground. I doubt their creators ever imagined they would become such a household hit. When the New York subway was being built at the turn of the 20th century, interior architects Heins & LaFarge wanted a clean, beautiful and luxe finish that would encourage people to want to go underground.

It was imperative that the stations felt bright and charming, but it was also vital that the surfaces were easy to clean and maintain (hygiene and a clean aesthetic was all the rage, as you can imagine). Although brick would have been ideal, as it can be laid in curves and is durable, it would absorb dirt and grime. They knew that a sterile feel, with pops of mosaics and colour to add the elegance, could be found in tile, but tiles were mainly square at the time and couldn't be used around the curved ceilings.

They worked together with several ceramic tile producers to develop the perfect tile for their needs. It had a ratio of 2:1, just like a brick, and could be laid in a brick pattern to ensure it could be used on curved or straight walls. It was glossy and bright, and easy to clean, and so they had their perfect tile. Swoon.

The subway was an absolute hit. People went wild for its charm and modern elegance. Other cities incorporated the tile into their underground design and soon a bevelled edge was added for people who wanted to use them in their homes. Before long they were adorning the walls of kitchens and bathrooms all over the world and are a top-selling tile to this day.

The subway and you

Subway tiles will almost always be low in price, so are great for keeping costs down. They also work if you want something that will not take over and will remain timeless in terms of style. A standard bevelled-edge, glossy, white subway tile, laid in a brick pattern, will never see you wrong.

However, never underestimate these girls and assume they are only for a low budget. Their low cost is down to their affordable production rather than their quality and they can, in fact, achieve many different looks. It's all in the lay.

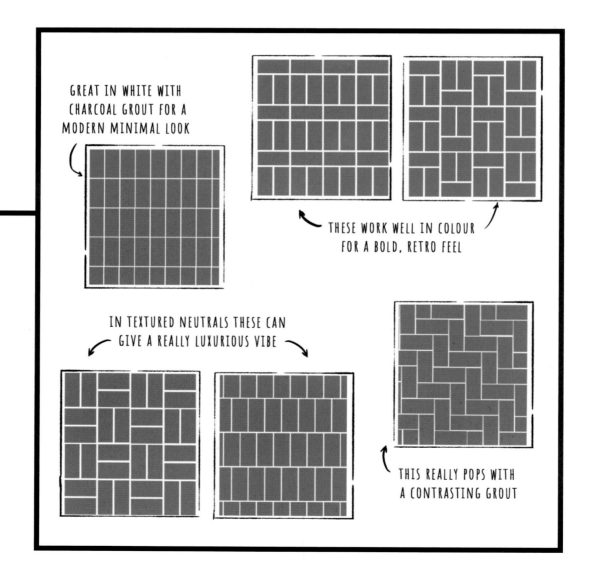

GREAT IN WHITE WITH CHARCOAL GROUT FOR A MODERN MINIMAL LOOK

THESE WORK WELL IN COLOUR FOR A BOLD, RETRO FEEL

IN TEXTURED NEUTRALS THESE CAN GIVE A REALLY LUXURIOUS VIBE

THIS REALLY POPS WITH A CONTRASTING GROUT

Flooring

Tiles

In a kitchen, the floor tile you choose is totally up to you. Some people like them loud and busy, others like them dark and glossy; some prefer them to create an illusion of space or hide marks in a high-traffic kitchen, others like them to fade into the background. Whatever you choose, here are some things to consider:

The tone

The kitchen is a busy area whose floor will naturally get dirty through the day. To buy you time between cleans, don't go for a flat-colour tile that will show dirt and streaks much quicker. Instead always opt for tiles with flecks and texture. Texture is also an excellent way to add more grip, if you feel that the floor is likely to be wet a lot. Keep grout colour in mind for the same reasons – darker grout will be better in such a high-traffic area than a pale grout that can dull over time.

Speaking of grout, the thickness can have a part to play in the overall aesthetic of your floor. Natural stone tile, for example, doesn't have even edges, which means you'll need thicker grout. If you prefer the appearance of thinner grout, a porcelain in a stone look would work better, as they are able to sit closer due to the straight edges. Rectified tiles are tiles whose edges are perfected after the kiln stage to make all the tiles the same size; this means they can sit even closer together again and use the minimum amount of grout required (underfloor heating will always require more grout).

Maintenance

A boring but very necessary consideration is the maintenance needed for your chosen floor, as there is literally no avoiding it once she is in.

A fine example is natural stone, which is porous, so needs to be sealed and have regular treatments to make sure she doesn't absorb any liquids or dirt coming into contact with her. If this sounds like too much upkeep, but you love the look, then go for something a little lower maintenance, like an imitation stone.

Size

Tile size will make a difference to how the floor looks overall, as well as the cost. You ideally want as many whole tiles as possible in the space for the best visual impact. Very large tiles are more expensive, due to their production costs, but can be cheaper overall, as they are easier to lay. If tiles need lots of cutting to fit a floor, this can increase labour costs. Large tiles can also help you pull off a poured concrete or terrazzo look, as less grout will be visible.

Small tiles can work well if you are going for a busy pattern. The more, the better! Or if you have a lot of fixtures interrupting the floor, they can be easier to install, as you'll waste less when cutting.

Durability

The kitchen floor is much harder to replace than doors, wall tiles and so on, so you want to make sure you are buying something that can stand the test of time. The Porcelain Enamel Institute (I live for a dedicated institute!) has our backs here. They have a rating system to make it easier to see how durable a tile is at a glance. They test the tile's glazing, not the tile itself, so they mostly deal with porcelain and ceramic tiles. You'll see the rating on the packaging or online description. Most interior wall tiles won't even have a rating, as they aren't designed for a floor.

Always look for the rating when shopping for tiles. Here is how it works . . .

RATING 5: HEAVY TRAFFIC OF A COMMERCIAL NATURE.
She's as durable as they come. Mostly used in places such as train stations.

RATING 4: MODERATE VERGING ON HEAVY TRAFFIC.
Able to withstand foot traffic to such an extent that it could be used in a commercial setting like a store or a restaurant.

RATING 3: MODERATE TRAFFIC.
Ideal for a kitchen.

RATING 2: LIGHT TRAFFIC.
Suited to lighter use by a barefoot gal. Think of an en suite.

RATING 1: NO FOOT TRAFFIC.
These are the kind of tiles you will have on an interior wall only. They can withstand rubbing for cleaning, but this glaze offers only light protection.

Tile alternatives

If tiling isn't your thing, there are some other great options for kitchen floors.

Vinyl

She is becoming more and more popular. She can be much nicer underfoot and not as expensive or labour intensive as tiling, but make sure she's at least 3.5mm thick or she will wear badly over time.

Solid wood & engineered wood

She can be gorgeous in a multi-use space, but water damage and warping can be an issue. If your room doesn't see too much action, she can be easily maintained.

Poured concrete

This is expensive (it could cost more than four times the price of a porcelain tiled floor) but you will get decades of use from it. I think it is a stunning addition and pretty timeless when done well. It can really work in harmony alongside older fittings, so don't dismiss it if you are not in a modern home. Concrete tiling is a more cost-effective option that can give you the look of poured concrete floors – just remember to keep the grout dark and minimal to pull it off.

Terrazzo

With the durability of concrete and the luxury of marble, terrazzo is an expensive but lovely choice. It can be poured and it also comes in blocks, or you can always go for tiles. Though an added cost, the addition of a slip-resistant glaze is a good idea here. Terrazzo will always give depth and warmth to a space and the fleck means it's easier to hide dirt through the day in a busy kitchen.

Rubber

Rubber can last for decades and can look minimal and modern in a large space. Textured rubber can also be fun if you're going for a mid-century look. You can also choose rubber tiling, which is less expensive but will still give you a great aesthetic.

Lighting

The kitchen is a room that requires different types of lighting, as it is used in so many different ways and at different times of the day. From preparing a bourguignon on Sunday evening and eating a soufflé with a lover to chopping celery for a morning juice, the right lighting can make it all the more enjoyable.

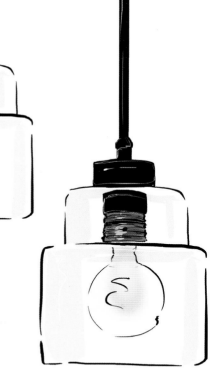

What you want to achieve is 'light layering', which plays with different types of lighting that work when used separately and also blend well together. One light you shouldn't forget to factor in is natural light. The kitchen has been designed to make use of natural light – for example, sinks in front of windows and reflective surfaces. Placing stations and items used in daytime near natural light is a clever way to make sure you get the best of it.

Task lighting

Every kitchen needs task lighting. This is used in areas where you will be prepping, chopping, cutting out mini pastry fish for the top of a pie and so on. It will be bright to allow us to see clearly and keep focused. These are best placed under wall units to illuminate the counter tops below and their kelvin should be around 4,000k plus.

Down lights

Down lights are fail-safe for kitchens. They sit neatly in the ceiling, won't require cleaning like a shaded Big Light and if dimmable can be all you need. If adding a task light is not a possibility, make sure bulbs in down lights closer to counters have a cooler temperature to help you out.

Pendants

Lighting for islands or tables should be decided at an early stage, as you'll need to be able to run power to them. Pendants are really popular for kitchens that also function as dining and living rooms, as they focus the light down onto one zone and can make the rest of the room feel 'turned off'.

For a flat island I love three large, dimmable glass pendants. When fitted with temperature changing bulbs, they can also be used for tasks and atmosphere. I prefer large pendants, as they are usually enough to light the whole surface. If the lights are too small, while they might add atmosphere to the room they won't be strong enough to light the counter space below – vital if it's also used as a prep space. If your pendants are going over a dining table, these can be lower and smaller with less spread, as it creates a more intimate affair.

Any surface up high in a kitchen will gather dust and grease, so the materials used in your pendants matter. Easy-to-remove glass bowl pendants can be soaked and wiped down every month to keep them gleaming. They won't rust like metal or absorb grease like fabric and they're also easy to tszuj if you want an update. Popping in a bronze-dipped bulb can give you a modern look, while a rustic-looking filament can suit an industrial vibe. You can also opt for a coloured bulb once they inevitably come back into style.

Plug-and-place pendants can be a great way to have a pendant without having to run wires through your ceiling. Instead they plug into a socket and can be hung from a hook above a table. Gorge. I also love rise and fall pendant lights. They can be higher and lower depending on what you want to use them for, so work great over any table or island.

Track lighting

Track lighting is something I love to use, as it means I can have one fitting installed but it can spotlight many areas. Ideal if you don't want more holes in the ceiling.

Accent lighting

In a larger kitchen accent lighting can be glorious, but it can veer into looking like a casino if overdone. I mean, not the worst of situations, but you do want to make sure that what you are highlighting is subtly adding to your vibe and not creating a whole new one. Large flat surfaces can give the feeling of space and minimal chic when lit, whereas light used to accentuate the curves of cabinetry can give a more ornate feel. You may also like to use lighting inside glass-fronted cupboards to highlight their contents.

The key with accent lighting is that she is not needed for function: she's there to delicately set a mood or tone. Go for soft, diffused light in a low kelvin that doesn't create intense shadows or take too much from the overall atmosphere.

Feature lights

You won't have to look very far to find interior advice that tells you a chandelier is simply a MUST for a stylish kitchen. A pop of glamour. While a feature light can be fabulous in a kitchen space, I can't get past the thought of being on my knees on an island unit, toothbrush in hand, scrubbing grease off each icicle. If you do go for a feature, keep her to a dining area away from cooking areas to make sure she is easy to maintain.

The kitchen sink

A sturdy bish that you will rely on heavily, it's a good thing to get right. The most common sink materials are stainless steel, composite and ceramic.

Stainless steel

Pretty straightforward and to suit most budgets and kitchens, but be sure to look at the gauge of the steel. Higher gauges will be weaker and more likely to dent, whereas something around a 16 will suit normal wear and tear. Also look out for things such as 'linen look', where the steel is embossed to mute scratches and wear. Go wild and go for gold (*screams*), black or even antique-look!

Composite

If you are looking for something low maintenance, durable, scratch-resistant, stain-resistant, heat-resistant and so on, a composite sink is for you. She is mainly made from things such as quartz and granite, which will give her a lovely finish and mean you can get a variety of looks.

Ceramic

She will mainly be a Belfast or Butler-style sink (there's an overflow hole in the Belfast – where they were less concerned about wasting water than London, the home of the Butler). Great for a heritage vibe, but she can chip, so you need to be careful with soapy hands and heavy pots.

The materials you choose will mainly be based around your aesthetic and budget, but, regardless, you need to consider her size and type.

Size

Three things come in to play here: the depth, the weight and the bowl. You need to be aware of what weight and depth your units can accommodate and what adjustments need to be made to your counter, if any. I will always go as deep as I can, rather than long and shallow. Deeper sinks are great for cleaning large roasting tins, hand-washing clothes, filling vessels and so on. A shallower sink will suit lighter tasks.

Sinks are referred to in bowls, so two sinks of the same size would be two bowls. I tend to find a 1.5 works best, as you have a second drain for when the main sink is in use, but it doesn't take up too much space. This is honestly priceless and an option you will never regret.

Type

There are three main types of sink: inset, undermounted and Belfast. Inset is dropped in to a hole with a visible rim, preventing it dropping through. These are the most standard kind of sink, but a great way to make a feature of the sink is to pick a great colour or material for her.

Undermounted means you need no rim at all, so she suits a minimal kitchen. Lastly, you have Belfast sinks. These are simply gorgeous and give an instant traditional feel to the space.

Tables & chairs

When choosing your dining set, it can be hard to know where to start. There are some pretty intense rules around the measurements of your dining table and the clearance around her. This, however, is based on people of 'average' size and assumes you have a lot of floor space in your property. Instead, I find it's best to exercise common sense around how much space each diner will need and how much you need to leave around the table and chairs to use the room comfortably. Don't forget, there is nothing stopping you pushing her in and out if space is tight. Just make sure you have furniture pads to prevent the floor scratching.

When it comes to shape, I adore the intimacy a round table brings and love that everyone can easily reach the centre at a dinner party. I also find that if you have empty chairs day to day at a round table it doesn't feel as odd as at a rectangular one. This doesn't mean a rectangular style won't always work – she can be absolutely brilliant in a long room, as she can cut out a very obvious dining zone.

Legs

Thin table legs are a great way to ensure such a large piece of furniture doesn't feel like she's taking over the room. Metal is great for this, as it's so strong it can be super slimline. It also comes in a high shine, which will make it reflective and even more minimal.

A central leg (or legs) will not limit extra chairs in the same way legs closer to the edge of the table will. These are a great option if you like to host a dinner party. Do be sure she can take the weight you intend, as a centrally placed support can be weaker.

Table top

The material of your table top is really important. The types of materials you'll find available will be pretty similar to counter tops: stones, composites, solid wood, engineered wood, metal, laminate and so on. It will be similar to a couch, in that the materials will increase the price significantly, but so will how it is put together. If you are going for an expensive table, you'll be looking for a lot of joinery and hardwoods, whereas lower priced tables will be laminate and screwed together.

Chairs

Your chairs don't need to match the table and they don't need to match each other. In fact, mismatched chairs can add a lovely charm to a dining area. Just make sure they have a high back and a wide enough seat to be comfortable. A bench on one side, against a wall, is always a great way to save on space, but have plenty of seats.

Common dining-set errors

Flat packs

If you are putting a dining table together, attach the legs while it is still in the box. You never want the table top to be on the floor during assembly, as it will scratch and dent. Don't forget to tape the tools supplied to the bottom of the table to use as the legs loosen.

Extendable tables

While you may feel like this is a no-brainer, heed my warning here. Go for a table that slides out to extend rather than having sides that lift up like wings. You see, you will most likely have the extension there for occasional use, so you need to be able to sit at it comfortably day to day. The latter style will stop you being able to pull your chair under.

Chairs

If you are adding chairs from another set, make sure they can fit under the table when they're not in use and that you can sit comfortably on them when they are. Dining chairs can come in so many widths, it is always good to double check they can be out of the way when you don't need them. The same goes for arms – always note the height in relation to the underside of the table.

A note on small kitchens

Planning a smaller kitchen can be a really satisfying project.
Here are my top tips:

- Flat surfaces are your best friend, as they work with light so well. Go for lighter colours and you'll add the illusion of much more space and natural light.
- Plan to use slimline units, such as 50cm-deep cupboards, and neater appliances. I would always recommend a 'half' dishwasher in a small kitchen, especially in an apartment with one to two beds; anything bigger can be a waste of time and money, and you'll take longer to fill a load. Same for a washer/dryer.
- Handles can take inches from your usable space. Go for something slimline or doors and drawers that just need a push to click open.
- Sliding doors are fantastic where you have minimal floor space. Folding doors are also great but can be more expensive and less durable.
- Roll-out and pull-out storage is ideal for awkward cupboards or where you don't have the clearance for full extension drawers.
- Plan a tall, thin cupboard for mops, ironing boards, clothes horses, etc. These go a long way in a small space.
- A hob with in-built extractor will give you back a whole wall unit. Just remember, this will benefit from a light fitting underneath and it needs to be suitable for steam, heat, etc.
- A clever way to optimize space is to make use of your plinths. Turning these into drawers is the perfect way to use up wasted space.
- Make sure you have plate storage up high. Most dinner plates are between 25cm and 30cm, so keep this in mind for wall units.

Kitchen linen

Before we leave, let's take a moment for kitchen linen? I love kitchen linen! She really doesn't get enough consideration.

Towels

What can we say about these girls? (*Swings over head.*) They dry, clean, wipe, protect hands from heat, waft smoke away from the smoke alarm . . . There really isn't another gal that gets quite as much use in the kitchen. We tend to go for the cheapest option, as we underestimate her importance and, of course, her different categories. Many people will have one towel they use for everything and I assure you this is not the way to go!

Dish towel

This is the towel you use to dry dishes and should *never* be used for anything else. She shouldn't hang from ovens or clean up spills and certainly should never be used to wipe hands. She needs to be a bacteria-free towel that is touching clean items only. For optimum drying, a dish towel should be cotton, but you can also use linen for more delicate glassware. The most common dish towel you will see is a terry towel. However, I prefer a soft, tightly woven cotton (usually called flour sack cloths, as it was what they were once made from), as it dries dishes immaculately without leaving streaks as terry would.

Wash your dish towels in a hot wash after one to two uses. They shouldn't stain, so it's safe to buy them in white. If they ever discolour, downgrade them to a chef's towel.

Chef's towel

Ever see a chef with a thin towel over their shoulder? These are my favourite type of kitchen towel and I find it is always great to have a rolled stack in a drawer. They are essentially what you should use instead of paper towels. You can pat down coriander after rinsing, wipe the rim of dishes before serving or grip the handle of a hot skillet. Ideally you want them to be thin and flat, so a flour sack style also works here. A chef's towel doesn't need to look pristine – most of my chef's towels are old dish towels, as it's a great way to keep using something that has lost its colour or is looking worn. *C'est bon.* These girls come into contact with food, so they end up with the most staining. I wash mine with a bio detergent on a very hot wash. The temperature will kill bacteria and the enzyme in the bio will help lift stains.

Tea towel

The tea towel got her name in the Victorian era, when serving your tea in your finest bits was a MUST. The presence of a tea towel was to avoid slips when handling expensive teapots and to stop hands getting burned. They were highly decorated to match the rest of the finery on show.

As time went on and tea customs changed, she would be the linen placed beneath pastries in a dish or folded and placed for decoration. Nowadays, she is that towel you could bring to the table that is not used elsewhere, perfect for helping serve, or lay in the bottom of a bread basket. Novelty towels are ideal here!

Hand towel

You'll need to dry your hands in the kitchen at some point and most people will have just one towel they use for everything, including this. Having read the above, I am sure you will now see the importance of a different towel for hands. A chef's towel is fine when hands are cooking, but after you have carried out other tasks and washed hands a proper hand towel in the kitchen is needed. This is where a terry-style cloth, with loops, can come in handy.

Oven mitts

I personally loathe a cloth oven mitt. This is mainly for the bacteria they harbour. They are rarely washed and are hung off the oven door, making them one of the last things I want to touch a dish, let alone my hands. They aren't great for grip and can lead to some dangerous spills. I will usually use a folded chef's towel or a silicone mitt, which is great for very hot things, like removing a Dutch oven. You can also find silicone gloves that can protect arms and hands when removing larger dishes and can be easily washed after use.

Napkins

Every kitchen should have reusable napkins and not just for 'good' use. Paper napkins are usually made from material that has been recycled many times, so it's not the worst, but it's still good to try to reduce household waste where there's an easy and fabulous alternative. Napkins are important, as they protect our outfits, furniture and lovers from a greasy paw. The first napkins were actually a soft dough that the Romans would dab their fingertips against.

When you are shopping for napkins, avoid anything with a hand wash only label if they're for day-to-day use. These are fine for special occasions, as you'll be more willing to wash well, press and box back up. What a stunning mindful moment.

Another thing to avoid for regular use is an ornate trim. Trims will fade differently from the base fabric and could leave them looking lacklustre after just a few washes. Napkins for special occasions can be as wild as your heart's content. I absolutely love a scalloped edge, and don't get me started on contrast hems or hand embroidery. Swoon!

Cotton and linen are the best options for daily use, as they are strong and durable, so washing won't damage them like it would other fabrics. They are also absorbent, which is vital. Polyester is very common now, as it holds on to colour and prints but it won't feel as nice.

Finally, check how the edges are finished. A double-turn edge is best to weight the napkin and for durability.

Cocktail napkin

These should be the most fun napkins you own. They should be a DELIGHT. They should bring a pop of colour as well as conversation. If a party has some camp cocktail napkins, I just know great things are to follow. The ideal cocktail napkin is square and 12.7cm x 12.7cm (5 in.) and is completely flat. No folds needed here. It will fit the base of almost every size of glass and it can be used to hold against the glass. Neat and chic.

Cocktail napkins are never going to endure much of a battering, so you can really go for it in terms of add-ons like trims and embroidery.

Tea napkin

A tea napkin is like an hors d'oeuvres napkin. Small enough to manage but large enough to catch a crumb. They will vary in size, but usually 30cm x 30cm folded in half will be about right. Just think about the kind of napkin that is perfect for a slice of birthday cake. These girls will wipe mouths and be left crumpled on plates, so go for linen or cotton and keep the decoration dialled down.

Dinner napkin

Dinner napkins need to be large enough to cover your lap with one fold. They need to protect clothing, as well as be available to dab a mouth or hands. If too small, you will see guests sitting more gingerly and gripping them to ensure they do not fall. To keep it relaxed and simple, go big. I have two sizes of dinner napkins. Informal affairs don't need as large a napkin, as there is usually only one course, so 40cm x 40cm works well. A dinner party with multiple courses would need 50cm x 50cm, giving the guest more cloth to use. It also gives you more space on which to place more cutlery.

Napkins are an easy way to add a little extra to a dinner party setting. (If you are starting to salivate at the mention of a dinner party like I am, there's an upcoming chapter that you'll love.) A great napkin presentation can set the tone alone. Some etiquette experts will say the napkins must match the tablecloth, but I think it's up to you. Go as wild as you please: you're the one doing the cooking.

When it comes to washing the stained tablecloth and napkins after a dinner party, it is best to leave them to soak in cold water overnight (separate colours!). This will loosen stains without setting them, as a hot soak would do. Once drained, check for stains. Rub a little washing-up liquid on them before popping them into a hot wash.

Napkin folds

Napkins are a great way to add some flair to your dining set-up. Here are some of my favourite napkin folds:

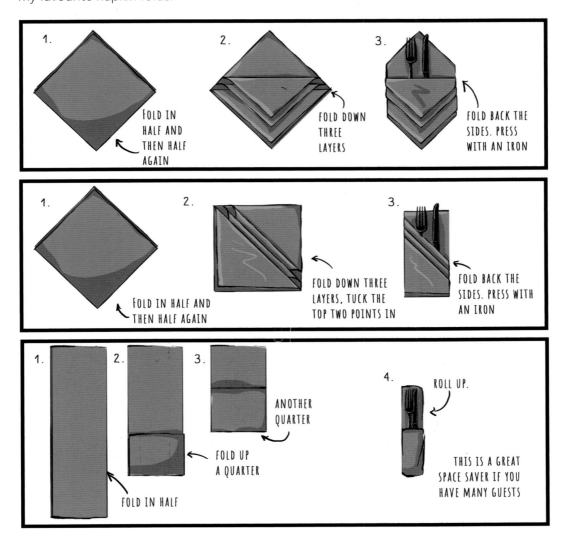

Now, let's pop our coupes down and take a strut through the hallway. She needs our attention as we sweep upstairs . . .

CHAPTER 3

HALLWAY

WHO IS SHE?

Let's stand back for a moment, shall we? We must take a little pause to assess the use of our hallway. Unlike other areas in our home, this space is impacted far more by routes, pit stops and zones, and less so by big furniture and fixings. This trio can really enhance or hamper the use and flow, and in a way hallway décor is essentially dictated by them. This is why it's a great place to start. It will ensure any changes work well with the flow and add to the use of the space.

ROUTES

The hallway is what will connect most rooms, so the routes here will be the busiest in the home. Two things that must be chosen wisely, due to the level of wear and tear she endures, are floors and walls. When it comes to hallway flooring, keep it easy to clean and durable. Material-wise, I would only advise carpets in an upstairs hall and not in the one connected to a front door, where possible. Tiling, solid/ engineered wood and poured flooring all work well here instead, as they are hard-wearing and long-lasting. Go for a fleck to hide dirt gathered through the day rather than a flat colour and consider grout colour well, if you don't want to always be cleaning it. Anti-slip is super important here to avoid slips, and keep rugs, mats and runners all fixed to avoid trips.

When choosing paint or wallpaper for a hallway, always remember what comes into contact with them frequently. Handbags, bin bags, bikes, little hands, big hands, pets, shoes, etc. A delicate paint or wallpaper just won't cut it here, but there are ways to combat the wear and tear and still serve style.

Dado, Dado

Wear and tear is why you will see a dado rail so often in a hallway. Far more than just decorative detail, they are a way to preserve the part of the wall that has to endure the most.

As lovely as it will look at first, if you decorate a busy hallway from top to bottom with an expensive wallpaper, it could end up being a nightmare. Let me give you an example. In a very large property I once managed, imported woven silk wallpaper ran through the entire main stairway, right up to the roof. I gasped when I first saw it. During one tenancy, a delightful wee tot made their way from the ground floor up to the office in the attic with two dark markers in hand, dragging a crisp, deep set of lines along the wallpaper. I also gasped when I saw this. A simple dado would have helped avoid such damage and would have looked quite gorge.

So, how exactly do you dado? For me, the ideal height is above the elbow. Anything lower is usually classed as a chair rail (from back in the days of great rooms). These were positioned at the same height as the dining chairs, which were pulled back against the walls when not in use. As well as not being practical for a hallway, they draw the eye down, making the walls look lower.

Above the dado can be as ornate and as decorative as you wish, though be careful about putting anything too precious near the door. Think about all the dust and dirt from outside, which can dull some papers and paintwork. Avoid anything that can be affected by prolonged sunlight exposure. This is why you will see some halls have the wallpaper at the top of the staircase wall rather than around the door. For the lower part, the dado, washable paints or wipeable wallpaper is ideal. As is wood panelling. If you want a period look, use tiles. I love it when the top, rail and dado all have the same tone but use different materials. It can look really severe, but elegant.

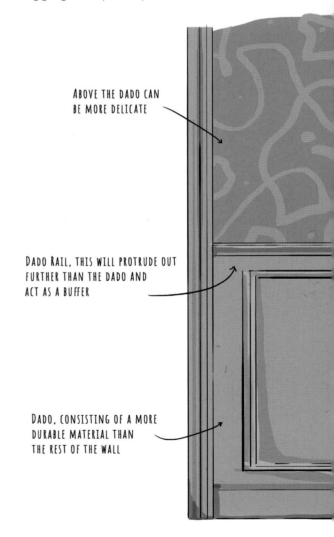

ABOVE THE DADO CAN BE MORE DELICATE

DADO RAIL, THIS WILL PROTRUDE OUT FURTHER THAN THE DADO AND ACT AS A BUFFER

DADO, CONSISTING OF A MORE DURABLE MATERIAL THAN THE REST OF THE WALL

ZONES

Most hallways, despite their size, will actually have different zones, even though we tend to think of them as one big zone in themselves. No matter what size hallway you have, a key zone is the entrance. How this is set up will really improve your departure and arrival each day. The ideal here is a slimline table with one row of drawers. This will be enough for you to pop something on temporarily but not enough to grow into a big pile. The drawers can house keys, sanitizer, accessories for commuting and anything else you use daily. Again, just enough to help you out but not enough to grow unnecessarily. If floor space is tight, go for a shelf. Above this I would opt for a mirror. Not only is it a chance for one last look before you're on your way, but hallways are one area of the home with very little natural light. A cleverly positioned mirror will bounce light through the space.

PIT STOPS

There will always be pit stops in halls, as we pass through them so often. For these to work for us and not against us, they really do need to be considered. You see, any items that lack an adequate, easy-to-use pit stop will end up as hall clutter, or indeed clutter in another room. Overloaded  hall tables, coat hooks or even floors can really impact the flow, so it is good to bear this in mind when decorating. What pit stops do you need here, and how can you accommodate them well? Before you set up a pit stop, think about when it will be used. Things we need for leaving the house should be easy to see and easy to reach to avoid a hectic rummage. Things we use at less time-sensitive moments can be housed in places that don't have as easy access. Most hallway pit stops will essentially be storage.

Under stairs

If you are lucky enough to have under-stairs storage, this is ideal for items we rarely use or for daily bits we prefer out of sight, like coats and shoes. If you are designing from scratch, consider pull-out storage instead of storage you lean in to. This will mean you can see what's inside far easier rather than only using what you can see. If you are not making any drastic changes but want to use it well, divide your under-stairs space into everyday and rarely used, with the everyday items being the easiest to reach.

Freestanding

Benches with pull-out drawers are ideal for storage in hallways, as they can house your day-to-day shoes and give you somewhere to sit when you put them on and take them off. If you do want to go for a shoe-only unit, avoid open storage, as these are almost always designed for inside cupboards and can cause scuffs on walls. If you are opting for high storage, make sure it is fixed to the wall to avoid topples. Handle-free doors and drawers are best in hallways, as they don't have anything sticking out.

Built-in

If you are going for a built-in unit, something slimline, floor to ceiling will serve you best, as it will fade into the wall and keep everything hidden from view. Even a 25cm-deep unit can be kitted out with a hook, shelving and drawer system that can house all you need.

Cupboards

People rarely make the most of their hall cupboards; instead, items will pile up inside with little to no system. You don't have to make any major changes to make them work better – even placing a shelving unit inside can create a shoe/linen/sports-equipment storage system that is easier to use. Tension rods are also a 'no screw' alternative for transforming a cupboard into a coat store.

Wall storage

Peg-board panels are a great way to create a getting-ready zone for children that can last years. You can simply move the hooks and knobs up as they grow. They can easily house schoolbags and coats for very little money or effort.

DÉCOR

Although it will rarely get much focus, a hallway is actually one of the most exciting spots to decorate. Once you have the practicalities covered around routes, pit stops and zones, it's a place where you can really go for it in terms of style.

So let's get into it!

Colour

The colours you opt for in a hallway needn't be focused around styling and you can let your wall hangings, lighting and so on do the work in that sense. Instead you can use wall colour to create atmosphere or a feeling of more space. A high-shine paint in a light colour will bounce light around to make it feel much more open, perfect if you want the light from the front door to travel further. If you have no natural light source, you can instead opt for dark tones to really offset this and achieve gorgeous depth. Again, as this is a space we dip in and out of, there is nothing to stop you being really eccentric in the hallway and playing with colour and pattern. Why not?

Your hallway is about flow; easy in, easy out. Keep this in mind with every addition and you will be just fine.

She's up the walls

It's rare to have such a large, uninterrupted wall space in a home as you get with a hallway. Usually the only things wall-mounted are radiators and the occasional entry phone or temperature dial. This gives us a perfect opportunity to inject some style into the space and make them a feature. Framed artworks or posters are a fantastic way to do this. Their low-rise nature means they won't hinder use of the hallway like a shelf would and they don't take up any floor space. They are easy to do yourself with either wall hangers or strips, if you are renting or likely to change it up often.

My favourite way to hang in a hallway is a row of A1 posters in thin black frames, as these can add a really gorgeous streamlined feel to the space. If you are looking for a less minimal touch, you could also go for a gallery wall.

MAGIC MEAUXMENT

I have a love–hate relationship with gallery walls but one space they can work well in is up a staircase or in a section of a hallway away from the entrance. These areas are not in the eyeline for long periods, so the busyness of a gallery wall can actually be ideal and really add some charm. The key to getting a gallery wall right is to decide what kind of hang you are going for.

The Organic Hang

This is when pieces are not hung in any set fashion or in rows but more organically to create an overall stunning visual display. This works really well if you have a range of sizes, as it will allow you to have fewer gaps where it looks like something is missing, giving it more of a balance throughout. Speaking of balance, it is important to work out your hang on the floor beforehand. You want to make sure, when going with an organic flow, that you are not making it too top or bottom heavy, or that the sides look uneven. Play around with it until you feel like it's aesthetically balanced. A great advantage of this gallery wall style is that you can add to it as time goes by.

The Grid

This is the style of gallery wall where you hang the same-sized frames in rows. It has a stunning visual appeal, as it instantly adds order to a room. It needs precision and dedication during the layout and hanging stage. It's up to you whether you wish to have a lot or a little space between frames. I personally find that the same width as that of the mount is a perfect visual fit. I would also make the space at the sides of the frames the same at the top and bottom. Content-wise the best grid walls you'll see are monochrome and this works particularly well for portraits.

The Organic Grid

This takes the order from the grid and the different frame sizing from the organic style. Here you will set boundaries as you would for a grid layout, but within that you can hang in a more organic way. It's best to keep the spacing the same, either vertically or horizontally, for a really great look. It can take a little work, but overall it adds a really nice finish to a room.

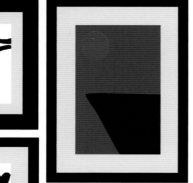

The Tonal Touch

This is my favourite style of gallery wall. It can be organic or organic grid, but its content is contained within one tonal family. The content can be anything from frames to ornaments, but it will all stick to the same variations of one to a few colours. This look can be eclectic whilst also looking chic and considered. You can also pull this off with similar imagery in different tones, for example a gallery wall of different leaves or coastal scenes works wonderfully.

LIGHTING

Lighting in hallways is usually only overhead, but this can feel a little like a fire escape if it's the only option, all the time. Just like other rooms, it is important to create atmosphere through lighting. Where possible, add a lamp, or two. The Big Light is always there if you need it, but lamps will guide you gently. Plug-in sconces are also great, if you have a socket but no surface to perch a lamp. Choose a warm white bulb rather than anything too bright. I love soft lighting in the entrance hall – it gives her that 'I'm home' feeling. Consider shades for hall lights well, even ceiling lights; go for something that can offer enough light to see well but also not cause glare by leaving the bulb too exposed.

Right, follow me. It's time to visit a space where you will spend a lot of time . . .
(*Click-clacks up the stairs and opens the bedroom door.*)

CHAPTER 4

BEDROOM

WHO IS SHE?

The bedroom! Such a unique space. How she is set up can be a true reflection of our relationship with our home and, dare I say it, ourselves. The reason I feel that this room is intrinsic to who we are and how we feel about our time at home is because the bedroom is ALL about its user/s and how they spend their private time. It is the one room where we don't have to necessarily consider a visitor's presence when setting it up; it's designed solely around us. How stunning.

Three things that impact our day to day heavily are the bedroom's routes, pit stops and zones. This is why the Min is actually one of the most effective stages here, as it's all centred around making them a joy. Zones in the bedroom will usually be for sleeping, dressing and downtime. Routes will take us to these zones and to important places like the shower in the morning or to our skincare at night. Pit stops will then decide how easy the routes and zones are to use. When we decorate or style our bedroom we should do so by enhancing our use of the room. For example, an air-purifying plant near the bed or a gloriously soft rug for your feet to touch each morning. It could be the scent of lavender pouches in drawers to greet you as you dress, or perhaps having everything easy to reach for the part of getting ready you dislike the most (drying hair, anyone?).

When I am kitting out a bedroom, be it for myself or someone else, I always start with the same shopping list. This covers the basics needed for someone to sleep, dress and relax in the space.

SHOPPING LIST

BED FRAME
SLATS, CENTRE BEAM

CONSIDER WIDTH
& LENGTH ADDED
TO MATTRESS SIZE

DO I NEED UNDERBED STORAGE?

BEDSIDE
CABINETS

A LITTLE
OVER MATTRESS HEIGHT
TO FORM BRACKETS

MIRROR,
FULL LENGTH

BEDDING
CONSIDER NATURAL LIGHT, WEAVE,
CONTENT

CURTAINS

BLACKOUT?
TRACK OR RAIL?

UNDER 3,500K
FOR NIGHT TIME

AIR PURIFYING

TRAYS UNDER
PRODUCTS

BEDSIDE LAMP

TALL, WIDE

DRAWERS

LOW ENOUGH
TO BE USED

MATTRESS

SLEEP
POSITION?

ON LEGS TO GIVE THE
FEELING OF MORE SPACE

THE MIN

As we know, the Min is mainly working with what we already have, so a great place to start for everyone is with storage.

Your storage system

How and where you store will pretty much impact the entire flow of your bedroom, so she is stop one. As we did with the living room, we first need to work with what we have, to see if we are actually lacking storage or in fact just lacking a good system. Take a step back for a moment and assess your zones, routes and pit stops. The bedroom storage system should work around all these and make them smoother. One of the main things here is to make it really simple; things you use in a zone should be close to it and things you use at the end of a route should be stored along it. An easy example is a hook for a dressing gown on the route to your bathroom instead of it being somewhere that makes you walk off it and back on again.

Clothing

The biggest storage zone you're likely to have is for clothing and accessories. If you find yourself always scrambling through drawers, no matter how neatly you've folded your clothes after a decluttering session, the problem is most likely *how* you're storing, not *what* you're storing. The first place we need to start in getting a wardrobe system going that suits you is correct grouping.

Grouping

Lay out all your clothing (this method can be applied to all accessories and cosmetics too), then group it into what you wear and when. Don't just group them by item or by colour. I know this goes against what most organizers recommend, but I think grouping by occasion is what is most important. Everyone will have different occasions: work, days off, dates, a glamorous walk, comfortable downtime. It's totally up to you what categories you have. There may be some items that work for all, so keep a group for this too.

Places

Now think about the places you have to store your clothes. Categorize into ease of use. There will be some that are super easy to access, like your rails and drawers, others that take more time to get into, such as under-bed storage. These can then be zoned into parts that are easiest and hardest to access. For example, while your wardrobe may be in the 'easy to access' category, the back and top will be harder to get to than the front of shelves or the centre of the rail. Whatever is at the front of your under-bed storage will be easier to slide out than what's at the back, and so on.

Placement

It is now time to store. Match your 'easy to access' storage with garments you need to get to in a hurry and save the 'harder to reach' parts for garments whose occasions have less time pressure or for overspill, like out-of-season clothing. That sharp-shouldered Alaïa dress will rarely be grabbed in a rush, so you can pop her to the side of a rail. Allocating according to access will hand you back some serious time each week. For example, I like my work and everyday clothing to be in my 'easy to access' zones, as it gives me more time to spend on my much-loved morning routine. It will also help you wear your clothes more, and when you shop your selections will be more considered, as you will be more aware of what you need.

Extra storage

Once you have everything in place, it will be easier to see what kind of storage you are lacking. If you are low on easy to access storage, fabric shoe-storage hangers to pop on the inside of the wardrobe doors or room doors are fantastic for spaces with minimal easy-access storage. They can host anything from socks and hair straighteners to belts and, of course, shoes. They utilize an unused, easy to reach area and make getting ready a breeze.

If you are lacking in hanging storage, tension rods can easily add other rails for shorter items like skirts and tops. If hanging in general is an issue for you and you – no judgement here – cannot for the love of Christ ever hang up your clothing right away, even with copious amounts of hangers and ample easy to access rails, there is a solution. Apply hooks to the inside of your wardrobe doors. You'll be far more likely to hang the clothes you've slipped out of from these hooks, and once you close the door they disappear from view. You can then face them the next morning or at the weekend and hang correctly. It is far better for your clothes and your headspace to keep clothing off the floor.

Cosmetics storage

Your products will usually be divided into ones you like on display and ones you like out of sight. For the ones you like to see, drawer units in a bedroom will usually be low enough to be able to create a dressing table or open storage for cosmetics you use often. Just be sure to protect the surface. Many will contain oils that will cause damage, so something non-porous like a metal or mirrored tray will be a both stunning and practical move. For the stuff you want more hidden, use the floor of the wardrobe. A small set of lightweight drawers here can be ideal. I would look at something like under-desk drawers, as these are usually really affordable and compact. The top can be used for you to stack handbags or shoe boxes.

Bedside storage

Anything you need in the sleep zone should be in your bedside unit, so both hidden and exposed storage is key here. I also find this a great spot to have a 'pre-sleep' zone. Just a little area on the unit top where you can do some soothing self-care to help you drift off. This can house calming oils to sprinkle on your pillow, a night cream or perhaps a lip balm. This will encourage you to do something soothing before you turn out the light.

Shoes

Before we leave storage, I want to talk about something I am asked so frequently about: shoe storage. Shoes need a little more thought before they are put away.

Storage prep

- Always clean shoes before you store them. A wipe-down of the areas your foot was against and a spot clean will do fine.
- Shoes should be completely dry before storage. So ideally you will give them twenty-four hours before you pack them away. All feet sweat, so this allows the moisture gathered to be released. Cedar shoe-trees are a way to dry them out quicker, as these draw out moisture.
- Remember to keep the shoes' shape in storage. Acid-free tissue is ideal here and can be molded to keep straps from creasing.

Shoe storage

- Don't store shoes in plastic long-term: they need to breathe. Instead, if you must use under-bed storage, for example, pop your everyday shoes in there, as it will be opened frequently and avoid mould or damp getting in.

- Shoe bags are designed to stop shoes rubbing against each other during travel. They also prevent colour transfer and protect your clothes from footwear within your suitcase. Don't store shoes in a bag within their box, as this will restrict airflow. Choose one or the other. Fold the dust bag on top of the shoes before the lid goes on to offer added absorption, if needed. Finally, don't use a polyester or plastic dust bag. You want natural, breathable fabrics, such as cotton.

- The best way to store an expensive shoe is in its original box, with tissue-stuffed toes, a silica gel packet to absorb moisture and the paper they came with.

- I'm not too fond of open shelving when it comes to shoe storage. Store-like set-ups are becoming more popular in homes, but these can leave shoes and bags exposed to things that are not great for them in the long term. Dust is one issue, but light is another. Artificial lighting around shelving can cause some materials to discolour or to yellow, and the heat can dry out the glue. One tip is to display shoes suited to that season only, as these will be worn most and prevent a build-up of dust and light exposure.

- Airing your occasional-wear shoes is also vital. Every time I swap out some summer and winter clothes I will also take out all my shoes and open the boxes. This allows them to breathe and I can inspect them to make sure all is well. When I strip my bed, I also leave my wardrobe open, so it breathes all day like my mattress. Leave the window open (unless it's pouring rain) or have your ventilation on high. The ultimate way to air your shoes is to wear them. Saving something for the right occasion or very rare occasions can actually mean the glue dries and becomes brittle. You don't even have to wear them out. If that's not an excuse for a heel over a bowl of granola, I don't know what is.

- It is often recommended that you stick a Polaroid of the shoe on the outside of the box, but what if your boxes are two deep? Instead, place the Polaroids on the inside of the wardrobe door with numbers. This way you can see what you have at a glance when choosing outfits and then find the box with the corresponding number. You can then also arrange the Polaroids in order of specific wear, like summer, occasion, etc.

Lighting

Bedroom lights are something we have to get right. Think about the impact they have on our lives. If we have the correct lighting before bedtime, when getting ready or even when working out, it will benefit us greatly.

Bedside lighting

Bedside lighting is a must. Having only the Big Light in a bedroom means we get bulb glare when trying to relax in bed and the trip to turn off the light each night will also hamper a smooth transition to the land of nod. A simple click into darkness is much smoother. If you have lamps already in place, opt for a bulb in the range of 2,700k to 3,500k. If you read often in bed, you'll want it on the higher side. If you do not have bedside lighting yet, I have her covered in more detail in the Tszuj.

Ceiling lights

Bedroom ceiling lights are best with a shade that covers the entire bulb and softly diffuses the light. This means, no matter where you are in the room, it's not going to bother you. It's a small but very effective change. Just remember to use an LED here for safety.

Accent lighting

One of the biggest treats you can give yourself in a bedroom, especially if you spend a lot of time in it, is accent lighting. I'm not talking about a string of fairy lights over a bedframe. Accent lighting creates ambience and a peaceful atmosphere rather than accent fittings, like in a kitchen. This can be as simple as lighting up a little alcove or corner for you to chill in, or you can opt to position light behind a mirror or furniture for a more diffused glow.

Task lighting

There will be tasks you need to do in your room, such as dressing, putting away laundry, working at a desk and so on. Lighting these areas can be a great way to separate different zones. Stick-on strip lights can be a glorious addition to a wardrobe or set of drawers. They highlight the contents as you open to help you see what's inside. Make these kelvins higher than the rest of the room.

Making your bed

Something else that can really enhance our bedroom, with literally no spend, is how we make our bed. Really. If you want to keep your sheets feeling and smelling fresher for longer, it's all in the way you leave your bed each morning.

While most people assume the best way to do so is dressed like a hotel bed, this method only really suits clean bedding. When we sleep, we shed skin, we sweat, we drool. Once we get out, the skin particles and bacteria, as well as odours, need a chance to be released. If you pull your duvet immediately back over that warm spot you just left, you're baking the baddies into the fibres and filling, and this is what causes bed linen to lose freshness and bedding, such as duvets, to hold odours.

Here is something you can do while your SPF dries each morning to ensure a fresher bed for longer:

- Pull back your duvet. Stand to the side of the bed where you slept and unhook your sheet from the top corner. Grab some of the side, too, and lift her up and shake vigorously. You will see dust come right off her. As fibres trap and absorb, this is a moment to release. Pop the sheet back in its corner and grab your pillows.
- Pillows need to be shaken and puffed after use to prolong their life. But there is another aim: all night you were breathing into that girl, so you want to get that stale air out. Pat her, fluff her and plump her up. Bonus points for flipping her in the air like pizza dough.
- Shake out your duvet, then fold it at the end of the bed. This will let parts of the duvet and sheet that were against your stunning body all night have a chance to breathe, air and release whatever else they need to.

THE TSZUJ

For this section, I want you to keep two things in mind as we discuss additions you can make: texture and colour. In a bedroom, we can use both to enhance our experience of the space. The colours of the bedroom need to make you go 'Ahhhhhhhh' when you walk in, lie down, get up. The pitch, however, is up to you. You may want it to be almost a relaxed sigh and go for whites, or an elated scream and surround yourself in hot pink. When in doubt, keep your base in neutrals. Pops of colour can be added later with less commitment.

For texture, this needs to encourage calm and comfort. Before you purchase anything new for the bedroom, consider its texture, both how it feels and how it looks. If you're going for a rug to soften hard flooring, why not make it feel like standing on a cloud. What a start to the day! If you cannot change walls or fittings you dislike, add a distraction through texture with macrame, tapestries or a large canvas in neutral colours to give warmth and depth instead of flatter alternatives that have no texture or fabric interest.

Layering with texture also looks great. Use knitted throws, cushion covers with prominent weaves, rattan plant pots, a sheer panel behind your curtains, layered rugs and so on. This will all create calm, but it will also help absorb sound and keep in heat.

The Tszuj here is all about enhancing the zones and their use, instead of just visual appeal. One of the first things you will see when you enter a bedroom is bed linen, so this is a great place to start.

Bed linen

Glorious, glorious bed linen.

Why does some bed linen cost over a grand and some under a tenner? How can you feel like you're floating in a milkshake with some, and with others like you've wrapped yourself in a sheet of sandpaper? Most of all, why does no one explain it in a simple way? Ring the bell, class is in session! Here is what you need to understand about the buzzwords on bed linen packaging.

Thread count

Thread count refers to the number of threads per square inch on a fabric.

Why does this matter?

Showing how many threads can fit in a square inch is a way to show off the yarn quality. Only a high-quality yarn can realistically be very thin, as she is strong and can stand alone. This means you can fit more high-quality yarn in each inch, giving you a high thread count. Inferior yarn is always thicker, as it will snap unless it's twisted with more yarn, so you'll get less in a square inch, giving you a lower thread count.

So, this applies to all types of thread?

No, thread count only really applies to cotton. If you see thread count on a pack of sheets that contain polyester, it's merely there for marketing. Polyester can be created super thin to achieve a higher thread count but that doesn't make it a better quality fabric for bed linen. Linen is almost the opposite – she has a naturally thicker yarn, so her thread count will inevitably be lower. Only pay attention to thread count on 100 per cent cotton sheets.

Why does the integrity of the cotton matter?

If you use a high-quality cotton, more of the cotton is exposed, making it softer to the touch, far more absorbent and more breathable. Ideal for bed linen.

So, the higher the thread count, the better?

Actually, no. This is where you can get swindled. There is a limit to the number of good quality threads that can actually exist in a square inch for it to be effective as bed linen. Most bedding experts say that a good quality cotton sheet will have a thread count of 300–500, as you still need the cotton to be breathable. Anything that's 600-plus should have you looking over your cat-eye spectacles with a raised brow. An inferior cotton on the loose.

Is low ply always best?

Ply will tell you how many yarns have been twisted together to make the thread. Only high-quality cotton can realistically be 1 ply. Single ply is your gal because, aside from a great hand feel, twisting cotton actually makes it less absorbent and also less breathable. Now here is where some tricks can also get played. Some manufacturers will produce a sheet that is 3 ply with 250 threads per inch and call it a 750 thread count. You have been warned.

Weave

The weave of your bed linen is another factor that can affect quality and price. There are two main high-quality weaves: percale and sateen. Why are these weaves better quality than a standard weave? Well, they can only really be achieved with a long staple (high quality) yarn. This is why they are used in more expensive bedding.

Sateen has the advantages of satin without the fragility. She feels silky, soft and dense. A sateen weaves four (sometimes three) over and one under, which exposes more of the thread surface and ensures this satin touch. Two sateen-weave, 300–400 thread count Oxford pillow cases are the greatest gift you can give to your bed, especially if you like to read. They are so soft but also structured to lean against and won't wrinkle in the same way as others.

Percale is soft, but not as soft or dense as sateen. She is better for people who get hot at night and need extra breathability. To achieve this, she is like a basket weave, so one thread over, one under. She's often likened to a good shirting material, so that's how I always remember her: as long-lasting, breathable, light.

Overall, if you were going to buy linen to match seasons, sateen is perfect for winter and percale for summer. Don't be too turned off by percale's hand feel in store; she actually gets softer as she is washed.

Other fabric options

Linen

This girl doesn't get a whole load of coverage when it comes to bedding, but she is quite a versatile choice. She is cooling in summer and has a natural warmth in winter. This also means that if you share a bed with someone who has a different temperature preference to you, in linen you both get what you need, more so than with other fabrics. She is actually more durable than cotton and is bacteria-resistant. If you are an allergy queen, she could be your ideal match. She is also a stunner if you are not into ironing, as she is best un-ironed and left naturally creased. This relaxed, boho vibe is actually quite gorgeous in a minimal bedroom (avoid in a cluttered room).

Polycotton

This is a blend of polyester and cotton. The synthetic fibres mean it's easier to iron and is more durable, while the natural fibres give some breathability and absorbance. I recommend making sure it's at least 50 per cent cotton. Pure polyester will feel rougher on the skin longer term, even if it feels soft in the store, as a finish is usually applied that washes off.

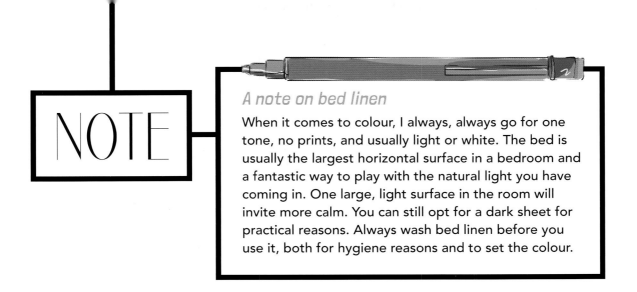

NOTE

A note on bed linen

When it comes to colour, I always, always go for one tone, no prints, and usually light or white. The bed is usually the largest horizontal surface in a bedroom and a fantastic way to play with the natural light you have coming in. One large, light surface in the room will invite more calm. You can still opt for a dark sheet for practical reasons. Always wash bed linen before you use it, both for hygiene reasons and to set the colour.

Bedside

A great bedside set-up is essential. If you are looking to add some styling and interest to a bedroom, this is ideal. There are two main elements here: the bedside light and bedside unit. Together these offer some needed punctuation to the sides of the bed and help to establish the boundaries of your sleeping zone. A lesser element I always include is some sort of framed artwork above the lamp. Not only will this stretch the boundary right up the wall, it also makes use of a free space in the bedroom that is rarely used. Fuss on the bedside walls is also better than other areas, as it's to your back when you are sitting in bed.

Height

For bedside units, an ideal height is between the level of your mattress and one pillow high. This will help with all bedside needs and tasks. You want the lamps to be tall. In luxe bedrooms, height here is almost expected and the more drama the better. If your room is otherwise plain or you cannot do much to change it, two belters of bedside lamps can bump the taste level up several notches.

One thing to watch with height: make sure you don't get bulb glare when sitting or lying down.

The shade of it all

When it comes to shades, ask yourself what you want your lamp to do before purchasing. Opaque shades will give you more light. If you have a large room, it will throw enough light for bedside activities, as well as for you to be able to safely navigate your way to the bathroom at 3 a.m. If the room is smaller, or multi-use, a shade that is dense will throw light above and below, which keeps the focus on the bedside and allows you to just 'switch on' the bed zone. Always ensure the shade is wide enough to light the whole unit top.

Distance

There is a lot of talk about the distance your lights should be from your bed and how far apart sconces should sit, etc. For me, the only rule is that you should be able to easily reach the switch from a sitting and lying position, and there should be no bulb glare. If you have no space for a table lamp next to your bed, you can still make sure you get the benefits of one. Clip-on lights that can slot onto your bedframe or a wall-hanging light that plugs in are both great options. If you lack the floor space for bedside units, consider alternatives like those that are held in place by your mattress or wall-hung units.

Curtains

Window dressing in a bedroom is about so much more than aesthetics. It can determine the hours you sleep and the temperature of the room, as well as adding a sense of space if done correctly. For this reason, I find curtains best, as they can help you achieve it all.

Before you think about curtains, you need to consider what they will hang from. A ceiling track is my ultimate preference. LOVE! You can cover from floor to ceiling with your curtain and literally shut the outside off. Zero light leakage. So relaxing. They also give height to the room, as the curtains are hung as far above the window line as possible. You don't have as much faff with a ceiling track, but you need to make sure the curtain weight matches the track. Anything too heavy will be a disaster.

For curtain rails, minimal is always better. Our eye almost always goes to the rail if it's busy, so keep the fuss to a minimum. Many people will place rails a mere 5cm from the top of the window, but this will do nothing for the room. Hang them as high as you can to make the walls feel longer and to add a more luxurious feel. Be it track or rail, ensure your curtains don't cover

the window when open. Blocking natural light is a no-no, and it also makes the windows look smaller.

Fabric

There are two things to consider when buying fabric: light and heat. If there is too much light coming in or too much heat going out, curtains are a brilliant quick fix. In fact, blackout curtains can help with both. It is such a dense fabric it is excellent at both blocking out the morning sun that can overheat a room and wake you up in the summer and keeping cold air out in the winter.

You can get curtains that are just all one layer of blackout fabric or they will have blackout lining behind the main layer. For optimum draught exclusion, go for curtains that are lined with a thermal layer as well as blackout. These are really great for single glazing. You can also buy these linings separately to add to curtains already in place.

Colour

The big thing to watch with curtains is colour fading. Especially patchy fading. For this reason, a neutral colour is always a good move. Fading will not be as obvious, and if your walls are light they will fade into the background and let the eye focus elsewhere. Keeping the curtains neutral will also help them to stay around for longer. Speaking of timeless curtains, I avoid grommet, tab and visible rings, as all of these tend to date the curtains themselves. You want a simple, neat finish to the top to ensure they can stick around. It also stops too much light flowing in.

Curtain crisis

My curtains are too light

If you have curtains in place that are too light in weight but function pretty well otherwise, you can do a simple but effective update. Blackout lining can be bought by the metre and is easy to find, so you can make your own lining. If you can't sew, you can buy blackout slips that are already hemmed and ready to be hung from your curtain. They come with clips to secure the lining to the curtain tape and make it look seamless.

My curtains are too short

I personally LOVE a panelled curtain. It's an easy way to transform the vibe of a short set. You can go for a completely contrasting shade or pick up a tone in the pattern. My only advice with these is to make sure you find a fabric of similar weight.

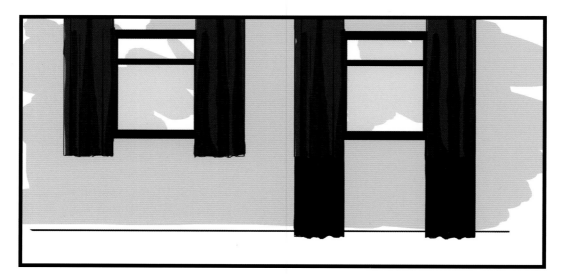

My curtains are vile

If you cannot change the curtains, for whatever reason, you can do a really cheap and easy update. Hand tack (a loose stitch) your preferred fabric over the original curtain to give her a new lease of life. It's kind of like putting a great coat over a bad outfit. No one will ever know. At the end of your lease, or when you get a new pair, you can just unpick the tacking stitch and they will be back as they were before.

For the best application, lay the new fabric wrong side up on the floor, then the curtain wrong side up on top. Cut the fabric so it leaves 10cm on the top and sides and 20cm on the bottom. Iron back a double hem (5cm, then 5cm) of the fabric, so it folds over the curtain, and do the same with the bottom (10cm, then 10cm). This gives a heavier hem, which is better. Once you are happy it is all in position, pin and then hand tack.

DIVAN DRESS UP

One of the quickest ways to give a divan base a tszuj is to wrap it. You can buy elasticated wraps that come in many different fabrics – ideal, if you are renting. If you have drawers in your divan, wraps are out as they prevent access, so choose a valance sheet. Don't go for the flouncy options; go for sharp box pleats and a textured fabric for a high-end feel. I love an oatmeal linen – it's chic and adds to a room rather than looking like a cover-up.

Almost every divan base will come with two large screws at the back for a headboard to slide on and sit in place. This is an instant way to bring the bed to the next level. Complement or match the wrap or valance sheet and consider the overall look of the room. If you are trying to make it look bigger, go light, as it will fade into walls.

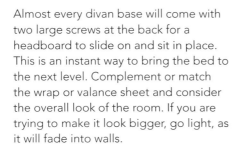
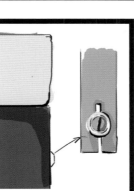

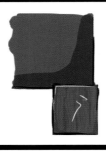

If you are tight on storage, being able to access under the bed is a major plus. Divan raisers will not only look great, they will give you enough room for some low-rise storage to slide underneath. Ideal for accessories or shoes. It's also a great way to make the room feel a little bigger, as you get a peek of the floor underneath. Wooden blocks are the sturdiest option. You will usually need to remove the wheels, but this is easy. Either a twist or pull.

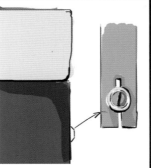

THE OVERHAUL

When bigger changes can be made to a bedroom, they will usually involve the bed, mattress and built-in storage. Daunting items indeed, but we can make it simple (*crosses legs, clicks fingers*).

The Bed

Our precious bed. Not only is she a centrepiece of the room décor-wise (I mean, there's no avoiding this, look how big she is!), but she is also a centrepiece in our lives. She is where we dream, where we stream on a Saturday morning, where we cry with heartache, lay our heads after life-changing days, and she always welcomes us, no matter what, or who, we bring with us. I am a firm believer that if we acknowledge how much our bed really is there for us, come rain, shine or PMS, we will set her up just right.

This gal was originally put in place to raise us from the floor and out of harm's way from damp, rodents and insects. She has come a long way from the days of grass and hay. She is an important element in the home and was once such an expense that noblemen would not leave her behind when moving from manor to manor. She was, at one time, considered such an asset that she featured in wills. On this point, not much should have changed. A bed frame really should last a lifetime, but our need for change and the cheaper materials now used in some frames means this is no longer very likely. However, as with all furniture, if we buy nice, we won't need to buy twice.

Placement

Getting the placement right is the first step to getting the most out of your bed and the bedroom itself. You will normally have two sockets on one wall, around six feet apart, for your bed to sit between, so lighting and charging is a cinch. This usually makes it obvious where the headboard should go. If you have a smaller space or no sockets, try to get your bed to face the door as much as possible. It adds to a calmer feel if you nod off in this position and it looks good too. Beds in guest rooms, for me, don't need to be centrally placed. It's the bed that is spare, not the room, so I feel you can use the space much better when the bed is to the side.

Size

Your placement will dictate what size of bed you can go for, but you should also make sure all doors can open as needed and that you include your skirting boards when measuring. Those extra few millimetres can really make a difference, so take in anything else that could push the bed out from the wall, such as sockets or radiators.

Bed sizing can differ around the world, so it is always worth checking the size guide if you are buying online. You may have heard some rules relating to bed size – that the recommended bed length is 10cm longer than the tallest person using it, or the minimum width for a couple sharing should be a king – however, you may want to use the floor space for something else, and smaller beds can, in fact, be better for intimacy. It's really down to you.

UK and IRE sizing

	Length	Width
Single	6ft 3in. / 190cm	3ft / 90cm
Small double or queen	6ft 3in. / 190cm	4ft / 120cm
Standard double	6ft 3in. / 190cm	4ft 6in. / 135cm
Standard king	6ft 6in. / 200cm	5ft / 150cm
Super king	6ft 6in. / 200cm	6ft / 180cm

One key note here: these sizes are for the mattresses; there are no standard sizes for bed frames. So when you see 'double bed frame', this means the frame will fit a double mattress, but the frame itself will sit around that, so it will be bigger. Always check the bed frame's dimensions. Some will add on 80cm to the length, for example, like a roll-front velvet number. Others will add just a few centimetres. Smaller frames are usually metal: as they are so sturdy, they can afford to be slimline. Many people will opt for a slim metal frame to get a larger mattress into the space rather than a thicker frame which hosts a small mattress. The choice is yours.

Bed frame

I'm not saying a bed frame should last you so long you'll be penning it into your will at ninety-eight, but if you buy well, it will last you decades. Your mattress, and parts such as slats, can be swapped out when they wear, but the frame itself should be able to stand the test of time. They can pretty much be broken into two categories: bedsteads and divans.

Bedstead

This is the most common type of bed frame. It's the one that a mattress will sit into, on top of slats and a mid-beam that runs down its centre. They are mainly made of metal or wood and either left exposed or covered with padding and fabric. The most expensive frames will be solid wood, featuring joinery and wooden dowels, while cheaper beds will be glued and screwed. In the mid-range, usually good quality metal fastenings and wooden dowels are used. Cheaper frames are fine in a guest room, but they can end up breaking and adding to your contribution to landfill within a couple of years if you buy one as your main bed. In general, if you see a bed whose price looks too good to be true, it probably is.

There is one failsafe way to spot a cheaper frame if you cannot suss the joints easily. Many high-street beds will feature really on-trend elements that cost more to produce, such as an upholstered back, velvet fabric, storage, etc. So, to lower the overall production cost they will have cheaper frames that need additional support in the form of a little leg propping up the mid-beam. A double frame should be strong enough without a central floor support, so I would always avoid a frame that has a leg underneath the slats.

Divan

The dreaded D-word. The landlord bed. When I say divan, the first thing most people think of is a cream brocade-effect base and matching mattress. While that style is very much still readily available, the increase in popularity of fabric bed bases means you can get some stunning divans now. They can really become a feature in the room in a bold velvet, or melt into a light carpet in a flecked oatmeal. They can also be a great option for small rooms.

No extra space is taken up with this type of frame, as the base is flush with the mattress. This means you can have a king divan in the same space as a wooden double.

Divans can come with some clever storage options, such as Continental (half) drawers to accommodate for bedside tables; sliding doors, if you have no clearance for drawers; and drawers on just one side, if the bed is up against a wall. If you really want to make use of the bed base, go for an ottoman bed, which is like a divan but the mattress lifts up and there is storage space underneath.

One thing to note is that mattresses wear out faster on divans, so go for a spring base, if you can, as it will last longer.

Whichever frame you choose, you need to decide early on if you want the bed to be a feature or a whisper in the room's overall aesthetic. If you have a set style, committing to a feature bed won't faze you. If you know that you like to change it up every few years, go for something more subtle. A bed that has a lower headboard and minimal frame will allow you to dress it to your taste at the time. It's much easier to style a room using bedding on a minimal frame than to try to work with one that is out of date. The height is also something to consider. I personally like a mid-sized bed: too low won't be the best for getting in and out long term, and they are harder to perch on when adjusting a slingback. High beds can really overpower a room and hide much of the floor, making it feel smaller.

Mattress

There is always that worry of getting this wrong and sleeping uncomfortably for years to come. But do not fear, once you are armed with what you need to know, you'll be able to wipe out two-thirds of the options at a glance and can focus on finding the right mattress within your budget.

What is in a mattress?

One of the main factors that affects how a mattress will perform, last and support is her composition: both her core and any filling on top. Technology and material development mean that mattresses have come a long way. Now, you can have one to suit your every sleeping need, from your preferred position and temperature to the allergies you have.

There are three main categories when it comes to what's inside your mattresses. They are spring, foam or hybrid, which is a combination of both.

Spring

Coil

Open coil or continuous coil are types of spring mattress. As with couch suspension, inside is a system of springs, either made from individual coiled springs tied together with one wire or a set of coil springs all made from one wire. This means that when you move, the system moves with you. For this reason, she is not great if you are sharing a bed, as you can end up rolling into your partner when the mattress dips or waking when they move, as you will move too.

As it is just a coil system inside, with some webbing on top, she is very lightweight and pretty affordable. She will be the mattress you usually see with an entry-level divan. As she isn't the most supportive and can wear out faster, she's most suited to a guest room. As she begins to wear, the coils will start to fail, causing dipping.

Pocket sprung

This is a step up from coil. With this type of mattress, each coiled spring sits within individual fabric pockets. The springs can then move separately to support the contours of the body. This style of spring mattress will last a lot longer than an open or continuous coil mattress, due to less wear during use. You also won't have the problem of the entire mattress moving when one person adjusts their position.

Hybrid will be a mix of both pocket sprung and coil. The pocket sprung layer will be closest to the top of the mattress for optimum comfort. No matter which type of spring mattress you have, she will need to be flipped often to avoid wearing out the coils in specific areas. They are also very breathable – just think of all that air inside. This means they are great if you like to be cool at night and find foams make you overheat. The downside is that coils may dip over time and once these go it will affect the quality of the support.

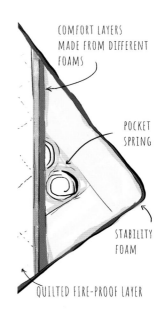

COMFORT LAYERS MADE FROM DIFFERENT FOAMS

POCKET SPRING

STABILITY FOAM

QUILTED FIRE-PROOF LAYER

Foam

Memory foam

Did you know that memory foam was developed for NASA? It was originally designed to improve seat cushioning and crash protections in aircraft, then it went on to be used in both medical and sports equipment, including the lining of professional American football players' helmets. It's an advanced type of foam that reacts to body heat. This is why it became an instant hit in the mattress world. As your body's heat is absorbed by the mattress, you'll notice that the foam softens and moulds itself to the contours of the body. Once you get out of bed and it starts to cool down, the foam moves back into its original shape. It used to be called 'slow spring-back foam' for this very reason.

The benefits of memory foam are many. Foams in general are better for those who suffer from allergies (except latex, of course). It can allow two sleepers to remain unaffected by each other's movements and can mould to any contour, unlike a spring mattress, which will only dip so far. This foam is quite cold at first, so it is great to climb into if you love that icy-sheet feeling. However, once she warms up, she is much warmer than other mattresses. This girl isn't suited to someone who sleeps hot. Many people will buy fans, leave windows open, change their duvets, but it may be that the mattress generating heat around their body is the problem. If you currently have a memory foam mattress which you have just realized is the source of your sweaty woes, there are things you can do. Don't use any polyester in your bedding, as it will trap heat. A cooling mattress topper will also help. Toppers don't change the support of the mattress, they just affect the comfort levels, so choosing one to sit between you and the memory foam is a great way to cool down. Make sure this is also made of natural fibres for breathability.

Latex

Latex foam comes in two varieties, natural or synthetic. They can be more expensive, as they are more costly to produce, but if you are looking for the contour support of foam without the deadening feel of memory foam, then latex is a more buoyant option. Latex mattress manufacturers also claim that she will last longer, backed up by lengthy guarantees. Certain brands also offer biodegradable mattresses that come from a renewable source.

Latex doesn't get either as hot or as cold as memory foam, as she is not controlled by body temperature.

You can also find synthetic latex mattresses that offer similar qualities to the real deal for less cost. These are obviously not eco gals.

Polyfoam

This combines a few different densities of cheaper foam to make a mattress that can support the body easily. They are not as durable or long-lasting as memory or latex, but that is reflected in the price. You will see a lot of poly as a top layer in cheaper mattresses.

Hybrid

A hybrid mattress combines springs and a variety of foams. They usually have a bottom layer of springs with a core of high-performing foam. These hybrid mattresses try to offer more than what you can get from a straight foam or spring mattress. This means you can find a lightweight or breathable mattress, along with great support.

Firmness

Don't be fooled into thinking that a firmer mattress means higher quality. Firmness is more about preference and sleeping position.

Coils, tense. Foams, dense. This is how I remember how firmness works in both foam and spring mattresses. Springs will have coils with a thicker gauge, be wound tighter and there will be more of them for a firmer mattress. Foam will have different levels of density deciding its firmness. The firmer the mattress, the more support it will give to certain sleep positions. What you're looking for is a mattress that will allow your spine to remain in a neutral position.

You don't need to actually sit on a mattress to know how firm it is. There's a scale for that. Mattress firmness is measured on a scale of 1–10, with 1 being the softest and 10 being the firmest. A medium-soft mattress starts around 3 or 4, medium-firm is around 5 or 7, and very firm is 7-plus.

Side sleepers would benefit from a medium-soft mattress: one that's soft enough to allow their hips to sink in, while keeping their spine neutral. Front sleepers will need a medium-firm mattress to ensure that the contours of the body can be supported. A medium-firm to firm mattress works better for back sleepers, as their weight is spread out. If you tend to sleep in different positions, go for a mattress that suits the position you sleep in for longest. For a mattress that'll work for two different types of sleeper, stick with a medium-firm. You can always top it with something softer, if you wish.

Testing

In store

If you have the opportunity to indulge in a test drive, be sure to do it well. Many people will make the effort of getting to a mattress showroom (they are never easy to get to) but have no idea how to test them properly. I get that lying down on a bed in a shop feels weird. Of course it does. I don't think we are designed to just lie down in front of strangers, out of pure cave-girl safety instincts, but you'll be fine in a warehouse on the side of a motorway. It is honestly sillier to buy the wrong bed for yourself than it is to lie on your side in a shop. Own it, henny.

The million times I have walked through a bed showroom, I see the same thing. People will gingerly perch on the edge of a mattress. Coat on, of course, sometimes even their bag. They'll do the sit, bounce and pat. Some will even go to the trouble of a horizontal test. Lie on their back, still in a restrictive coat, staring at the ceiling, moving their hands as if making a snow angel.

Ask yourself, have you ever done this once in your actual bed? The answer is no. Unless you plan to start sleeping in these positions, you need to test her correctly. Slip off that stunning trench, get someone to hold your bag and lie in the position you sleep in. Do not be mortified. How does that feel? Does your spine feel neutral? If you are really into this, there is nothing to stop you getting someone to take a pic, so you can analyse your spine's position. You could even wear a vertical stripe top as a guide, if you want to be really extra.

You also need to turn over. I mean it. Whenever I see someone turning over in a bed showroom, I think 'she knows'. Testing correctly can save you money, always a great look. When you are turning, note how it feels and if that is OK with you. It's a lot easier to turn on a sprung mattress than on something like memory foam. For some people, a difficult turn is a no-no. The effort or even the bounce can be taxing on their body. If you do a lot of reading, even on your phone, pop yourself into that position. Should you have the person you may be sharing this mattress with beside you, you need to test at the same time. Lastly, you need to note what it's like to get in and out. This can be something that will cause stress on the body when it doesn't need to.

Online

The great thing about most 'bed in a box' mattresses is that they usually have a stunning return period. So you can unbox, let it rise, test it out for a week or so – some you can try for several months. This is a great way to test a bed properly.

Any great mattress company will give you in-depth info into the mattress you are considering. In my experience, if there are not many details on what is in it, you don't want it. If you are going for a more expensive spring, these don't tend to roll up very well, so be wary of any spring that is rolled up and very costly. Bed in a box mattresses are usually one-sided, which means you can't turn them. Some companies say this makes them less durable; however, if made of the right stuff, they will last longer than a poorly made flippable option, so don't go on flippability alone.

When opening any rolled mattress make sure it is already on the bed, as these unfold really quickly and can literally spring out. There should be directions on the packaging for what part of the packaging to cut but, I guarantee you, someone has that exact mattress unboxing on YouTube, which is always handy to watch first.

A bed in a box will usually need twenty-four to seventy-two hours to rise, depending on its content. This is because all the air is sucked out of the foam for transport. Once you unbox, it will start to rise again, as it fills with air. If you have no other option, it is safe to sleep on your mattress before it rises. It won't be at its most comfortable when not fully expanded, but you won't be doing any long-term damage to it.

Mattress topper

Though they won't drastically change the level of support provided by your mattress, toppers are pretty amazing. They can help you tweak a mattress already in place to your preference. These are great for rentals, as you can make some minor changes to the way the mattress feels without any major drama. Some toppers can be as expensive as a mattress, so make sure you know what you want from it. Is it to cool down the bed? Soften it a little? Add comfort? Add height? You get my gist. Write down your reasons for needing a mattress topper before you shop. If you like your mattress but it's been in the rental for a while before you, note why you like it and get a topper that serves you in the same way. If you have a freezing cold room, adding a memory-foam mattress topper can help you keep warm during the night.

Mattress care

To keep your mattress in great condition, you do need to do more than change the sheets.

- Flipping: Do this once a season. If it's one-sided, then just rotate. This will prevent areas of heavy wear.

- Breathe: You need to care for your mattress as you would a couch. Leave her exposed for as long as you can when you do a linen change and lightly vacuum before you put the fresh set on.
- Bed slats: Always make sure the slats are in the correct position when you change the sheets. If they have slipped out of place, it can result in pressure on parts of the mattress where it shouldn't be.
- Mattress protector: I cannot tell you how important it is to have one of these. Owner, renter, landlord: ensure there is a mattress protector in place from day one. It will increase the life of the mattress, as well as prevent odours and stains.

Built-in storage

Everyone will use built-in storage differently and have different budgets, so sizing and materials will vary, but when buying there are some things to keep in mind:

Interior: You'll have already done the Min and know what you need as regards shelf, drawer and rail space. Don't forget to consider easy and hard to access points, as this is what will ultimately affect how smooth your storage system is to use. Lastly, drawers from the elbow down are great, as you can view the full contents more easily than a shelf, so try to plan these in where possible.

Measure well: Make sure you are counting skirting and anything else on the wall that will reduce the overall width of the unit.

Clearance: Always check the doors and drawers are able to open fully and don't interrupt the flow of anything else. If you feel that doors could hamper the use of the space, go for sliding doors. These will also give you room for a larger unit.

Go as high as you can: It's better to store out of sight, instead of on top of a wardrobe.

Mirror, mirror: The doors of your wardrobe doubling up as a mirror is a great space saver. It also makes the dressing zone more efficient.

While we are here, our wardrobes and drawers are items we use daily, but we don't make a fuss about them. A shame, when you think about it. Something that can really add to their use, as well as keep our clothes smelling fresh and act as a repellent to moths (*grasps cashmere cardigan against chest*) are lavender pouches. Glorious! These are so easy to make yourself and will ensure you are greeted with a wonderful burst of fragrance every time you dress or put clothes away.

MAGIC MEAUXMENT

The pouch

You can use anything for the pouch, but I find a pair of tights best. We all have a pair that laddered on the first wear and this is an ideal way to reuse them. I also like to use black tights, as my wardrobe is mainly black, so they look great nestled among my clothes with dramatic black ribbons. If you have some sheer fabric, you can also cut this in a circle and just tie it into a bundle.

Method

The first pouch will be the easiest. You just need to cut off the foot, fill and tie up. As you get further up the leg of the tights, you'll need to knot the bottom, turn it inside out and then fill to hide the knot.

You can lay pouches in drawers, or hang them from hangers or the rails themselves. I do enjoy them nestled among out-of-season clothing, too, to keep it smelling great.

The lavender

You can dry it yourself, but a bag of dried lavender works perfectly. It will usually have some added lavender oil, for extra fragrance.

Tie

For hanging, I like to use ribbon. Twine is also fine.

As we leave the bedroom, I hope you have a deeper understanding of what you want to get from her and how she can make your days feel smoother and more relaxed. It's a room you can really take your time with and add to slowly, décor-wise.

CHAPTER 5

BATHROOM

The bathroom! A glorious and vital room in our homes, she is heavily depended on by all who use her, yet is often so overlooked. She's usually the last room we visit before bed and the first when we wake. In the morning, she helps set us up for the day ahead: cleansing, sprucing, brushing, preening. Evening wind-downs are enhanced by her soothing baths or hot showers. As our time with her is private, we often find a sense of peace and calm in our bathroom that is not found elsewhere in the home. Lovely, isn't it?

Before we pop inside, let's take a minute to do our assessment. Routes and pit stops will have less of a focus here as bathrooms, en suites and toilets tend to be so small. However, they are great to keep in mind for towel storage and bin placement. The zones here are what will need most of our time. Unlike other rooms in the home, there are two zoning systems we will run through. The first we all know and love, and that is zoning the room into areas of use. We tend to use these rooms for so much, it is important that these are really clearly defined and easy to use to make our bathroom activities more enjoyable. There will usually be a bathing or shower zone, a sink zone, storage zones and so on, depending on how many are in the household. Then we will have electrical zones. These help us to make sure that we have the safest placement possible for lighting, shaver sockets and other electrical items. More on that later.

WHO IS SHE?

Her true function is to offer us a place where we can carry out personal hygiene moments in private and in a sanitary fashion. This means a lot can go on behind these walls and to truly get the most out of our bathroom we need to understand her a little, as it really does impact how we decorate as well as use the space.

We rarely learn about the bathroom in this way, unless it's in a repair or despair scenario. So, I feel it is vital to have access to this information and for it to sink in during a relaxed time. This means, should we need that knowledge in the future, we are plucking it from a positive place in our minds and are able to make more confident decisions.

WATER

Let's begin. For a bathroom to function as it should, it will need to be able to bring water in for bathing and washing, and let water leave when flushing and draining. These two set-ups are not only vital for function, they also affect what we can have in our bathroom and where it can sit.

Water pressure

One of the most important elements in a well-functioning bathroom is water pressure. Why?

Low water pressure means not only that at times washing your hair with your own tears feels more effective and your bath loses heat while taking longer to fill, but also that some shower types cannot be installed.

Let's take it from the top (*raises a satin-gloved hand*). Water pressure is the force that pushes the water through your pipes and out of your taps and shower heads. What a gal. Most homes get their water from a public water supplier, but some homes have a private water source either just for their own home or shared with a group of houses nearby. These are usually located in more rural areas. This is why your friend in the countryside has a well, glorious tap water and shiny hair.

If you have a public supply, there are some factors that will affect the water pressure to your home. Here are the most common:

Demand

Water pressure can be lower in the morning when many people in your supply area are washing at the same time. Think of all your neighbours also popping in the shower before their six-step skincare routine. In warmer climates, it can also decrease when sprinklers or garden hoses are in frequent use. Basically, when everyone is pouring from the same source at the same time there will be a noticeable drop in the pressure.

Proximity and elevation

If your home is at the top of a hill, you will most likely have lower water pressure than those at the bottom. That's just gravity, bish. The same can be said for homes further from the water supply. She needs to work harder to get there, so she will be weaker when she arrives.

Water pressure standards

Thankfully, there are standards which must be met when supplying water to homes. Although most countries state that water suppliers must be able to supply every storey of every building in their area, they don't make them meet a pressure standard for every floor. Instead, the 'height requirement' must be met at the boundary of the property, where the supplier water enters the home and here only. How it flows once it's in your home is not the supplier's problem, it's yours. This will be affected by things like:

- Pipework: older homes will have thinner pipework, resulting in lower water pressure.
- Limescale: shower heads, taps and appliances can become blocked with limescale build-up, affecting their performance (there is a stunning solution for this in chapter 10, Hauskeeping).
- Stopcocks or shut-off valves: if these are knocked and slightly twisted closed, it will affect the water pressure. This is why you should frequently check that the valve is fully open to ensure you are always receiving optimum water pressure.

The standard for water pressure coming into the home is 'one bar'. This means its force can reach ten metres, which is fine for most showers. However, this force can weaken the higher you go in the home, so additional pumps may be needed to keep pressure up for showering.

TIP

How to test your bathroom water pressure

Pressure can be different between kitchen and bathroom, so make sure to test this with the bathroom sink. You will need a one-litre container and a stopwatch.

Start by running the cold tap (we won't test the hot tap, as it will almost always have a different pressure, but we will chat about that later on). Get your stopwatch or phone ready, and once the tap is in full flow, pop the container under the tap and press go at the same time.

Stop the clock when the water fills one litre. If it took longer than six seconds to hit the mark, this gal has low pressure.

What to do about low pressure

If you have a sudden drop in pressure and you're in an older home, the first thing you should check is if the dishwasher and washing machine are running at the same time. Many older homes have thinner pipes and if multiple machines are using water at the same time, this can slow down your supply. Then check your stopcock. If these aren't causing the issue, check if your neighbour is experiencing a drop too. If they are, it will be caused by a supply issue, so you should alert your supplier to the problem. If they aren't, you may have a leak or a blockage somewhere within your pipe boundary.

If the rest of the house is fine and the shower is the only problem area, there are some great options. The most extreme is hiring a plumber to fit a power shower or pump. This is suited to showers on a higher level where the pressure is lower as a whole. If installing one of these is not an option, look into shower heads designed for increasing water pressure. These are great for renters stuck with a low-pressure shower. If you have a shower that has low pressure on a level that has generally good water pressure, the fittings themselves may be the issue. Shower head filters wear out over time, so a particularly old shower head may need to be replaced.

If you have low pressure in your home and are having a new shower or bathroom fitted, a plumber will be able to advise on the best shower and boiler to suit your needs. You do have options, like refitting the cold-water tank to a higher position, or fitting pumps and boosters to your water system.

Now that we're more aware of the force of the water coming in and why it is important, we can move on to what the water does once it's in our property. For her to come out of our taps, hot or cold, she first needs to go through the water system. Buckle up, this is a life lesson.

Water systems

There are two types of water systems in the home: one will bring you water (supply), the other will take it away (drainage). Then there are two types of water supply systems: direct and indirect. You know when people say it's fine to drink the water from the bathroom tap? Well, I would only trust them if they can tell me they have a direct water system. This is also why I am a little uneasy when people say it's grand to drink hotel room tap water.

Indirect water systems deliver fresh water to your property. This stops off at the kitchen sink, but the rest gets sent to a cistern. This cistern stores the water that is supplied to the rest of the home. Water that comes from the cistern isn't classed as drinkable, but it's fine for bathroom taps, for example. The advantage of a cistern is that she has a store of water should the main supply be temporarily off. Also the higher pressure from a direct mains supply is said to be more trying on some fittings.

A direct system is more common in new (read smaller) homes, as there is often no space for a cistern. The cold water sashays into the property directly from the mains water supply and can be called for from any cold tap, making it all drinkable. For hot water, the cold water supply will run through the water heating system in place before it comes out hot.

Hot water supply
From these options, you then have your hot water systems. The water in your bathroom will first come from the mains supply, then go through your water system, then the heating system, and then out your shower or taps. Glorious! There are different types of hot water systems and it's good to know which one you have.

To the right are details on how the most common water systems work. It is important to know which one you have. Once you have taken her in, you can mop your brow. The heavy lifting will be over!

Gravity Fed System

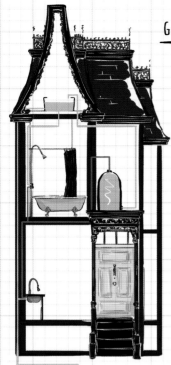

Common in bigger homes, water is supplied to an attic tank before feeding to a cylinder.

Inside this cylinder is where the water gets heated up either by an electronic element (immersion), by a boiler or by solar power.

They are low maintenance and a cheaper option, but they take up a lot of space. They can also have low pressure issues, as they are reliant on how high the tank is in the loft. A plumber can advise on how to boost pressure with a pump.

Unvented Water Tank

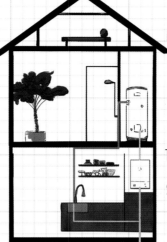

Her water comes straight from the mains and there is usually a wall-hung boiler, immersion, solar power or other sustainable source that controls her.

These are more expensive to install and when something goes wrong it's more costly to fix.

● Instant/ Mains hot water

These work by water coming straight from the mains, going through a heating system and then out of a tap or shower. People tend to prefer these as the pressure you get is usually higher. However, if you have low mains pressure you cannot add booster pumps.

Combi Boiler

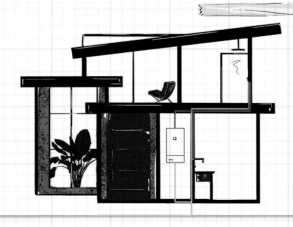

Usually hung on the wall and doesn't need a hot water tank to supply hot water to the home.

They are found in smaller properties, as they require little space and can have issues supplying hot water to two bathrooms at once.

WASH

Let's begin with something practical. I keep it in mind for every bathroom purchase, from tiles right through to a vessel for tampons. It helps make sure that what I am buying for her suits her and can withstand bathroom conditions. She is unlike other rooms in the home due to her high moisture levels, so buying for her needs consideration of this. It doesn't mean we cannot have fun – as long as the item matches this criteria, it's good to go. Say it with me. WASSSSSH.

Water: A bathroom uses a lot of water and this needs to be considered from the early stages of kitting her out right through to the smaller décor details. This will ensure safe use of the space (for example, non-slip elements and safe placement of electrics), reduce damage to walls and floors (for example, tiles, shower trays, shower curtains), and of course avoid any leaks into other parts of the home (through silicone, grout, etc.). The wonderful thing about the bathroom is that all of her practical elements can also be styling points in themselves. Tiles can be a talking point, grout can be painted, shower curtains can be utterly fabulous. She can werk as well as work.

Access: Access is important to keep in mind for the flow of the room as well as for repairs. If you are in the design stage of your bathroom, make sure you're considering access to piping, cisterns and drains. You'll also need to make sure there is clearance for doors and drawers when it comes to shower tray, toilet and sink shapes. Access also applies to smaller details. If you're looking into freestanding units, shelving or hooks, for example, make sure doors can open fully, you have room to step out of the shower, and use of the sink or toilet is not restricted.

Steam: There is nothing like a long, hot shower. Hair mask in, exfoliation, circular scrubbing, all while swinging your hips to Jocelyn Brown. Oh, I love a steamy moment. With the key word here being 'moment'. Steam, as atmospheric and alluring as she is, is not something you want hanging around for longer than necessary. If she does, she will eventually encourage damp, mould, flaking paint, warping and other condensation-related issues. Even with the most stunning extractor systems in place, what is sitting in the room during the use of hot water needs to be OK with daily exposure to steam. You want to make sure your non-tiled areas are adorned with paints and paper that are designed for bathrooms. Any storage, fabrics, mirror . . . everything right down to your toothbrush holder should be made from materials that don't rust easily or warp if exposed to moisture. For example, a shelving unit made of MDF will chip at the corners over time or that rose gold basket you bought for your bath bombs will rust quickly.

Hygiene: A lot happens in a bathroom that needs to be dealt with appropriately. Toilets are designed to carry away toxic waste and drains whisk away waste water, but little thought is given to rubbish bins, toilet brushes and other accessories in the bathroom that come in contact with waste. Certain materials encourage great sanitary conditions (living for you, stainless steel and chrome) and some materials don't (I'm looking at you, wooden handles). It is essential to consider hygiene when shopping for your bathroom to ensure she can carry out her duties well. The easiest way to ensure something is hygienic is to make sure it is not porous or likely to absorb bacteria. This also matters when it comes to bathroom cleaning accessories. They should have minimal details and be able to be washed down without damage.

Whoever the user – a single occupant or a large family – if you consider the above elements in your purchases, you are guaranteed a bathroom and contents that will live and last well. Never forget: your bathroom can be a fun, chic reflection of your style, if the basics are working well.

Every bathroom needs certain things to function well and in a sanitary fashion. This is why the shopping list for this room will have a little more guidance around it.

Bin

I am passionate about getting the right bin. You're assuming pedal metal bin, right? Well, I actually avoid them. I want a bin that can last years, be submerged for cleaning, have little interaction with footwear and doesn't wear out or break easily. This is why I like to go for a resin or plastic bin that has a swing top. This requires minimal touch, comes apart in two bits and can get a thorough wipe down each week with ease. Most importantly there is a lid; open-top bins are to be avoided. It should be small. If it is large, it doesn't get emptied as often, and people are more likely to throw in items for recycling, like shampoo bottles.

Toilet brush

Every bathroom needs a toilet brush. For me, silicone is the only way to go. When buying anything that has plastic parts, I want them to last years and years, and silicone can help with this. It's also more hygienic, as it is non-porous, so doesn't attract germs in the same way. It's hard-wearing, and you won't get that horrible discoloration you get on bristles because it dries so quickly. Some brands do open pots to aid drying, but I like the pot they sit in to be vented. Wall-hung sets are great, as they're less likely to have spills, can save on space and eliminate having to store anything on the floor around the toilet. Shudder.

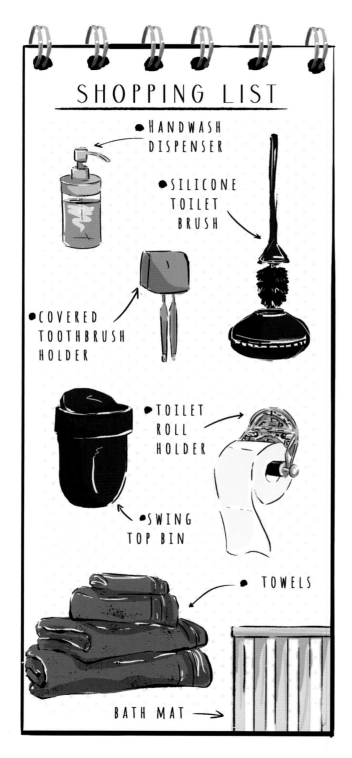

SHOPPING LIST

- HANDWASH DISPENSER
- SILICONE TOILET BRUSH
- COVERED TOOTHBRUSH HOLDER
- TOILET ROLL HOLDER
- SWING TOP BIN
- TOWELS
- BATH MAT →

Handwash

I like to have a refillable handwash pump. We are getting closer to being able to buy items like this by the litre to reduce our plastic consumption, so these are great. Visually they are a lot better than the word antibacterial in blue staring at you every morning. These are best opaque or see-through, so you can keep on top of refills.

Toothbrush holder

OK, we really need a solid chat here. I don't think enough of us are aware of what a toothbrush holder needs to be in order to serve us well. As interiors have taken over the high street, matching soap dispensers and toothbrush cups have been an easy way for brands to add an interior product that can change with the seasonal colours and prints. If you are currently in possession of a toothbrush 'cup', I urge you to repurpose that bish now. If she matches your dispenser, fill her with cotton pads. If she's a colour or pattern you love, make her a wee vase. If she's glass, why not throw in a candle and leave her on your bath . . . You get the idea. Whatever you do, avoid using her to house your toothbrush after use.

You see, after you brush your teeth, that water runs down from the bristles into the bottom of the cup. And it stays there. Then it starts to smell. Toothpaste sometimes gets added. It discolours, the smell gets worse, and mould grows in the cup and on the end of your toothbrush (hygiene nightmare). Have I convinced you to get an open holder yet? There are so many open styles to choose from, but my favourite is a pebble-style holder (just make sure it has bumpers on the end to allow for draining), as it can also be popped in your wash bag for travel. There are wall-hung holders with covers, too. These usually come with suction cups. You pop them up and the cover protects the bristles. Again, great for every day but also fab for travel.

Toilet roll

I like to make sure there is a toilet-roll holder, as well as some kind of storage for spares. Holder-wise, off the floor, and I recommend it is 66cm from the floor and around 25cm from the toilet rim. However, I think it is more important to have them suit the actual user, so play around with the placement. Storage-wise, I like something that conceals them completely.

Towels

Start with two bath, face and hand towels per person. If you choose a pattern, make sure that any colours present can go in the same wash, as they will nearly always run on their first wash. I like hand towels to be a bit more eccentric than bath towels, so will always go for something bold and keep the bath and face in plains. If you think I am going to leave it at that when it comes to towel shopping . . . never! We have a stunning section on her coming up to help you choose well.

Bath or shower mat

It's essential that these are hung to dry after use and aren't left on the floor. Polyester dries quickly, but bamboo mats are great as they don't encourage mould, dry quickly and are raised from the floor.

THE MIN

The Min here will be like other rooms but can make a really big impact to the look and feel of the space. Just like the kitchen, even if you are thinking of an overhaul, carry out the Min first. It could really change how you see the space and want to alter it.

A deep clean

Nothing, and I mean nothing, can be done until we can see the true condition of the bathroom. A deep clean will allow you to see what is working well, what is worn and what needs some TLC. A deep clean also gives you time to reflect on what really isn't that bad and what needs to change. If you are unsure of how a deep clean should go down, I go into detail in chapter 10, Hauskeeping.

Fittings

Toilet-roll holders, shower fittings, hooks and so on are usually held in place with grub screws. These are small screws without a head and you can use a small Allen key to tighten them up. If you have any loose or tilting fittings, check the underside for the grub screw and tighten. While you're at it, tighten up the shower hose to avoid any leaks.

Shower curtain

Replacing the shower curtain, if one is in place, is a tiny change but an easy way to set a certain aesthetic in a bathroom. These come in two forms, completely waterproof plastic or water-resistant fabric. The latter is usually what you will have if you go for a pattern and these are most likely to get mildew and mould. For this reason, a shower curtain liner is a must to keep them from getting heavily soaked. I personally love the liners alone. Clear curtains won't cut off the room and you can keep them open to drip dry after use without overwhelming the space. You can also get ombré clear curtains which are divine, especially in deep greens.

Repair plugs

Broken plugs can really impact your use of the sink and bath. Don't live with a plug that doesn't work as it should. Often there is a simple remedy. Here are the three main types and their fixes.

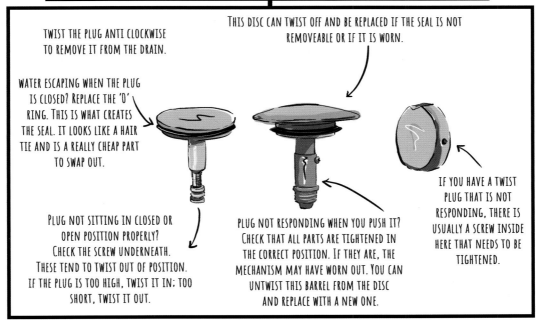

PLUGS UNPLUGGED

TWIST THE PLUG ANTI CLOCKWISE TO REMOVE IT FROM THE DRAIN.

THIS DISC CAN TWIST OFF AND BE REPLACED IF THE SEAL IS NOT REMOVEABLE OR IF IT IS WORN.

WATER ESCAPING WHEN THE PLUG IS CLOSED? REPLACE THE 'O' RING. THIS IS WHAT CREATES THE SEAL. IT LOOKS LIKE A HAIR TIE AND IS A REALLY CHEAP PART TO SWAP OUT.

IF YOU HAVE A TWIST PLUG THAT IS NOT RESPONDING, THERE IS USUALLY A SCREW INSIDE HERE THAT NEEDS TO BE TIGHTENED.

PLUG NOT SITTING IN CLOSED OR OPEN POSITION PROPERLY? CHECK THE SCREW UNDERNEATH. THESE TEND TO TWIST OUT OF POSITION. IF THE PLUG IS TOO HIGH, TWIST IT IN; TOO SHORT, TWIST IT OUT.

PLUG NOT RESPONDING WHEN YOU PUSH IT? CHECK THAT ALL PARTS ARE TIGHTENED IN THE CORRECT POSITION. IF THEY ARE, THE MECHANISM MAY HAVE WORN OUT. YOU CAN UNTWIST THIS BARREL FROM THE DISC AND REPLACE WITH A NEW ONE.

Storage

Just like the bedroom, the storage system here is one that can really make or break the space. The first place to start is to divide the items into things you use often and things you use occasionally.

For daily use items – cloths, cosmetics and creams, etc. – these should be in easy to access areas, like counters, unit tops or the first shelf of wall storage, kind of like a dressing table. However, this can also leave them exposed to the less favourable conditions, which can damage them, and they also don't exactly look brilliant, do they? Popping them into suitable containers is key, but they needn't be boring. Glass, metallic and mirrored vessels with lids are great here, as they are non-porous and can withstand the bathroom's conditions, as well as protect the contents. Practicalities aside, lifting the lid of a vintage sugar bowl in the evening to pluck out a muslin cloth is far more enjoyable and stunning than rummaging through drawers. If you have the space, vessels like this don't just need to be for day-to-day items; pop in anything that is for bathroom use that can easily fit. Tampons, hair ties, bath salts, lipsticks . . . go wild. If you need to store a lot of make-up in the bathroom, I recommend clear drawers. It's easy to see what you have, and they are also easy to clean and the products are protected.

Three-tier shelving units and other small sets of drawers are so common in bathrooms, but while they can be useful they are a magnet for bacteria. If you have one, the best place for it is at the bottom of the wardrobe. You can house your more occasional-use items here and free up your bathroom storage.

Plants

Plants are a great addition to bathrooms, as they become the feature and can soften a room full of hard surfaces and no soft furnishings. They can also take the eye away from décor in places that you don't adore.

When it comes to choosing plants to live in your bathroom, here is what you must remember. They need to be OK with fluctuating temperature, love humidity and be suited to little or low light. All that moisture in the air will be a joy for some plants and an absolute mare for others.

So now we know succulents are out, as they need a dry room, but ferns love humidity. They come in so many varieties, you can find one to suit your bathroom. Some don't need a lot of light and others need a window sill, so be sure to check her light requirements. One thing about ferns is that they aren't ideal if space is an issue, unless they are hung (how fabulous around a shower!). If you have a small bathroom, go for something that grows tall rather than out, so it can sit on the floor but never touch it.

Don't forget, just because a plant suits your steamy main bathroom, don't be tempted to put the same plant in a downstairs loo, as this won't have the same humidity levels and needs a plant suited to drier conditions.

If you have a windowless bathroom, there are lighting options that can help plants along, but they are not the most relaxing to bathe to. You can find solar-powered lights that you can charge up and pop in to spend time with the plants without the need for plugging them in.

Now, I mentioned previously that I was going to talk more about towels. I LOVE talking about towels.

Towels

Towel shopping has been influenced by 'fast' interiors, as they are items that can instantly add a style to a bathroom with minimal cost or effort. If bought purely with a lewk and not their true purpose in mind, you can, in fact, end up wasting money, honey. You're not only affecting your pocket but the environment too.

With easy tweaks, high-street manufacturers can update their towel range each season to match trends and encourage customers to buy more frequently. They can do this using dyes, pattern, print, embellishment and so on. These processes can increase the production cost and therefore the unit price unless something gives and that is usually the fabric content and the weight. By compromising on these (vital) elements, they can deliver a luxury look at a low price.

There are some glorious things you need to know about towels to help you make the best choices for your bathroom. My aim is that when you see something stunning that will serve a look to dai for, you will be able to take a quick glance at the description and know if she's the one for you. There is so much talk about towels needing to have the fluffiest or purest cotton or be really expensive to be a really good towel, when in fact a towel is only a winner if it suits the user. Towels are like tea: there's no ideal that suits everyone.

Composition

When it comes to what a towel is made of, absorption, feel and durability are key. This is why cotton is the preferred yarn of choice and why you'll see her on almost every bathroom towel label.

Cotton on

Cotton is the original towelling queen because she is naturally absorbent (she can hold around twenty-five times her own weight), durable yet also incredibly soft to the touch. These stunning characteristics make her ideal for a towel but also mean she is usually more expensive than other yarns. Another reason for her higher price is that she is a natural fibre and the manufacturing process is more costly than that of manmade fibres such as polyester.

When you are looking at a cotton towel, you may assume that she is high quality without even touching her, but it can in fact depend on what type of cotton she is made of and if she is blended at all. Cotton is grown from the seeds of the *Gossypium* plant, but there are many *Gossypium* plant species around the world. Different places produce different types of cotton with different characteristics that affect its price. Have you ever questioned why exactly 'Egyptian cotton' on a product description drives the price up?

Egyptian cotton: Where the cotton is grown affects its quality. In the same way that Italian marble is best because of the minerals present, Egypt's humid conditions and glorious soil mean she grows a stunning cotton variety. The reason Egyptian cotton is so renowned is that it produces a *finer* yarn. A finer yarn means a higher thread count per square inch, which makes the towel more absorbent, softer and, of course, more durable.

Although people argue that some crap cotton can be grown in Egypt, it is how their cotton is made that really makes it good. Egyptian cotton is hand-picked, meaning that by the time the cotton goes to be carded it is more intact and has been through less stress. Her fine, long fibres have little damage and will therefore be less affected by washing compared to other cottons.

Turkish cotton: I bet you haven't heard about Turkish cotton, but I'm going to let you in on a secret. You get all the softness, absorbance and durability of a longer and finer thread, as this is also mainly hand-picked, but with one key difference. Egyptian cotton is so absorbent it is not advised as the towel of choice in humid countries, as it can actually attract moisture in the air and become damp without even being used. *Mon dieu!* Turkish cotton has a much faster drying time, so if you have humidity issues in your home, you don't have a towel rack or you soak the bejesus out of your towel after a shower, this is the gal for you. Another thing to note is that Turkish towels are said to get softer with use and washing.

If you have Egyptian cotton towels already and find they smell after little use, keep them as a winter towel and dry quickly on a radiator after use.

Cotton and polyester blend: To reduce the cost of producing a towel that still delivers on thickness and look, polyester is often mixed with cotton. Polyester is cheaper and retains dyes for longer than cotton, so there's less fading. It is also less absorbent, so while it won't dry you like 100 per cent cotton towels, it will dry much faster after. If the humidity in your home is causing a really damp-smelling towel, this can be a great option.

Now that you know why composition matters, what about all the other jargon we see on packaging?

GSM

One thing that is always visible on towel packaging is the GSM. This stands for grams per square metre. This is actually how all fabrics are costed. A specific-sized circle is cut from a roll of the cloth and weighed, and this weight is then applied to a formula.

GSM is particularly important for towels, as it relates to how thick the loops are, which implies how luxe and absorbent the towel is overall.

300–400: This is for a super quick-drying towel, say a gym towel or a dish towel.

400–600: The absorbency and softness is better. This is quite a good standard for a bath towel. They are easy to launder and quick to dry.

600–900: This is where we get into your wants rather than needs. These are the higher quality, thicker towels that some people love but that don't suit all homes.

Manufacturing processes that add value
Combed: When a towel is combed, it means shorter fibres that would inevitably come loose during use are combed out. This means what you buy won't shed and reduce in weight or look.

Zero twist: When a premium cotton is used, it is so long and strong that twisting it isn't necessary. When you see 'zero twist' it basically means it's a very high quality, strong cotton.

Double-turned edges: Inspect the edges of the towel and rub it between your fingers to see if it has been turned twice. This will make it far more durable. You want your towel to last a long time, right? Don't be tempted by trims that are too fussy to last long, like a pom-pom or tassel. These are best on an occasional hand towel that is rarely used, thus not washed often.

Borders: Knowing what border you prefer your towels to have can be an interesting way to link your towels regardless of brand or colour. Cam borders are flatweaves and Dobby borders will have a pattern. I personally love the timeless essence of a thick cam border. It's very '90s Manhattan hotel.

Washing towels

The first wash you give your towel is important. You should wash the towel thoroughly before use to set her colour and to clean her before she touches that gorgeous body. She also will most likely have been set in a product to make her feel even softer than she is, but this will hamper absorption potential. Washing will remove it. On this note, do not use fabric softener on towels, as it too coats the fibres.

Don't overload the machine; ensure towels have enough room for a thorough rinse, so the detergent doesn't stay in the fibres. Use a mid-heat tumble dry to ensure a fluffy, fully dried towel ready for storage.

If you don't have access to one, before you hang a towel to dry shake her first. This will loosen the loops and allow them to puff as they dry.

THE TSZUJ

If you can make some deeper changes, here are the ones that will make the biggest difference.

A fresh coat of paint

A new coat of paint on all woodwork can really lift a bathroom. I always find that keeping the woodwork white helps keep it topped up and fresh over many years. It is a room that benefits from a lot of white due to the connotations with hygiene and great sanitary conditions. It is always good to also have the main bathroom in lighter colours, so it is easier to see if there are any damp or leak issues early on. Save the more extreme décor for a less steamy bathroom.

Fresh silicone

Even the most worn-out of bathrooms will benefit from fresh silicone. This also doesn't need to stop at the bath or shower. Your bathroom should be sealed at every joint that could get splashed, so a new bead of silicone around the floor, skirts and fixtures will be divine.

Toilet seat

You don't need a new toilet to give a whole new vibe. The toilet seat is the way to go if you are not doing a new suite. I also find that a discoloured or poorly functioning toilet seat can let the whole room down.

You can make an older style toilet look more up to date with a modern seat, or if you want a more vintage or traditional look, black wooden toilet seats are the perfect way to get that vibe. I find these great in general, as they look so chic.

Tiles

If you really hate the tiles in place but are not going to change them, then enhance them. I wouldn't advise painting or putting tile stickers on large tiled areas in the bathroom due to how it will wear. As lovely as it would be to completely cover the tiles, here is what I would do instead.

- *Brighten or repair damaged grout.* If the grout is still intact, but the deep clean didn't lift the discoloration, use a grout pen for a quick fix. These don't last for ever but are great for a wee top-up.
- *Borders*: If you have a wall of tiles with a border or strip that you hate, this will be small enough to paint over. Either match it to the other tiles to make it disappear or use it as a feature. I find that you must go with the same type of tone to really pull this off. If your tiles are a warmer tone of white and you want to add a pink strip, go for a pink with a yellow undertone; if your undertone is grey, it won't gel as well.
- *Colour change*: When I have tiles that are all one colour and the grout is in good nick, I will stain the grout to make it a feature. It allows me to update the walls with very little spend. This works especially well on subway or square tiles; the effect can get lost on larger tiles. With staining, I prefer to use products that smear on and then wipe off, leaving the grout with a new colour. Painting grout is a mare: you have to have a very steady hand and it can drip while drying. I cover this in more detail in the kitchen chapter. Charcoal will give a sleek look that suits both industrial or art-deco vibes. Pastels like mint green or pale pink can give a fun pop to the room, and then bright colours like orange or red are great for a kitsch feel. Floor tiles always look more modern with a deep grey update, as it takes down yellowing that happens over time.
- *Research*: If the tiles are particularly offensive all over, search the tile description on something like Pinterest for inspiration. You'll find lots of images of how the tile has been styled, usually with other colours being used to enhance its tone. For example, a dark beige natural-look tile that you think looks old-fashioned can be styled to create a really on-trend earthy sanctuary vibe with some clever use of colour and plants.

NOTE

A note on flushing the toilet

If you flush your toilet without popping down the lid first, we need to have word, hen. First, let's start with the word 'lid'. Lids close things that need to be closed when not in use. Lids are put on toilets to close them, as this prevents anything getting dropped in the water by mistake (RIP blusher brush), and keeps children and pets safe, but they are mainly there for when you flush. Have you ever heard of a toilet plume? She sounds like a plush duster but is in fact a bacteria-infused mist that is released when you flush. Have a wee read over that again. It is impossible to flush without creating this mist and studies have shown it can travel a few feet from the toilet bowl and stick to surfaces (yes, even toothbrush bristles). While it doesn't make you ill, it's still best to avoid allowing this mist to breeze around your bathroom, so pop the lid down before you flush.

Heads, hoses, holders

These play a huge part in the overall styling of your room. They can transform a clunky electric unit into a more glamorous affair and help you achieve modern minimal in the oldest of bathrooms. If you are sticking to the shower you have but have the budget to swap these out, they can do wonders for the room.

Riser kits

These are great for a household with people of varying heights or those who may not always want to get their hair wet (hello, Tuesdays). When going for a riser kit, I personally go as minimal as possible – true metal or metal plating. I like the top and bottom to appear floating rather than anchored, so look for kits that have them attached from behind. I always, always also take the soap dish off. They are rarely well designed and look quite dated. You can instead create your own system based around what you use in the shower.

Mains and hook

You will sometimes see this kind of shower in older properties or, again, above a bath. It consists of a shower hose attached to the mains tap, with the head attached to a hook on the wall. All you'll need here is a replacement hose and head.

Shower heads

Speaking of heads, in this wonderful age we now have shower heads that can transform water. No, really. They can change the quality of the water before it gets to you and I am not just talking about the LED ones that change the colour of the water to make you feel like you're at a foam party on your sixth-year summer holiday. Some are designed to help combat hard water and others can add more water pressure without using more water. There are also heads that do both. If you are having a hard time with hard water, look into these.

Shower units

These can often look quite dated, but as they don't tend to wear badly, they remain in properties for a long time. If you are craving a more modern look in your bathroom but have a white plastic unit, you can paint the frames of the doors. Just make sure you use the right primer and paint for the surface, and lots of tape!

Fittings

Swapping out wall fittings for a new look can really lift the walls. A huge trend at the moment is to change all hardware to black, which followed on from golds, and I have a feeling we will see white silvers next and even pastels will have their moment. Whatever you go for, ignore what's hot right now and pick something you genuinely love and want to see every morning.

THE OVERHAUL

If you've been dealt a particularly bad bathroom and have the budget to overhaul, the best place to start is understanding what can go where and growing your décor plans from there. The two girls deciding most locations are water systems and electricity. Not exactly two things that mix well.

Where your toilet, sink and shower can be installed will be based around pipes, both supply and waste. Bear in mind here that moving a toilet is usually a lot more expensive than a sink, for example, as you need to consider sewage as well as other piping. It is usually already in the best location for connection to the soil stack, so this is why many people will leave them in the same location. Drains can also be costly to move, so instead people will change the size of the bath or shower and not move it.

Electrics

We all know I love a good zone. LOVE! However, as mentioned at the start of the chapter, there's another zoning system to consider in a bathroom along with zones of use. Enter: Bathroom Electrical Zones.

Electrical regulation divides bathrooms in to four zones, depending on their proximity to water. This is to guide us in our installation of electrical items, from fans to sockets, and make sure that the right IP is being used in the right area so we are not put at risk.

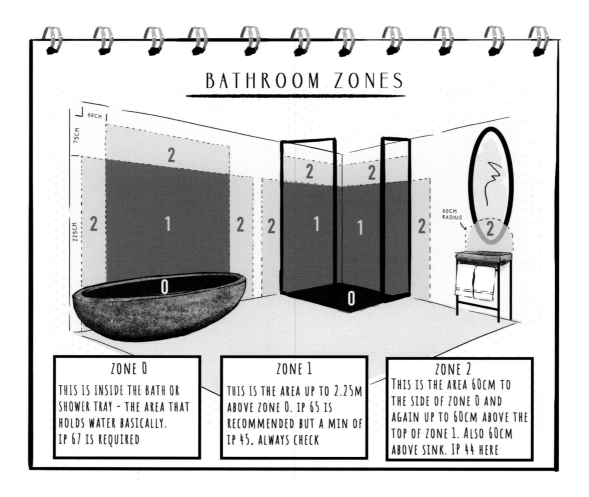

BATHROOM ZONES

ZONE 0
THIS IS INSIDE THE BATH OR SHOWER TRAY - THE AREA THAT HOLDS WATER BASICALLY. IP 67 IS REQUIRED

ZONE 1
THIS IS THE AREA UP TO 2.25M ABOVE ZONE 0. IP 65 IS RECOMMENDED BUT A MIN OF IP 45, ALWAYS CHECK

ZONE 2
THIS IS THE AREA 60CM TO THE SIDE OF ZONE 0 AND AGAIN UP TO 60CM ABOVE THE TOP OF ZONE 1. ALSO 60CM ABOVE SINK. IP 44 HERE

IP stands for Ingress Protection and the number accompanying it is a code used to specify the level of protection an enclosure or area provides the electrical equipment within it. The first number indicates how she will fare against foreign objects like dust and the second indicates how she will do against moisture. The first number goes from zero to six and the second from zero to eight. The higher the rating, the more protection provided.

Getting to know which electrics can safely go where will not only impact electrical items, it can also influence other décor, so it's great to be aware of it early on. For example, you may want to make a sink wider, now that you know she's the only thing that can go on a particular wall, or maybe your mirror needs to be bigger so it can run right up to a light fitting. It will also help you decide where tiling is best placed and if there is optimum protection from splashes.

Tiles

Speaking of tiles, we've already talked a little about tiles in the kitchen chapter, but bathrooms have different needs and styles, so here is some top-up info:

- You can use floor tiles on the walls, but not wall tiles on the floor. When you see a bathroom with the same tile on the walls and floors, they will be tiles that are specifically designed to be light enough for a wall but non-slip enough for floors.
- More tile and less grout is visually more appealing in a bathroom, as grout is harder to clean. This means real stone is out, but a stone replica, where the tiles can sit closer together, can work well.
- It's best to avoid tiles that are cold underfoot, which is another reason to avoid real stone. If you are opting for underfloor heating, make sure the tiles you want will suit it. Some cannot take the heat.
- Remember access when planning tiles. If you are covering pipework or cisterns, always ensure your tiler has included inspection panels that can be easily removed. I've come across many leaks that resulted in walls and boxing-in being cut open as there was no access to the pipes.
- If you want to make the room look bigger, you can use tiles to help you. Tiling a bath panel the same as the floor can make the floor space look bigger; same goes for the strip under a raised shower tray.
- Don't make your floor tiles too light and plain. Lighter tiles need a light grout and this can mean it ages quickly. A plain tile with no texture won't be as good for grip.
- If you have an old, coloured suite (you lucky duck!) and it functions well, consider keeping it. These are priceless in my eyes! Choosing tiles that really play with the colour or the era they are from will be head and shoulders above anything you could put in instead. It takes the most exquisite taste to make an old suite look contemporary. Search your old suite colour online and see how others have made theirs work.
- Colour blocking with tiles can look absolutely gorgeous and is an easy way to create a really expensive look with just plain tiles. For example, subway or square tiles, which are always the most reasonable, can be used throughout, but the shower unit or sink splashback can be another colour, or you can do a 50/50 top/bottom split. Divine!

Showers

The water pressure and water system are what will essentially decide what type of shower will work in your bathroom. It is only once you know the shower type you can have that you can go on to choose the look you want. People will often start with the aesthetic, only to realize it's not a shower type that can be installed. To avoid disappointment, let's get into it in a little more detail.

Mixer showers

Visually, these are my favourite.

They are what you will see in most shower inspiration boards, as they give the most visual appeal. All that needs to be seen are the shower head and controls, and their placement is not too limited, as all the bulkier stuff can exist behind the tiles. They also give you the most freedom when it comes to types of shower fittings, as the head doesn't need to be linked to a wall-hung unit via a hose and the controls can be where you please.

If you have the option of a mixer shower, really take advantage of the freedom they give you and make a feature of it.

On a more practical note, these work best in homes that have good water pressure and access to instant hot water. They are easily installed, as they don't need any electrics or pumps. To avoid the risk of scalding, your mixer shower should always have a thermostatic mixing valve (TMV). This usually sits in a barrel or similar between the levers and stops too much hot water being delivered at once. These are a must, in my opinion. They can suffer limescale build-up over time, which affects their performance, but with regular maintenance they will serve you well for a long time.

Power showers and electric showers

Power showers and electric showers are often confused, as they look so similar. Both are essentially a plastic box with dials and buttons that sit inside your shower unit.

Power showers are for low-pressure bathrooms and their internal pump is what increases the flow of hot and cold water. They are ideal for boosting the power of your shower but need hot and cold water present. Electric showers, on the other hand, use cold water and will heat it themselves. These are more economical to run, as you only heat what you're using, and they're cheaper to install, which is why they are usually the option when adding a second shower to the home.

Visually, wall-hung units are rarely that gorgeous and people will assume you can only buy the white box with silver accessories. However, I can free you of that curse and assure you that you can find wall-hung units that fit most tastes. The higher you go in price, the further you get from boxes and to more streamlined or feature units.

The controls and head must be attached to the unit. They'll also usually come with a riser kit that allows you to raise the head up and down, but these can be bulky and not the most appealing if it's an older set.

If you have one of these in place and have your heart set on a matte black ceiling-mounted shower head with sleek levers, you can work towards it. Replacing the riser kit is one way to really update the look of an old wall-hung unit. Just make sure your replacement has the same screw placement to avoid more holes in tiles. A sleek, minimal riser kit and larger shower head can draw the eye away from the unit and become a feature in themselves. It's also an easy way to update the bathroom for very little.

Shop around and you will find something with the visual appeal of a mixer shower. A more extreme option, and only something I would recommend if you are doing a deep overhaul, is to have pumps fitted to work with your water system, so no wall-hung unit is needed, but this is costly and not always possible. Check with your plumber before browsing.

NOTE

A note on showers

If you are adding a second shower to your home and are choosing between electric and power, here is my best advice. If you have a low-pressure gravity-fed tank, you may be better going electric, as that takes water straight from the cold mains, rather than a power shower that draws water from your tank. Some tanks take an age to fill back up after a power shower has been used and it can be a mare.

Digital showers and smart showers

This is like the Prada of thermostatic showers. Imagine being able to turn your shower on from your bed and step into it at the perfect temperature? Imagine! No waiting awkwardly to the side while the water warms up, no wetting the top of your head as you lean to reach the controls on a day you're not washing your hair. Instead, you flick back the duvet and a steamy, stunning shower at your desired temp awaits. They need good water pressure.

A smart shower is effectively a digital shower with added customization that can be controlled by any smart home system. 'Alexa, I want a level five power shower for four minutes then ice-cold for a minute and a half, then a light spritz.' Smart showers can be the new complicated coffee order. Be as obnoxious as you wish.

On a more practical note, they can be really handy for making sure children and older people have a shower suited to their needs.

Shower trays

Getting the tray right is extremely important when it comes to practicality and a bathroom's overall lewk. Sharp and thin will help you achieve minimal chic, while rounded and thicker trays will give a more traditional appeal. Shower trays come in standard sizes, so it's not a complicated shop, but there are many shapes to choose from. Some will add to your styling, some will help you save space and some will help with access.

Square and rectangle will give you more door options and are the easiest to replace if you ever need to. Corner showers come in the form of a quadrant, which is like a large slice of quiche, and pentagon, which is more like a diamond (or a square with a corner cut off, if you're a glass half-empty gal). These are great for saving on floor space, especially the quadrant shape, but when you're in one you don't notice a difference in size. You can get large versions of both if space saving isn't the main aim; perhaps there's a gorge view opposite or it's where the plumbing is easiest. Other shapes include P and D, curved and pentangle. These can help you make the most of a small bathroom.

Buying a tray

When it comes to buying a tray, you need to make sure your measurements are precise to avoid large gaps. This is pretty easy if you already have one in place; if you don't, just make sure all doors can open fully with the new tray in place.

Height

Be future-focused when choosing. A walk-in shower tray is one that can go down and stay down. The easy access of a flatter tray or wet room will mean as people in the home age or their mobility changes, you don't need to replace the tray. To have a low-rise tray, your pipework cannot come up above the floor level, so you may need to have this redone to accommodate a flatter tray. While flatter trays are becoming more popular, if you do need a raised tray to hide the pipework, you don't have to opt for garish plastic along the side – I always prefer to have the floor tile worked into the plinth so it looks more streamlined.

Material

Ceramic: Think Belfast sink. This will be called a ceramic or fireclay tray. They are heavy and can look quite luxurious, but they may chip. Also, even though charcoal ceramic trays are to dai for, they can be cold underfoot. Some people love it, but if you're not into cold feet, beware.

Stone resin: These trays are made of minerals mixed with resin and then coated with acrylic to create a solid and durable tray which is warm underfoot. They are becoming really popular; in fact, composite materials like this are now also popular for floors and counter tops due to their versatility and visual appeal. Instead of the tray simply being a practical item, it can become a feature in the room, as they are much easier to colour or pattern. My favourites are stone marble or granite effect. They can be really easy to care for, keep clean and they're lightweight too, unlike real stone. You get all the visual wonder without the maintenance and they can go on most floors.

Acrylic: Affordable and widely available, they are a very popular choice for homeowners who want something practical and easy to install. They are usually reinforced with wood underneath and come in standard colours.

Wet room

Not to be mixed up with walk-in showers, as these have trays; a wet room instead will have a floor that inclines ever so slightly towards the drain to help water leave the room after showering.

A wet room is great for space saving, if you need level access or if you want a really minimal look. There can be a screen but still the whole room needs to be tanked (waterproofed) in order for it to work well. To do this, the floor around the shower area and usually the lower section of the walls are primed with a membrane to make them waterproof, the floor is sloped and then the whole lot is tiled over.

If you do decide a wet room is the gal for you, here are some tips. Consider the rest of the room well. I would suggest wall-hung sinks and toilets, as this will stop water gathering where you don't want it. Opt for underfloor heating if you can, as this will dry the floor much quicker. Make sure your drain is pretty big. Long rectangle drains to the side are best visually, plus you then have a more comfortable place to stand. Make sure the drain is as far from the door as possible, as the floor will slope towards the drain. In smaller rooms, you don't want shelving in your way as you shower: inset shelves into the wall instead of having them jutting out.

Baths

Baths, glorious baths. My favourite item in a bathroom. There are many different bath shapes, but your decision will be mostly based on what you can fit and how you want to use the rest of the room.

Don't overlook add-ons and details beyond the shape, as these can kick it up a notch. You could make it a whirlpool bath with jets and pumps. Double-ended can add some visual drama, as well as a practical edge, as you can choose either end to rest against. 'Walk in' baths have a door that reduces step-height, which is great if you don't want to get rid of the bath entirely but access needs to be easier.

Sit-and-soak bath

This style is inspired by the Japanese ofuro bath, which is a shorter but deeper bath that allows the whole body to soak while you are in a seated position. The idea is to first shower and then, once clean, you take a seat inside and soak in hot water. How mindful. A sit-and-soak is a great way to have both a shower and bath in a smaller bathroom.

Materials

Acrylic

The low-cost option. She is made from sheets of vacuumed acrylic, then a layer of fibreglass, which means you get the pros of a fibreglass bath without warping or absorption of water. The material is sturdy, affordable and warm to the touch, which some people adore. She is lightweight, so you don't have to worry about a reinforced floor, and the bath will usually sit on a timber frame. You can pretty much use all general cleaners, as she is not porous.

Stone resin

You guessed it, this gal is your stone look and feel without the drama. She is on the pricier end, but the durability and ease of care makes her a really great option.

Steel

As you can imagine, she is super heavy. A sheet of steel is moulded into a bath shape and then coated with enamel. She gives a really high-end look and can achieve sharp lines, which many people like. She's cold to the touch, but when she's filled she retains heat really well. This is something to consider if you're going for a shower bath, as it'll be colder on the feet.

Toilets

The style of your toilet will enhance your overall bathroom look. No, really. If you are trying to create a traditional bathroom vibe, popping in a square wall-hung bowl will visually fight with the overall vibe. When choosing a toilet, think about the shape and aesthetic. Here are some handy snippets to keep in mind when toilet shopping.

Minimal: If you want a minimal look, go for a back-to-wall toilet. This will have the cistern hidden from view, as it will be boxed in. The bonus of these is that you can make the most of the space above the cistern and have a large mirrored cupboard and shelving. It's a brilliant way to keep things clean and streamlined. I would also choose wall-hung. These allow you to sweep a mop underneath, so are great from a sanitary point of view, but also being able to see the floor beneath can give a feeling of more space.

Traditional: The right toilet will really elevate your look here. You don't have to go for the full whack of a raised cistern and chain flush, but you can opt for something with curves and a rounder look to keep the tone. Wall-hung won't work as well here, but you can still go for back-to-wall and add some traditional hardware.

Flush types

If you have a close-coupled toilet, it will have come with a button or handle flush already attached. As a lefty, I always appreciate a centrally placed button. Sensor flashes are getting more and more common now in the home. These provide ease and a more hygienic set-up, as you don't have to touch the flush at all. They are also great for anyone with decreased mobility.

Sinks

Sinks are another way to set a tone in a room and it's not actually a must to have a fully matching suite. Once you get a similar aesthetic, such as modern, minimal, traditional, etc., it will all sit in harmony. I personally love a sink as a focal point in a bathroom, with the rest of the suite more muted.

Pedestal

All plumbing is hidden behind the pedestal. These are pretty standard, so you'll have a choice of sizes, styles and colours. Great if you feel like you want something that isn't going to stand out or date too much.

Vessel

Like a bowl upon a counter. Taps will usually be freestanding or wall-hung. These are not the style of basin you would have if you are tight on space. They are more suited to a bathroom where they can be a feature. These come as dramatic as you please, from painted and glass to concrete. *J'adore*.

Wall-hung

Gives the look of more space and a more minimal vibe.

Washstand

Brilliant if you need to maximize space but don't have the room for a full counter. These will have some rails and perhaps a shelf to form a unit for the sink to sit on, or it will be part of a unit that has doors and drawers.

Corner

For when you are super tight on space. They really suit hand-washing only. Ideal for a toilet under the stairs, for example.

Slimline

Again, ideal for a second toilet or if you have clearance issues.

Semi-recessed (and recessed)

Quite popular for counters, as they serve less sink and more counter.

Bathroom wastes

When buying a bath or sink, you will hear about wastes. A waste is the system that drains the bath or sink when you are done. It is often overlooked, so it's good to be clued up in advance.

The waste consists pretty much of the plug, parts that drain the water away and some include an overflow or connection to an overflow to stop you overfilling if a tap is left on. Some parts like the drain and overflow (this may sometimes just be a hole near the rim) are visible but there are also parts behind the bath and sink that connect the overflow and drain to a pipe that leads to the main drainage system in the home. Bath wastes are always wider than sink wastes.

If your sink has an overflow (I think it makes a LOT of sense to have one, so I would always opt for this) then certain wastes are not compatible. You will need a slotted waste with a hole, so even when the plug is in a closed position water from the overflow can head away as it needs to. It's like having a second constantly open drain for the overflow only. Some overflows need different connections so make sure you know what you need for yours, as choosing the wrong one can lead to a disaster. Heed my warning, hen.

There is one more thing to bear in mind when you are buying wastes – your taps. Many people forget about the waste when buying the taps and vice versa, which leaves your hardware mismatched. This can be OK for something like a vessel sink, but when it's a bath or regular sink try to get them matching.

Bathroom taps

When it comes to taps in the bathroom, you'll be limited to certain types if you already have a sink or bath in place, as these will have holes that dictate the type that can go in.

- A single spout to mix hot and cold water usually controlled by two handles or a single lever.
- With two holes, you'll have separate hot and cold taps, or a mixer tap which has two taps with a single spout that can also have a shower hose connection.
- Waterfall taps are mixers with a trough instead of a spout. Be careful to position these correctly so the water doesn't overshoot the basin.
- Bath filler taps are on the wall of the bath and have a hidden spout. So it will look like a handle or an overflow cover but this is where the water will come from. Best for minimal bathrooms.

We also have the option of a freestanding tap: long thin taps that come from the floor and curve over the bath to fill her. Delightful.

Many new baths will have no holes at all, allowing you to choose the type of tap and where to drill.

Heated towel rails

Towel rails are a fantastic way to save space, as they do two jobs at once: heating the room while acting as a towel rail. These are great for keeping damp and mould at bay, as they allow your towel and the room to dry faster after showering. Here are some factors to consider.

Size

Towel radiators don't give off as much heat as normal radiators, so if it's the only one going in you should ensure it can provide enough heat. If floor space is an issue, go for one that is tall rather than wide. To work out the best size of radiator, you can use an online heating calculator.

Placement

Aim for as close to the bath or shower as possible to add ease to your routine. If this is not possible, have them on the opposite wall, so it's a just few steps over a bathmat.

Fuel

If possible, go for a dual fuel option, which means it can be powered by central heating or electricity. I love this option, as it means you can dry and have warm towels throughout the year for less cost.

When it comes to the design and finish, this will depend on personal taste, but once you have ticked the practical boxes, it's sure to work well.

Lighting

Bathroom lighting can make such a difference! To cover the basics, have a light over the sink mirror and then a central light if possible. This allows you to opt for a warmer light, which is more flattering than the cooler ceiling light.

Ceiling lights

These can range from downlights to dome lights but all must be suitable for bathroom use. Most bathroom ceiling lights will be flush, recess or low rise, so they work well with low ceilings. Bathroom chandeliers or over-bath pendants are becoming more common, which can add a luxurious feeling, but do remember you need safe access for cleaning.

Accent lighting

I find this lighting great for bath time, as it provides light without the glare of the ceiling light, which can be quite distracting when you are trying to relax. Vanities, mirrors or skirting can be lit with soft glowy lighting to give the room a spa-like vibe.

Mirror lights

Some mirrors come with lights, so you won't need to give lighting the sink area too much thought. However, if you prefer the idea of sconces to sit either side of the mirror just be careful when fitting them. Stand in front of the mirror and have someone hold the fitting to the side or above to see what distance works well.

Lamps

Sockets are not permitted in bathrooms in the UK and Ireland (excluding shaver sockets) unless they are three metres from the bath or shower. As most bathrooms are less than three metres wide they're rarely seen.

Storage

Homes are getting smaller and, with more combi-boilers in place, hot presses are becoming a luxury of the past. This means you may need to store a lot more in your bathroom than it is designed to take. It is natural to go for the largest storage option possible for a space, but instead focus on what exactly needs to be stored. You'll have worked out how much exposed and display storage you need from doing the Min, so this will help you choose wisely and avoid a tall shelving unit full of clutter that is hard to use.

Wall space

Wall space is often overlooked in bathrooms and can really help you out when it comes to storage. Adding shallow shelving to a wall is a great way to use up wasted space. Even the addition of a small floating shelf for your morning and night skin routines can really enhance how you use the space. Ladder shelves are great for a rental, as they don't need to be hung and will simply perch. Hanging storage on the back of a door or from a towel rail can also make the most of smaller bathrooms.

New bathrooms

If you are lucky enough to be starting fresh and can add what you like, mirrored cupboards that run really high are a great addition to any bathroom and kill two birds. Look out for wall units with built-in shaving sockets, so what you charge doesn't have to be left out.

Keep handles to a minimum and go for 'press to open' doors. Flush fittings with minimal details are easier to keep clean.

Fitted storage in the bathroom can save a lot of space and can even make use of areas that are not usually used. As discussed in the toilet section, having a 'back to wall' toilet means you can build storage into the cavity wall behind it. This is clever, as it usually houses an exposed cistern.

Children's toys are always best stored near the bath. A netted bag held over the bath by suction cups is ideal, as it can drip dry after use and be within arm's reach when bathing.

Multi-use storage

Towel rail hooks, bath panels with doors, and mirror cabinets are all examples of multi-use storage for smaller bathrooms. If something new is going into the bathroom, look at options that also provide storage. The under-bath storage option is great for cleaning products or spare toilet roll, out of view in otherwise unused space. I also like that it gives access should you need to inspect under the bath.

Under-sink storage

This doesn't have to be a vanity unit. If you have a pedestal sink, you can buy freestanding metal units that can sit underneath and house towels and other linen without taking up space elsewhere.

Elevating bath time

To enhance your time in any room, all you need to do is appeal to your senses. The bathroom is no different. Before bathing, take a light shower: you want to use bath time for relaxing rather than washing and it's better to be sitting in clean water.

Touch: Before, after and during your bath, touch is super important, as it can help draw out the experience. If you wait to begin relaxing when you get in the water, you will have a very short period of time to switch off. Stretch this out. Relax into the prep: the staging, the practical and the impractical. Roll a washcloth behind your head for a softer support, ensure there is a bathmat ready to go, use your softest towels and have them nearby for a smooth exit. When it comes to bubbles, any bubble bath is fine or consider adding salts. Soaking in salts has incredible benefits for your skin. You can always make your own.

Smell: Opt for candles that have lavender or chamomile, which both promote relaxation. Light these before you start to fill the bath, so the room can also fill with scent.

Taste: I personally love a bath snack. I'm not talking a burger here, rather something that can be placed on a thin waterproof tray and placed to the side. You will also want a large glass of water – a steaming bath means you need to top up your water intake.

Sound: Take inspiration from a high-end spa. Forest, rain, water playlists help people relax and get in the zone. These will add more calm and Zen than a podcast.

Sight: Soft light is essential. If safe to do so, cut ceiling lights. They can stop you properly switching off. Battery-powered lights, accent lights or candlelight can all create the perfect glow. Before you get in, remove everything resting on the edges of the bath. Bottles of shampoo or shower gel can be quite distracting to your eye, so pop these out of sight.

MAGIC MEAUXMENT

BATH SOAK

2 CUPS OF
EPSOM SALTS

1 CUP
OF PINK
SALT

FEW
DROPS OF
LAVENDER
ESSENTIAL OIL

1/4 CUP
OF DRIED
LAVENDER

- MIX ALL TOGETHER IN A BOWL & THEN DECANT INTO
  A GORGEOUS GLASS VESSEL WITH LID FOR STORAGE

- FOR YOUR NEXT BATH, MAKE A BATH BOMB USING A
  MUSLIN CLOTH. FILL WITH YOUR MIX, THEN KNOT
  THE ENDS OR USE A HAIR TIE TO SECURE. BON!

I hope this time spent with the bathroom has given you some food for thought. She may be a small room in our homes, but her impact on our day is mighty.

Speaking of little spaces, let's pop along to the home office, shall we? This isn't an actual room but her set-up is so important that we should treat her like one (*click-clacks down the hall past a gallery of vintage lipstick prints*).

CHAPTER 6

HOME OFFICE

MHW – MAKING HOME WORK

Now that working from home has been experienced in such a different way, by so many the world over, I am sure you won't mind me referring to it as 'making home work'. It's rare that homes are rented or bought based on their home office potential, so many of us really are making it work rather than it simply working. Until recently, any online search for home office inspiration would lead to images of seats with fur throws, positive quote prints (there was always a positive quote print) and vases of pink roses. There was little to no focus on the space actually having to function for an entire working week or what impact sitting on a little velvet pouffe would have on your back. A home office was more of an aesthetic space than a functional one: somewhere you would have if you could, not because you had to. Now, we are all too aware of what we need in a home-working space and aesthetics are the last part of the puzzle. We need it to help us keep focused, keep comfortable and keep going.

'WFH' plays down the absolute mission it is to create an area like this in a modern home. One where space is tight, other people exist and rooms are multi-use. It can feel impossible to have a zone that can tune out 'home' when you are working but can also later tune out work when you aren't. I'm here to tell you that it is possible. The first thing you need to know is that you don't need to have a whole room to permanently dedicate to an office; you don't even need a large area. If you have these things, then great, but your WFH space can be small, temporary and have another use. It can be at your dining table, or your dressing table. It can work well if you set it up right. Ready? Let's make home work!

SHOPPING LIST

• WORK ONLY

KEEP EVERYDAY ITEMS LIKE GLASSES AND MUGS SEPARATE FOR WORK. DON'T CARRY THEM INTO YOUR OFF TIME

• DESKTOP LAMP

THROW LIGHT ACROSS YOUR WORK AREA. MAKE SURE YOUR EYE IS NOT DISTRACTED BY THE BULB

• BULB

4,000 - 4,500K TO KEEP FOCUS BUT NOT OVERDO IT. ALWAYS REMEMBER TO SWITCH IT OFF FOR DOWN TIME

• AIR-PURIFYING PLANTS DESK OR FLOOR, JUST CLOSE TO WORK SPACE

• MAKE IT EXTRA

Lighting

If there is one thing you take from this chapter, let it be the importance of lighting when it comes to a workspace. We rely on it to work well and we need it to help switch off from work when we wish. It is one of the smallest and cheapest changes you can make

and, importantly, it is one of the most effective. This is where we revisit the matter of kelvins (k) – for a general guide to the temperature of the bulbs in each room of the home, see Hauskeeping, chapter 10.

High kelvins mean brighter light, lower kelvins mean soft, warm light. Ensuring your colour temperature matches what you want to do in the space will help with things like sleep and resting, as well as keeping active. Think about an airport, a production line, even a large office. Their cooler lighting keeps people focused and alert, with the office being ever so slightly warmer. Higher kelvins also actually lower your melatonin. From 3,500k up, we tend to be in a more perky state, but I would not go beyond 5,500k, as this will quite frankly keep you so wired that you'll be wrecked after five hours of it. Instead, a happy medium of around 4,000k or 4,500k is ideal for working. This can help keep you focused without wearing you out.

The ideal lamp is one which throws light over your working space, so you can see what you are doing. I live for a banker's lamp, which were designed for working, right down to the green shade. They allow you to see what you're doing with no glare from the bulb. Ideal. Bear this in mind when you are choosing your office lighting. Don't just go for a 4,000k bulb in the Big Light, as you will then have to live with that temperature outside of working hours. You will never really switch off from work mode. It will also cast a shadow over your workspace. Instead, choose a lamp that sits on your desk and throws good light over your keyboard or notebook. Its bulb should never be visible while you are sitting – or standing, if you are up and down a lot, or walk around taking phone calls. Bulb glare is tiring for those stunning eyes, so get rid of it completely.

If you have just the one lamp for the room, you don't necessarily need to buy another one. You can use a smart bulb that allows you to change its temperature, or you can hold on to the box and switch the bulbs (always let it cool, of course) when you switch from work to relaxing. This is especially important if you work in your bedroom. Keeping a cool light on in the evening will affect how you sleep. You want to get the kelvins down for the evening and get the melatonin up. I personally like to turn my work lamp off a half-hour before I intend to stop working so I can start to wind down to it.

The main takeaway here is that you don't want to feel like you are working in a home space even if you're working in your kitchen or bedroom. You want to create a work bubble that you can walk in and out of that feels and looks different from other areas of your home. A bubble that keeps you alert and focused, and one that can disappear at the flick of a switch. I bladdy love lighting.

Work zones

Have you ever considered not working in the one spot all day? Usually not all moments of the working day require the same level of focus or the need to be at your keyboard. Taking video meetings, brainstorming and phone calls away from your core workstation can really help you to break up the day when working from home. Being able to look at the room from another perspective, even for a phone call, is much better than sitting in the one spot all day.

In an office, you change location all the time and the day rarely feels as long. Whether you are working from a bedroom, flat share, kitchen, diner or lounge, this is something anyone can do. Look at your week's schedule and commit to sitting somewhere else for your phone calls, for example. Having a chair in a corner of a room, in a hallway or facing a window can provide a casual work zone, one that serves you another angle throughout your day. There will also be times that you just need a moment away from your desk. Perhaps you have a week with lots of video meetings. Why not set up a zone for this, even if it's just a different chair at your dining table. It will divide the day up and prevent that long stretch in the one spot.

I would also always advise having somewhere, anywhere, to have a laptop-less lunch. It is so important to have somewhere away from a screen, even if it is just while you eat.

Power zone

This is the core workstation and one that needs more focus, as it's where you will be sitting for the longest periods. It should be set up with comfort and focus in mind. A phone call or video meeting can have a more casual setting, but this needs to support you in different ways.

Most power zones will have a screen of some sort and its position is very important. You want natural light, but you don't want your back to the window – this will cause glare on the screen, which in turn might strain your eyes. Try not to have your back to the door. By nature we will automatically have our senses tuned to it. Position your desk away from the wall, so you are facing the room to make both of these happen. When you finish work, you can push your desk back

YOUR SCREEN SHOULD BE ARM'S LENGTH FROM YOU, WITH THE TOP OF THE SCREEN AT EYE LEVEL. DRAWERS ARE A GREAT PROP.

KEEP YOUR SPINE STRAIGHT AND LOWER BACK SUPPORTED.

MAKE SURE THAT CABLES HELP, NOT HINDER, YOUR SITTING POSITION. USE EXTENSION LEADS AND CABLE CLIPS TO PREVENT TOO MUCH LEANING AND STRETCHING.

THE ONLY ANGLES YOU NEED TO SERVE IN THIS POSE, MY DEAR, ARE RIGHT ANGLES. ADJUST YOUR ARM RESTS AND SEAT TO KEEP THEM SUPPORTED PARALLEL TO THE FLOOR.

KEEP SPACE UNDER THE DESK CLUTTER-FREE TO ENSURE THAT YOUR LEGS AND FEET HAVE ENOUGH ROOM.

against the wall to recover your floor space. Altering the workspace slightly after the working day can really help you 'switch off' from it.

To set up the space itself, start with a completely clear surface – desk and floor. We often remove clutter from the desk, only to place it underneath, which can throw your spine out of shape if your legs are then cramped. If it is easier to have a box into which you can pop items to take out again after work, this is better than fitting

TIP

Avoid light-coloured chairs for the workspace. White leather and pink velvet are huge trends as I write, but they can dull really quickly. All you need is a newish pair of blue jeans and the dye transfer will leave you weeping. Opt for dark tones, and fabrics that can take friction. If you sit daily in trousers tougher than your seating fabric, what do you think will wear out first?

yourself around them for eight hours a day. It will also help you to switch on and off. Getting up and walking away from your desk is great if you then have a commute, but if you're only walking a few feet to spend the evening, you will need more of a breakdown. Have a 'set up' and 'shut down' ritual each day, even if it is just clearing the space or wiping it down.

Plants

As humans, we naturally don't get distracted by plants. Our eye is more likely to be searching for fur than alarmed by green leaves. This is one reason why plants can be a gorgeous addition to a working area, but another is their air-purifying qualities, which help reduce the toxins in your space. Spider plant, aloe vera and peace lily are some low-maintenance plants that will also work on gently cleaning the air while they serve some aesthetic joy. Plants also require routine, so a morning spritz can really add to your switch-on.

Stimulation

If you feel like working at home is one long stream of caffeine to help keep the mood up, I have a solution for you. There are so many alternatives that can perk you up without inducing anxiety. First up is lemon. Lemon has been proven to help with clarity and focus. Peppermint is also fabulous for a perk-up. I find both of these sipped in a tea can lift me out of an afternoon slump and they are better for the gut (so often referred to as our second brain) than a hit of caffeine. You won't experience a crash afterwards, so you can calmly keep going.

If you find you get a bit restless during the working day, jasmine or lemongrass can help with stress. Just roll it on your wrist. My overall favourite for a mood lift and some focus is ginger. Thinly sliced (to give you more surface area) into a teapot and sipped mid-afternoon. It never fails to perk me up without the worry of it affecting sleep later.

Décor

When it comes to décor for your workspace, tap into what you know about the psychology of colour. Greens are stunning for calm and decision-making. Think banker's lamps, a green leather-topped desk, green law books and so on. It's a colour that can stimulate focus. If you were to add one main colour to a workspace aside from a white, a green or a deep blue will have a steady calming influence. Pink can actually be too calming, so if you are craving a bit of a kick, a brainstorm pink is to be avoided. Yellow can bring on a great creative spark, while red will get your adrenaline going. While I don't suggest painting walls to suit your train of thought during the working day, I do find it helpful to keep in mind the effect of colours on one's mood when planning your workspace.

MAGIC MEAUXMENT

When it comes to the little bits and pieces, I have three rules: make it fun, make it fabulous and make it feel different from downtime. Always have one or two things that spark a bit of joy near your workspace.

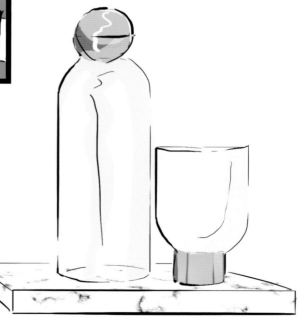

It can be a painting, a place you want to go to or maybe a wee picture of a furry friend. Office décor can be quite stark and impersonal, so having something that brings you some positivity and your own interpretation of glam is a must. You don't need to have a load of plastic and metal around you to create a 'professional' environment. Standard office décor is like this because it is designed for a large office and to largely go unnoticed. At home, once you know you have the basics correct, such as your positioning, posture and lighting, you can then add your own taste level. You can be an absolute icon, even when on Excel, so why not try to make the ordinary extraordinary?

If you are going to do the same things each and every day, they should enhance your time at work, right? For example, if you are going to have water on your desk, make a meauxment of it. Do I like mine in a minimal pitcher on a gold tray for practical reasons? No. But I drink a lot more water now than when it was in the plastic bottle I use for workouts. 'Workout' me occupies a different headspace from 'work' me and their water breaks are treated accordingly.

Making meauxments of the practical bits on my desk has become a way for me to tszuj up an otherwise boring but essential part of the day. Another reason is because I want things at my desk to feel different from elsewhere. I live in a flat in a big city – it's not like I can walk to another wing and kick off a great heel to feel like I have clocked off. My little meauxments are what actually help me to do this. The tray is only for work water, a certain mug is only for work coffee. They don't get used on weekends, so I associate them with work and it doesn't all feel the same. Try it.

Now, pop off that cool light for me and let's slink outside. There's a pitcher of Arnold Palmer with our names on it.

CHAPTER 7

OUTDOOR DÉCOR

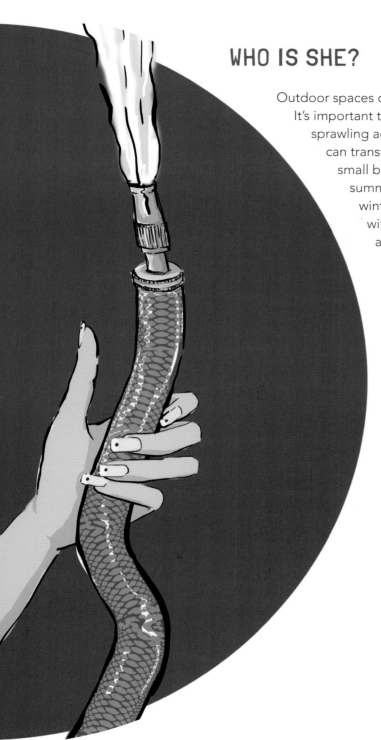

WHO IS SHE?

Outdoor spaces come in many forms and many sizes. It's important to remember that you don't need sprawling acres to make the perfect oasis. You can transform a few feet of concrete slabs or a small balcony into a haven to enjoy a balmy summer night or to cosily stargaze with a winter mulled wine. The 'who is she' here will mostly be related to the user. To achieve the perfect outdoor set-up, this is who needs to first be assessed. Before you begin even the Min here, make a list of what you need from your outdoor space. Think about everything – from storing to relaxing to anything you may like to grow. Too often we will arrange or buy for our outdoor space and forget we needed to leave room for winter storage or a bike, for example. Having this list from the beginning will help us avoid this.

THE MIN

Here we will spend mostly time rather than money, but it will create a lovely clear space for us to either enjoy as it is or to add to. If your outdoor space is making you feel a little overwhelmed, this is the perfect place to begin.

Clean & repair

It may seem minor but a deep clean of an outdoor space will work wonders visually. As you clean, note what could be repaired to save it from being damaged further or thrown away. Outdoor furnishings are pretty durable and often a small repair can make them last for many more years. For fixtures and floors, cleaning with warm soapy water and then a rinse will be fine. Use a soft cloth for things like wall fittings or glass, and a hard, bristled brush for something like concrete slabs and walls. For furniture, well, that depends on what you have . . .

Plastic furniture

Warm soapy water and a soft cloth is perfect for cleaning, as it won't scratch and will lift all dirt, sun creams and dust.

As you clean, look out for cracks, usually found in the legs. These should be dealt with right away with a glue specifically designed for plastic garden furniture. This can help the leg to last for years to come. Catching these cracks early will help you avoid any breaks.

If you are dealing with sun-damaged plastic or have some that you don't like the colour of, you can actually change this quite easily. Larger DIY stores sell paints that are suitable and safe to use on a plastic set.

Rattan

Due to its woven nature, this will hold a lot of dirt and dust. Use the upholstery setting on your vacuum and give her a light going-over to lift anything stuck in the weave. Next wash down with warm soapy water and a soft cloth, like a microfibre.

If you have plastic rattan and spot some fraying or tears, you can glue and stick these down or replacement strips are available to buy online.

Wooden furniture

You'll need a brush to clean down wood – just make sure she has lovely soft bristles. A non-scratch sponge would also do. Use warm soapy water and go with the grain. Make sure she can dry out well and quickly after. Softwoods will need a protective layer applied – think like a nail varnish top coat. On this side of the world, with the winters so damp, many hardwoods will benefit from this, too.

Metal furniture

A wash-down with soapy water and a soft cloth is the job here again. As you clean, look out for signs of rust or chipped paint. Top up with paint or a protective coat to prevent rusting.

If rusting has started, you can call on my favourite acidic queen: vinegar. The most common feature to rust is the feet, so you can pop undiluted vinegar into tubs and let the feet sit in them to remove the rust. The vinegar needs thirty minutes minimum to work her magic. The worse the rust is, the longer she will need. If the area is further up and impossible to submerge, soak a cloth in undiluted white vinegar and wrap around the rusty part, again leaving for at least thirty minutes. You can then just wipe it off.

If you have stiff hinges on folding chairs or umbrella poles, add oil at the start and end of summer.

Cushions and umbrellas

Hoover all cushions with the upholstery setting to avoid wear and tear. Then wash according to their instructions. It is better to put covers back on when they are very slightly damp and allow them to finish their drying around the filling so it can set into place properly. Always make sure cushions are bone dry and clean before you put them away and never store on the floor. Store 'em high to keep 'em dry.

Clear

Outdoor spaces tend to gather items that don't belong there: old mop buckets, broken ceramics and other miscellaneous bits and pieces. Before you think this all needs to go, think about what can be repurposed. It doesn't need to be as obvious as daffodils in wellies; it can be an opportunity to get really creative and chicly upcycle. Can anything be used as a planter, to spruce up pots or to section flowerbeds? If in doubt or despair, type what you have and then 'in garden' into Google and you will be simply charmed by what others have done with theirs. Don't stop the clear at rubbish like this – weeding, pruning and reducing anything overgrown is one of the easiest ways to free up space. It can also help you get more sunlight in certain spots.

THE TSZUJ

You may have all you need in place but feel like you're lacking some styling or pizzazz in the area. For this, we can use the Tszuj. Small changes that don't require too much time or spend but can add a real wow factor if done well.

Soft furnishings

This is a great way to spruce up an outdoor space, but the key is not to buy as you would for an indoor room; there are more elements at work here, so keep these in mind:

- *Sun*: Check that soft furnishings are UV/fade-resistant. It can be hard to make a fabric both completely fade-resistant and comfortable to touch, so this is why so many outdoor fabrics are light colours. That way some fading can occur, but go unnoticed.
- *Wear*: For outdoor cushions, especially seat cushions, you want a thick fabric. Anything too thin will fall to bits over time.
- *Comfort*: Vinyls can be super durable but can get hot and a bit sticky – after all, they are a plastic. You want something that will be durable but comfortable, like a canvas.
- *Moisture*: Being water-resistant or waterproof is important for two reasons. Do you want your sweat to seep into the filling? Also, when she's in storage, you don't want her growing mildew and mould. If a fabric states it's suitable for outdoor use, it will repel moisture, as it will usually have a coating applied to the fabric. 'Waterproof' means zero absorption but can sometimes be less comfortable than 'water-resistant', which will repel liquids that spill but when in a washing machine or in a large amount of water will absorb it.
- *Filling*: The best filling is a foam wrapped in fibre for seat cushions. This has the durability and the sink of the foam but the comfort of the fibre. Foam on its own can wear out quite quickly and just fibre is more suited to scatter cushions, as it will go flat through use.

Rugs

I love an outdoor rug. She can really add to an outdoor space, especially a small one. Balconies are ideal, as they will have their own drainage set-up and a textured floor, so she is not lying completely flat against it. This is perfect to ensure some airflow underneath. Balconies are a great fit for a rug because they are usually less exposed than other outdoor areas.

Like all outdoor fabrics, you need to select a rug that is UV-resistant and is suited to outdoor use. You can also find indoor/outdoor rugs which you can swap throughout the year as you please. I like to go for an intense pattern rather than a flat colour, always within a palette that sits well with the outdoors, such as greens, sands, animals or tropicals. A geometric or a polka-dot pattern can look a little too 'indoor'. The pattern will hide dirt and stains that are bound to happen outdoors, but it will also add some depth to an outdoor floor which is usually boring, as it is so practical.

You want to treat her like an indoor rug – spot clean, hoover often and ensure the corners are stuck down to avoid trips. To reduce wear and tear, I roll mine up and place it to the side on days of heavy rain and wind, as they can get blown away or knock over furniture. If she does get soaked, I lie her over the outdoor furniture to thoroughly dry out. It's not a big deal; it's just that walking on damp fabric a lot can wear out the fibres.

Lighting

If you plan to use your space after sundown, lighting is essential. The right light will create the most wonderful ambience and enhance whatever you are doing. You can, of course, choose to install lighting that is connected to your mains, and there is the option of low-energy lighting, but I love solar-powered. Fuss-free and using nature's gorgeous power is something that cannot be beaten, in my opinion.

You want to go for a warm glow. Anything white will make it look like a football stadium or an interrogation. You're aiming more for sunset in the Sahara. Unless, that is, it's a security light. Before you choose, be very clear about what you want to do with your light. Do you want to avoid evening meals feeling like a reservation at Dans Le Noir? Or do you want to make sure your route to the back door is easy to see? Maybe you want to light the whole space as you would a living room. Or it might be a pair of topiary urns. Gasp! Lighting can either hang, stand or be mounted and all give a different effect, so it is important to know which will match your needs.

- *Festoon lights* are brilliant if your idea is to add a light with little effort or expense. If you want to stick to one style of lighting, these can throw light without bothering the eye, unlike other choices. You can light up the whole outdoor space if you wish or just a selected area. They can be draped or hung easily, in so many different styles, with zero drama, and most of all they don't really take space away from anything else, as you are not using the floor or walls. You can cross two lengths above the desired area to brighten a large space. You can line a balcony railing, thread through a trellis, fashion a chandelier effect above a table . . . the possibilities are endless. When it comes to styling, however, I would suggest avoiding the bunting hang, where it dips in the middle. This shouts Christmas. Instead, go for sharp straight lines for a more modern effect.

  If buying online, look at the bulb size and take in how long the length of cable is. Pictures can be quite deceiving, so it's good to know the spec inside out. Also check that it has a still setting. Some just come with a flashing mode, which is not exactly going to add to a rioja around the firepit.

- *Stake lights* are light fittings that sit upon a stake stuck into the grass. There are so many options and shapes. Some are designed to light the floor around them, so are ideal near steps or along pathways, as they can safely guide you through the dark. I also love that you can stick them into plant pots near a front door, which is a chic way to be able to see your keys in the winter months. You can get some that are more for decoration and are popped around flowerbeds to allow you to enjoy their contents even at night. Others come in novelty shapes, though I have never been too fond of an oversized glowing snail on a rod.

- *Uplighters and downlighters* are usually placed quite close to what they need to be enhancing, for example said topiary urns. They are also great in a small space, like a courtyard, should you want it to feel bigger. You can place them above or below a white wall to make the space feel much bigger by night. Make sure their bulbs are not exposed to the eye when sitting and for this I find ideal those whose focus can be adjusted.

- *Lanterns* with solar-powered bulbs rather than candles are excellent if you use the space in different ways. They can be propped on a table while you eat or on the floor next to you as you read. I also like them for adding some atmosphere to the parts of the space that are not in use, as they are not usually too bright and can add a soft glow to a corner.

- *Hanging lights* usually come individually and can be hung from trees, walls, balcony ceilings and so on. They will rarely give you enough light to make a radical difference but are great dotted around for a soft-lit vibe.

Paint

Paint is another way to take your outdoor space to the next level. From furniture and walls to fences, paint can instantly transform most of the elements of your garden that are holding it back or help take the eye away from anything less favourable. With sprayers now more widely available to non-professionals, large outdoor areas can be covered quickly and evenly, making it an enjoyable project.

No matter what you are planning to transform, when it comes to painting anything outdoors you must ensure that you have selected an outdoor paint suitable for the surface and always prep properly and prime. If you fail to prep well, you will know all about it. Make sure that you clean the surface well and remove any loose debris, mould and cobwebs. Use this as an opportunity to fill any impurities and carry out any repairs. Primer will help your paint to bond, as well as protect the surface, but make sure it is OK for outdoor use.

Go for a warm, dry day with little wind for a better finish. Rain and humidity are obvious no-no's, but people will often overlook wind. This will blow dirt and dust against your wet paint and it will stick.

I like to create a blank canvas with white or off-white and then add pops of colour with furniture and accents on fencing. This will help you to achieve a look that will stand the test of time, as you can easily update a fence or chair for a whole new look. If you are not keen on white, or it's too bright for you, look into a plaster pink shade, as this works really well in outdoor settings against the sky's blue tones and foliage.

Walls

A garden wall is one that is easy to tackle yourself, but I would leave the walls of the house to a professional. They can spot any rising damp, ominous cracks and other issues that we may not. They will also know what can and cannot go over it.

Furniture

This is the one outdoor element where you can really go for it, as it can always be painted over next year. Wooden, plastic or metal furniture can all enjoy a fresh coat of paint. If you are not sure what to go for, fuchsia, bright yellow and orange are super popular choices against white walls, as they add a vibrant feel that is playful and in keeping with the tone of summer. If you are after a sleeker look, opt for charcoal, mocha and sand tones.

Fences

A fabulous way to add some drama to the space. I personally love a dark shade on a fence, as it acts almost like a frame. Sprayers are such a huge help with fences but avoid for trellises unless you can take them down to spray. Next door may not take too kindly to the patchwork you apply to their foliage.

THE OVERHAUL

The potential for an overhaul in some outdoor spaces can be endless. However, one major change all outdoor spaces can benefit from is new furniture. From large gardens to small balconies, the addition of some great furniture can really elevate the look as well as the time spent there.

Just like a living room, kitchen or bedroom, there will be limitations as to what can go where, ideal positions for larger furniture and directions in which things can face.

Users

First off, note the number of people who will be using the space. This will help you decide on seating, table size and how much free floor space you need. If you have children, you may want more floor space than seating. If this is going to be a place to lie in the sun in a wide-brimmed hat and a great lip, or have a date over (again, in a great lip), more seating, less floor for you.

Non-negotiables

There will be things already in place that will affect where you can place your furniture, hang baskets, lay rugs, position barbecues and so on. Things that are vital to the space that need to do their job properly for the space to thrive. To avoid mistakes, like placing floor cushions in drain paths or positioning a couch over a vent, you need to avoid the common error of only noting the amount of floor space available and instead note the amount of *usable floor space* you have to work with. Here's how you can start to uncover that usable space.

- *Function:* Are there drains, pipes, taps, electrics or vents in the area? What needs to be kept free for these to be able to function normally?
- *Flooring:* Is the ground sloping or uneven? If you plan on having something like a hot tub (I'm warning you, these are making a comeback), a large table or a gas heater, a level floor may be needed. It is also good to note any trip hazards that may be masked by furniture height or length. You don't want the furniture to create an obstacle course for the user. If you have uneven flooring or gravel, you'll want sturdy, wide legs. If you want to add a large rug, you need to ensure the floor can drain as it should with it *in situ*.
- *Supply:* If there are items that need power – heaters, lighting, hot tub – their placement will be determined by access to a power source, which can have a knock-on effect on the position of other items.
- *Clearance:* Are there doors, windows or cupboards opening out onto the space and how much clearance do they need to be able to do so? Open everything, then assess what would be open often and at the same time to determine the floor space you actually have to play with. Having to squeeze through a half-open door to get outside is a fire hazard, but you'll also end up resenting the set-up quite quickly. For me, you need to be able to carry a tray of margaritas to the table with zero risk.
- *Tasks:* Are there any workstations outside, like a clothesline, compost area or herb garden, that will be affected by what you have in mind? You need to make sure you can still carry a heavy load of washing to your line, hazard-free, or that the only place for your rattan sofa isn't next to a compost heap . . .
- *Sun:* Noting where the sun is at different times of the day will ensure you're getting the right sun exposure at the right time. This is also good for clothesline and compost placement.
- *Direction:* What do you want to face when you are sitting? What don't you want to face when you are sitting? This is often missed when planning, but it's important. Do you want to be able to watch the sunset from the couch? Perhaps it's more important to face the morning sun, or do you want both and need something lightweight enough to be able to flip around?
- *Privacy:* As well as eyes, consider ears during your placement.

Now that you know what space you have to work with, it's time to consider the style of furniture you would like. Sets are the most common way to buy garden furniture. They usually consist of seating and some sort of table. Many people will type in 'garden set' and choose by price and aesthetics instead of assessing what type of set will actually meet their needs. We actually must look at what we want the set for first – some sets will be more comfortable for dining but not work well for lounging, for example. Let's get into it in more detail . . .

Bistro set

A CLASSIC outdoor set, she comes as a small table with two matching chairs. This style came from Paris, where Parisian bistros needed to fit as many diners as they could along thin pavements. This makes her, by design, perfect for use in a smaller outdoor space, though you can get bulkier versions too. They come at every price level, so have multiple uses.

Use

Bistros are ideal for outdoor dining, or if you want to work outside in the warmer months, as she is pretty much set up like a dinner table, just smaller.

Styling

They are absolutely gorgeous in a colour pop with a bright or striped cushion. A black bistro set can add some gloss to the space, but avoid if you're placing her in a very sunny spot, as she can get quite hot. Opt for Miami-inspired pastels instead.

Pros

These are usually metal, wood or a mix of both, which means you can change the look easily with a splash of paint. Foldable options are great, as you can pull out extra chairs for guests when needed but keep them tucked away when it is just you.

Cons

These can be uncomfortable if you are looking for something to lounge on, as you are so upright. But if you are tight on space, you can create your own cushion pads (see page 188) to make reading a book in the sun more enjoyable.

Rattan sets

Natural woven cane is simply gorgeous, but for outdoor use it is only really suited to places where the weather is dry and not very humid. In the UK and Ireland manmade rattans are popular for outdoor use, as they can withstand the weather conditions better. They give you all the visual glory without the headache. Rattan sets usually come styled much like indoor furniture. Think couches, armchairs, coffee tables, dining tables and so on.

There are three main types of manmade rattan out there: PU, PVC and then PE, with the latter being the one you want.

PU and PVC are coated plastics, so you will get chipping, warping and sagging, and it won't be resistant to UV. It is also crap for the planet and you will almost certainly only get a couple of years out of it before it is brittle and snapping from outdoor conditions, as well as, literally, coming apart at the seams. I would avoid these as I would a lipstick that bleeds.

Polyethylene (PE) is the queen of rattans. She is a resin designed to look just like real cane rattan and the more eco-friendly option, as she is recyclable. Yas, bish. This means she can turn the look of rattan but also has the durability and sturdiness to last in any climate. PE will usually be weatherproof and UV-resistant, which adds to its long-lasting allure. You won't get chipping, as the strips are one colour the whole way through.

Before we get ahead of ourselves and think PE is all we need to look for, there are different grades of PE. These range from low (LDPE) to high density (HDPE), with higher of course being better, but any grade of PE is better than plastic rattan.

The quickest way to spot a PU or PVC rattan is to see if it is all one colour; PE will have darker and lighter tones running through it, as a natural cane rattan would. The guarantee is also a huge giveaway. If it's just for a year or two, it's a cheap plastic rattan.

Frame

Another thing that can help or hinder the life of your rattan furniture is the frame. She is usually made from steel or aluminium. The long-lasting and more expensive frames are aluminium, which can also take rain and moisture without rusting. Steel can rust and wear but is cheaper, so can be found in lower priced options. If the piece is not going to be rained on, steel may be OK, but it's

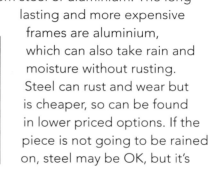

also a lot clunkier. Also, if you plan on moving the furniture around, be careful about the feet. Rubber gliders can get damaged when they are dragged on concrete.

Use

If you're after an outdoor lounge or dining room, this could be ideal for you. For an option that you can also dine at, there are sets that come with adjustable tables, low for coffee or dining height to suit your needs.

Styling

The weave of a rattan set makes all the difference. For a more chic and airy feel, look for rod or half-round weave, whose look has a more rounded, raised appeal than the flat-weave sets seen more often. A lighter colour will always look best in rattan, and have a little fun with your cushion choice. Avoid white or light colours, as the fabric will come in contact with a lot of food, liquids and sun cream.

Pros

These offer the most comfort and you will use your outdoor space a lot more with a rattan set in place. When bought well, rattan is one of the most low-maintenance styles of furniture you can buy and, with the exception of her cushions, can be left out all winter.

Cons

These sets are bulky and rarely foldable, which means they will be a bit of a hindrance in a smaller space where doors need clearance, etc.

Trestle tables

These sets are great, as they completely fold down flat and allow you to slip them into the back of a cupboard for winter or to the side when you want to use the space to, say, dry clothing, tend to your herbs or dance barefoot to 'Club Tropicana'.

Use

As these are so lightweight they are great for balconies. If you like to have people round for a BBQ, these are a perfect solution, as the benches mean you have options. If you want foldaway garden furniture for parties, this is also ideal.

Styling

Most will come unvarnished, so, before you do anything, seal her when she arrives. These can look great in pastels, deep colours or bright tones. They suit it all! Just bear in mind that darker table tops need a tablecloth in the sun to avoid retaining heat.

Pros

These are super lightweight, made from metal and wood, and are inexpensive in comparison to other types of dining sets. A lick of paint can transform these and they will last years, if cared for.

Cons

No back rests mean they aren't the ideal option for lounging and can get a little uncomfortable after a while. However, you can always cushion these.

Materials

There are many different materials available when it comes to furniture and it's good to know what to expect once they come to live with you. This will help you choose a set that suits your set-up all year round.

Wood: Wooden garden furniture is great if it is a hardwood, especially teak. This will have its own oils and is good at battling the elements. If you love a makeover project, you'll be able to pick up a quality set for a low price to restore to her former glory. Softwoods get damaged by water, so these need to be treated.

Plastic: While plastic furniture isn't the most stunning of choices, she is usually the most affordable. If you need to move your furniture around a lot to chase the sun or out of the way for other activities, plastic is lightweight, usually stackable and easy to store. She is water-resistant, though she can get blown around. She is also prone to fading.

Metal: Metal furniture is super durable. Most will be coated to prevent rusting and this needs to be kept intact. It is best to keep it dry during winter, so go for a great cover that allows for air circulation.

Aluminium: This is a rust-free gal and she is lightweight enough to be able to move her around with ease. But like plastic she can be blown over. She can hack most weather conditions, so she can be great if you have zero storage and need to leave her stacked outside. She can discolour over time due to oxidization, so if her colour is important to you keep her dry all year round.

Wrought iron: This is the kind of garden furniture that has a decorative look, ideal for a quaint bistro set. She is quite clunky and hard to move, so it should be a set that can stay put. This can be brilliant for a garden that gets a lot of wind. Like all metals she can rust, but you'll buy her painted and, as long as she doesn't chip, the metal underneath won't rust.

Small space saviours

Small spaces can be enhanced with the correct furniture and accessories. If you don't choose carefully, you can end up with a space that is hard to use. Here are some things to look out for if you are working with a small outdoor space.

Furniture

If you opt for a set, this will take up most of the space, so go for something neat. The arms of the chairs in some dining sets can use up a lot of room, so go for a thin arm and back. To avoid feeling like the space is overwhelmed by the set, opt for a low back, and preferably not a solid one, so you can see through it. Always ensure that the chairs can fit under the table. This will save so much space when not in use.

Fold it up

Folding furniture is the best option in a small space. It's highly likely you won't have storage for your furniture, so being able to stack it in a cupboard or to the side during the winter months is a real bonus.

Up the walls

When you are low on floor space, you should always use the walls. Fold-down tables that can be fixed to a wall or hung from a balcony rail are a brilliant way to save on space.

You can also opt for a hanging chair. These will need a pretty sturdy set-up to hang from but can be a fab space-saving accessory, not to mention they are extremely relaxing to sit in. This is an ideal piece if you wish to utilize a corner that is too uneven for chairs or has a drain in it.

Ladder shelves are a gorgeous touch, as you can use them as a herb garden. These are also fab if you need to keep anything you are growing off the ground due to night-time visitors to your garden.

Multifunctional

As with any small space, furniture that has multiple uses is the way to go. Anything that can be adapted with a few moves will help you make the most of it.

A good use of a corner in a small space is two low benches (bonus if they offer storage) lined along the walls in an L-shape. By adding seat and back cushions it can make a slimline couch by day. The addition of a folding table can twirl her into a casual dinner setting, and placing benches either side gives you a more formal set-up. Three different looks from three pieces. Stunning.

Look out for things like picnic tables that fold back into a bench, and of course my favourite: seats that have slide-out tables to perch a martini on, if needed. The storage side of outdoor seats can make stunning ice boxes for parties or can house gardening equipment for your macrame planters, but I would avoid filling it with cushions in winter months, as it can become a pest and mould palace.

Play with light

Garden mirrors work so well in a small area, as they create the illusion of more space. Go for mirror sheeting instead of a heavy mirror that can be knocked over or broken. It's super lightweight, so you can move it around easily to get the perfect placement. Sheeting is less likely to suffer from weather damage the way a true mirror would. An antique-style look will have flecks and marks on the mirror and this dulled look will stop birds flying into it, lower the glare and will mean you don't need to clean it so often, as the dust and streaks won't be as obvious. It is always a great idea to hang and place plants near your mirror, as you will double up on greenery visually. Always ensure she is securely anchored.

Hanging accessories

Hanging planters and rail pots (plant pots that are moulded to sit safely on a railing) take up zero floor space but add so much to a balcony or courtyard. If you have no grass, being able to add your own greenery is a way to add a warm and soft flow to the space. Even if you have a small balcony, adding to the space with hanging accessories can really bring it to life. Before you hang, ensure that all doors can open and that there is headroom over the paths people will walk.

Barbecues

Adding a BBQ is a stunning use of outdoor space, in my opinion. When it comes to these gals, you can be left scratching your head at all the choice and it can be hard to know where to start. Get to know the types of BBQs out there and you won't take long to realize which category is best suited to you.

First, check out how they are fuelled. When it comes to cooking outdoors, you'll have the choice of using gas or charcoal.

Gas

If you want an extremely quick set-up, full control of cooking the food and low-maintenance cleaning, this is great for you. A gas BBQ is essentially like a gas hob, as you will have knobs to turn the heat up and down as you please, which means you can also cook one side at one temp and the other at another. Again, as it is like an outdoor hob, it can come as big as you need, with as many add-ons as you like (there are SO many add-ons), which can pretty much turn it into an outdoor kitchen.

You don't need to be as savvy about cooking over fire as you would with a charcoal BBQ and you won't have the same clean-up after, but – and I must stress this point – you don't get the same taste. This is the kind of BBQ to suit someone who wants to cook outside and is not too fussed about the charcoal flavour.

Charcoal

This is my BBQ of choice. I love cooking over fire, as the taste cannot be beaten, and while the high-end gas BBQs can create smoked food, for me it's not the same. I just enjoy the whole process, from start to finish. Yes, they take more time to get hot. Once hot, you can't just lower it when needed. And don't mention the clean-up. But for me it's all worth it. A summer evening spent setting up and cooking over a charcoal BBQ is simply glorious. I also find it better if you are going for a meat-free meal, as the flavours are much deeper (baby gem sliced in half, cooked inside down, then drizzled with lemon is a big fave in my home). Instead of storing gas canisters, a bag of lumpwood charcoal is all that you need, which also makes it more economical. If you really want to kick things up a notch, have a peek at smokers.

MAGIC MEAUXMENT

CUSHION COVERS

THERE WILL ALWAYS BE AN AREA OF A GARDEN, TERRACE OR BALCONY THAT GETS SOME GORGEOUS HOURS OF SUN BUT CANNOT BE KITTED OUT WITH FURNITURE DUE TO CLEARANCE, AND SO IT OFTEN GOES TO WASTE. *MON DIEU!*

TO MAKE THE MOST OF THESE SPOTS, ALL YOU NEED IS SOME CUSHION PADS TO HELP YOU CREATE A LITTLE NOOK FOR READING OR RELAXING.

AS EVERY NOOK WILL BE A DIFFERENT SIZE, HERE IS HOW TO CREATE ONE TAILORED TO FIT YOURS. . .

YOU'LL NEED:

- FABRIC SUITABLE FOR OUTDOOR USE
- FOAM (GO FOR AS HIGH A DENSITY AS YOUR BUDGET WILL ALLOW)
- THREAD AND NEEDLE (IF HAND SEWING) OR SEWING MACHINE
- SCISSORS
- MEASURING TAPE

OVERVIEW:

YOUR CUSHION COVER WILL BE MADE UP OF THREE PIECES

1 - FRONT: THIS WILL COVER THE FRONT AND SIDES

2 + 3: BACK: THESE WILL FORM AN 'ENVELOPE' OPENING FOR THE PAD

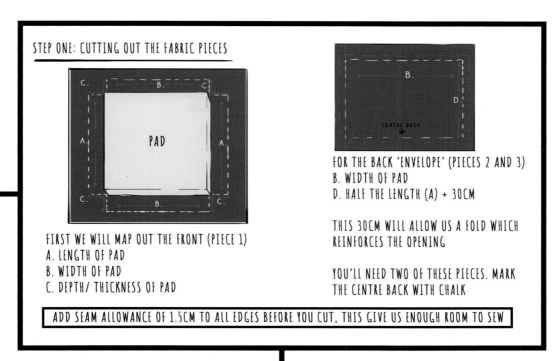

STEP ONE: CUTTING OUT THE FABRIC PIECES

PAD

FIRST WE WILL MAP OUT THE FRONT (PIECE 1)
A. LENGTH OF PAD
B. WIDTH OF PAD
C. DEPTH/ THICKNESS OF PAD

B.

CENTRE BACK

FOR THE BACK 'ENVELOPE' (PIECES 2 AND 3)
B. WIDTH OF PAD
D. HALF THE LENGTH (A) + 30CM

THIS 30CM WILL ALLOW US A FOLD WHICH
REINFORCES THE OPENING

YOU'LL NEED TWO OF THESE PIECES. MARK
THE CENTRE BACK WITH CHALK

ADD SEAM ALLOWANCE OF 1.5CM TO ALL EDGES BEFORE YOU CUT, THIS GIVE US ENOUGH ROOM TO SEW

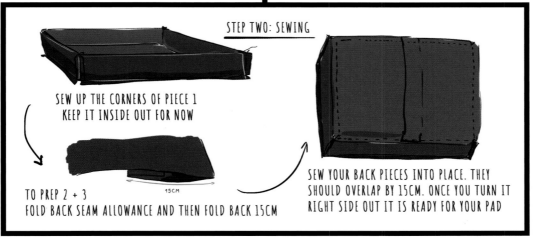

STEP TWO: SEWING

SEW UP THE CORNERS OF PIECE 1
KEEP IT INSIDE OUT FOR NOW

15CM

TO PREP 2 + 3
FOLD BACK SEAM ALLOWANCE AND THEN FOLD BACK 15CM

SEW YOUR BACK PIECES INTO PLACE. THEY
SHOULD OVERLAP BY 15CM. ONCE YOU TURN IT
RIGHT SIDE OUT IT IS READY FOR YOUR PAD

An outdoor space is a gift and I hope you have learned in this chapter that whatever you have can be turned into a sanctuary. Take your time considering what will suit yours and the rewards will be endless. (*Pulls back wide straw brim and raises an iced tea.*)

We may have come to the end of the tour, but I have a surprise for you. There is one thing we have yet to discuss. Once your home is set up just the way you like it, there is something that becomes even more enjoyable . . . Events!

Dinner parties and Christmas, to be exact.

CHAPTER 8

THE DINNER PARTY

I'll make an event of any dining affair, big or small. Be it a breakfast with flatmates, having someone over for a bowl of pasta or a pho delivery on my own on Friday. It may be a linen napkin added, a lovely plate, perhaps a candle will be lit. There will always be a lot of consideration and a little fuss to enhance the experience. So, you can only imagine how I feel about a full-on dinner party! It's like a high. Let's head to my dining table and discuss the finer details of how to pull one off with minimal stress and maximum enjoyment. Take a seat (*plucks napkin from table and slides over lap*). Some chocolate mousse?

Before we get stuck in, I must assure you that your dinner party can come in any form you like. Over the top, casual, big or small, but she must, and I repeat MUST, have a great ambience to be a success. It will also take the heat off you as you do your bits. We've all been to parties, weddings and events where someone has spent a fortune but the atmosphere was as dull as a Yeezy colour palette. Then to another soirée where it was done simply and cheaply and the atmosphere was one to remember. It's really not about the spend. For me, if you want the best chance at creating a great atmosphere that is as easy for guests to slip into as a pointed-toe Roger Vivier mule, it is all down to *CHAIRS*.

C - Conversation
H - Hydration
A - Anticipation
I - Illumination
R - Relaxation
S – Salivation

Conversation

Good conversation will enhance any party and is a huge part of the dining experience. No matter the food you serve, the year of the wine or the colour of the napkins, one thing that will make everyone feel full is connection through free-flowing conversation.

If you are having close friends over, conversation will usually flow without your aid. However, if you are having a group that has not met before, or perhaps you're meeting your in-laws, you may need to have some subtle things in place to start, encourage or move along conversation. This can be as simple as having a few fail-safe questions about upcoming trips or memorable meals.

It's also important to remember that you are not Geppetto. I loathe a dining experience where there is an expectation to converse, perform or act in a certain manner and especially if you feel like the host has every moment decided for you. Guide people to topics but don't drag. (*Pulls spoon across plate.*)

Hydration

Water, water, water. If you do anything with gumption for your dinner party, let it be the water. For many reasons, keeping everyone hydrated is key for a great night. While you may think this is as simple as a glass of water per guest, it involves so much more. An ideal serving of water is 250ml per person, so use a large glass to enable you to make sure each guest has at least one serving to start, without having their glass filled to the brim. I love a 400–500ml stemless wine glass. I know, I sound like an arsehole, but bear with me. I love the water and wine glasses to have the same shape and you can also fit a really large glass of water in them without looking like a pint glass you'd find on a bedside table after a night out. The shape is also good to avoid spills. I've done the tall, thin water glasses and they always end up getting knocked. This way you have a chic but sturdy way to keep a guest in great supply.

For serving, a table jug, with a larger jug (or Brita) kept in the fridge for topping up makes sure the water is always cool. This means no one has to get up for water and you can keep the table jug topped up yourself between courses. Thin slices of lemon in the jug add visual appeal, but are also good for your breath and gut.

Anticipation

A hint of anticipation is always a stunning addition to any event and can be created with one thing – a set dinner table upon arrival. It will encourage a lovely sense of 'can't fucking wait' in your guests. It also means you can enjoy the setting process and not have to work around people sitting at the table.

You can be as extra or as simple as you like when it comes to this setting. Menus, name cards, candelabras, floral arrangements and so on are all optional extras, not necessities. Consideration with a twist of creativity is richer and more alluring than any expensive dinnerware could ever be. It's all about how you work with what you have, not about what you have.

To begin, lay out the things that your guests will definitely need to wine and dine with ease that evening, from glassware to cutlery. If it looks lovely at that, then leave it there. If you feel it needs a little tszuj or you want to incorporate a theme, then add, but only slightly, as people need room for reaching, passing and gesturing. The best decoration at a dinner party is relaxed guests, so keeping it simple will ensure this. Too often, people try to create a dinner party table setting with grandeur and add-ons that actually hamper a comfortable dining experience. Start with the necessities, then build with the user in mind.

Illumination

It's important to have enough light to be able to see what you are doing but not enough to feel like you're at a bar in Gatwick at 6 a.m. Not everyone has a light fixture above the table, so instead we have candles. Tea lights and low-rise candles can lead to burned wrists or napkins going up in flames, so go for a tall candlestick with a long dinner candle. Go for tapered – stunning and less likely to knock. I like two candlesticks to spread the light. Always opt for an unscented candle for the table, as scented candles while eating can throw people off. Light them shortly before people sit and then leave to burn until everyone has left the table.

When it comes to lighting the rest of the room in a multi-use space, I find that under-counter lights are a godsend and having a lamp or two but no 'big light' on is a must. You want people to feel they are in a little cocoon, so removing distractions by literally turning off the rest of the room is a lovely way to do it.

Relaxation

A calm atmosphere starts with you. Be aware of body language and rushing, even if you are feeling stressed. Take a moment to remind yourself that everyone loves to eat something they don't have to cook themselves, so you just need to lean in and relax.

Music will guide you well in setting tone. My personal favourite, and it gives me chills writing this, are 1960s/70s cocktail lounge or mid-century martini lounge playlists. They make me feel like we are all at a bar on *The Love Boat*, sequinned sharp shoulders glistening in the moonlight. It's upbeat without being distracting, with an undertone of romance. I dai.

Comfort is a huge part of relaxation, and this is one of the main reasons I like to have a lot of room on the table, so people can rest their arms as they please. A wobbly chair or table can throw this off. This is where letting a red wine breathe before the meal comes in handy. Keep the cork and cut it down to fill the gap. It can be glued or taped in place to keep any rocking at bay. This is also a great moment to consider if the nuts need tightening on your flat pack furniture. A quick tszuj will tighten her up and resolve any creaking.

Salivation

Food is the last thing mentioned, as I wanted it to be clear that food is only as big a deal as you wish to make it. You don't have to serve an eight-course meal to make a dinner party memorable, but it does help to think about the food as an orgasm in the desire, arousal, orgasm and resolution (a nod to Masters and Johnson here) sequence of events. Desire is the set table. Arousal is where you serve a little something away from the table, before people sit. This can literally be chips and dips, an amuse bouche, or, my fave, a vol-au-vent. Something fuss-free that you can serve on a tray, ready to be popped in the mouth while having a cocktail. The orgasm itself needs no explanation: this will be the seated main course and starter. And lastly, you want resolution. This would be a dessert such as a sorbet or some cheese, and tea or coffee.

Keep this light structure in mind to avoid overloading yourself by thinking every bite needs to be a huge effort – and to also avoid overloading your guests.

So, the next time you host, don't forget your CHAIRS.

HOSTESS ANXIETY

We all get it. If you had an Irish upbringing, you get it more. Don't ask me why, I don't make the rules. (*Pours sherry into crystal glasses.*)

Fed & watered

While I can't unpack the origins of your anxiety around hosting, I can offer some advice on how to minimize it. First, hydrate. The one thing a dinner host will always forget to do is to keep themselves fed and watered that day. It's too easy to forget your needs in the rush of it all, but you are the most important thing in all of this, and keeping yourself balanced and hydrated is key. If you are nervous about the workload, there will always be one guest you can rely on to help you clear away or serve. If I am having a big dinner party, I will have one friend I always ask to come early so we chat through the flow and I know they have my back for the night.

Lists

Even if you're not a fan of lists day to day, pouring yourself a lemon and honey tea and taking some time to create a few lists will keep you on track on the day. It will also help you realize where you may be stretching yourself and, most importantly, where you can really switch off and enjoy yourself. Here are the four lists I make.

Food & Drink

Compile this in the week before the party. It will help you tease out things like when to shop, when to prep linen, candles, choose and buy wine, borrow a crock pot and so on.

If there is something I particularly want to cook – say, for example, beef or something that is in season – I almost always google suggestions for a one-pot recipe. This saves so much time and energy and is the easiest thing to prepare and serve. Trust me, a coq au vin or a vegetarian curry from scratch is easier than something with a lot of moving parts. Being able to start a dish earlier in the day and allow it to slow cook until you need to serve it is one of the greatest dinner party gifts you can give yourself.

Another thing that will help you decide your mains and starters are the types of serving you wish to do. Large-format dining or family-style dining, where people serve themselves from dishes placed on the table, is ideal. You don't need to worry about individually plating, food going cold, people not getting enough or getting served too much. The main reason I adore this style is because you all get to sit together for longer. I also like it for starters and desserts, if the head count is over four.

All you will then need to do is consider sides. These can be as complex as you like, but a starch, like a potato or grain, is a must and then you want a healthy crunch like a green bean or salad. I have never failed by adding something purple. A slaw, beetroot, purple carrot, purple potato and so on. I tend to go for texture and colour, then make it simple but plentiful. It's nice to choose sides you can mostly prep in advance. I will prep my salad, wrap and refrigerate, so it only needs dressing before serving. Or you could prepare a dauphinoise that only needs to be baked and so on.

Remember, starters can be cold if you wish to prep beforehand and plate later, giving you more time at the table. A fish or meat-free starter is always a winner. Remember, you want to ease into this. Dessert can be as you wish – cheese, affogato, cake, whatever takes your fancy – but you'll be wrecked if it involves a lot of work on the night. While it may be nice for guests to see individual flaming flans arrive at the table, I am sure they would much rather spend more time with you and something simpler.

A platter for dessert or starter is something I nearly always fall back on. These need very little cutlery, small plates and people can choose how much they want to eat. Key for a relaxed evening! They are super easy to throw together and the entire course can be brought to the table on a lazy Susan (a fab investment, if you love to host). One note here if you are serving a platter of any kind: I would always try to refrain from making it look too 'fiddled with'. The board should look like it had the most minimal amount of handling possible. Should you be serving both meat eaters and vegans or vegetarians, you need to make separate boards. As a host you don't want someone trying to figure out what hasn't touched meat or cheese.

Order of service

This list keeps track of what you'll need for cooking, serving and eating. It's incredibly helpful and ensures you avoid the panic of realizing you don't have enough pots or oven room or that you need to borrow a larger platter in advance. This is where you can start to edit. If you realize something won't work with your set-up, you can swap it out before you go shopping. You may only be able to fit two large oven dishes at once, so if your recipe requires a third, now is the time to rejig.

Shopping list

This will centre around your recipes. Take each course and note every single ingredient in the recipe, even if you think you already have it. Don't forget the drinks too – you'll need lemons or cucumber for water, ice, mint leaves for tea, and so on. Then go through your cupboards, crossing off what you do already have. This makes sure you have enough of what you need in stock, that it is in date, and it helps you use up what you have instead of doubling up. Don't forget things like washing-up liquid and dishwasher tablets, as well as what you'll need for your bathrooms.

I like to divide my list into stores. My local corner is better for lemons, for example, and a nearby supermarket is much better value for my cocktail ingredients. It also means I have a few small lists instead of one mammoth trip where things can go amiss.

Schedule

Glorious. This is where you note down when things can and need to be done. Do this over the week before the dinner party. When to clean areas that people will be in, what can be prepped the night before and what is crucial the morning of. Here are some things people forget to schedule:

- Double check dietary requirements and attendance in the week before.
- Take out the bins before you prep so you have fresh and empty bins.
- Do a full dishwasher load and put it all away before people arrive. This gives you space on the night and ensures everything you need is clean.
- Take meat out at the required time to get it to room temperature before serving or cooking.
- Set up your cooler.
- Wobbly chairs and table check.
- Clean linen check.
- Your time. You will need to eat, watch *Real Housewives*, get ready and so on. Remember to make sure you have time to do all of these.
- Fresh hand towels in bathroom, top up handwash, etc.
- Prepare the space for people to throw their coats, bags and inhibitions.
- Open red wine to breathe.
- When to put plates in to heat.

A GREAT LAY
Selecting

When it comes to a smooth and enjoyable dinner party from a host's point of view, preparation is your best friend. Aside from food and drink, your setting, cutlery, crockery and glassware should all be considered in advance. This will make sure you can seamlessly host without having to wash or rummage last minute. Washing in a rush and inevitably smashing something will stress you out, so it's best to have all of this out of the way, early doors. You'll have an idea of what you need from your service list and will already have noted that it is all present and correct, but now you need to make it accessible and ready to go.

I tend to pull everything I will need out the morning of, to make sure it's all washed and as I need it. Then I group it into when it will be used. For example, crockery and cutlery for each course, serving dishes with their utensils, dessert plates and so on. This makes sure I'm not rummaging or fretting to find a bowl for the potatoes when I should be joyously sipping as I hear every detail about a guest's fling with a baker on a recent weekend away.

This is one of my favourite times of the prep. Silence. Order. Creativity. Once I have figured out how much of everything I need, I then try to reduce it down as much as possible by doubling up where I can to avoid any mid-party washing or cramming stuff onto the table. Really, it's all well and good having mountains of crockery and cutlery if you have hired in someone to assist you with service, but too many moving parts can end up being a nightmare and take you away from your role as host.

When I was younger I used to waitress and wash up at dinner parties for wealthy people. (Yes, it was the Celtic Tiger era and at times a pain, but it kept me in glitter eyeshadow and frosted lipstick, so it was a win.) My rate would have been cheaper than a babysitter, but my gawd did I see the value it added to the evening. Our presence freed up the host, which added so much to the evening. This is why I choose to keep my kitchen duties during a dinner party to a minimum. I'm not going to hire someone to help me, but I can be clever about what I have to do and when.

To host a stunning soirée, you don't necessarily need to have cupboards of serving platters, napkin rings and stacks of crockery. Necessity is the mother of invention, they say. Don't be afraid to repurpose and get creative. I used to create a two-tier charcuterie board from chopping boards and ramekins, as my dining table at the time was tiny. It always went down a storm because it was fun, resourceful and did the job. Your dinner party doesn't need to look like a restaurant, because it's not a restaurant.

Now, where were we? Oh yes, grabbing all you need for a smooth service. Put your mid-meal accessories, like serving spoons and spare napkins, on your 'spares table' (more later) and then divide the counter space into sections. Put these sections in order of which course they are for, with the tea and coffee bits and pieces to the end, so you can move down the counter in order of course. I like to keep the area near or on the draining board completely free to stack used dishes. Keep a space next to the hob with boards or heat pads already down so you can place anything hot to the side. I have always had a small kitchen and this method has worked a dream for me.

What, where

When it comes to setting the table, start with the guest settings before anything else to ensure that each person has enough space. Always, always have the large plates and serving dishes to hand to see if everything fits.

Finding out the plates, sides, mains and glassware don't all fit during the dinner is a tad more stressful than working through it beforehand.

Everything doesn't have to match, all you need to ensure is that each setting has the same layout and is made up of the same items. If you have odd plates, glassware and cutlery, but it is all placed in the same sequence per setting, it will look glorious.

First up, the cutlery

How simple or how complicated you make your cutlery is up to you. Guests will start from the outside and work their way in, so knives and forks are placed accordingly, with the cutlery for the last course closest to the plate. We've all seen *Pretty Woman*. However, most people will be working with one or two sets, due to space or cutlery restrictions. This is OK.

Changing cutlery between courses is a choice. If you have only enough cutlery to set the table once, I am sure your guests would rather have you at the table than listening to you hand-washing in the background. There is zero pressure to swap them out – it's not a hosting crime for guests to keep the same cutlery. If you do have multiple sets, make sure you group them before people arrive. Having the second setting on a folded clean dish towel waiting in the wings will help you grab and reset with ease.

When it comes to layout, the advice is to place the forks to the left and knives to the right. However, there's something about the negative space between spread-out cutlery on a table that irks me. Perhaps it's guests sitting with arms meekly between the little gap until dinner begins; it's like the space between the knife and fork becomes the boundaries in which they must sit. I personally prefer the cutlery on a napkin to the right or centre, if using a placemat and plate. It's simple and chic and appears more considered than a spread-out affair. It also gives you and your guests more room to work with. Most dining tables are smaller than those of a restaurant, so freeing up space is key.

You can be as casual as you wish when it comes to cutlery; dessert spoons can be placed after the main meal, for example. Don't feel under too much pressure. As long as everyone has what they need to put food in their mouths, it's all good.

Now, set out your glassware

Glassware should sit just above the cutlery to the right of the plate or where the plate will be. Water glasses should come first and sit closest to your guest, while the wine glass should sit to the right of that. It encourages more water consumption than wine and, most importantly, the wine is less likely to be knocked over. Another tablecloth saved.

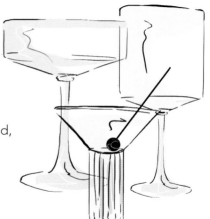

You don't have to go crazy when it comes to glasses. A water glass and a wine glass (if wine is being served) per guest will be perfect. If anyone is not drinking alcohol, still always serve what they are having in a similar glass to others.

If you have red and white glasses to match the wine being served, great. If not, don't overthink it. Most hipster restaurants serve wine in tumblers right now, so if you're out of stemmed glasses, don't worry, you're on the same trend as a French–Swedish fusion restaurant in a warehouse somewhere. Try to make sure these tumblers for wine are all a similar size.

Crockery

If you're serving bread, pop a smaller plate with a bread knife above the dinner plate to the left, in line with the glassware. If you have a small table, don't sweat this.

As with glassware, not all your plates need to match. If you have almost a full set but one plate has broken, instead of having one odd plate, make them half one kind and half another. Placing them every second plate will look more considered. If you have a complete mismatch and you want to hide the fact, place a folded napkin on the centre of each plate with cutlery on top to bring the focus there. Your plates won't be empty for long so they don't need to cause too much stress.

Spares

As I have mentioned, I love giving the table as much space as possible, but I also hate to leave the table often. A nearby sideboard or a wee table is the perfect 'spares' table. It can also be a bookshelf. It can house cutlery, plates, serving spoons, decanters, spare napkins and anything else that doesn't need to be on the table the whole time.

Wine

When it comes to wine, keep white or anything that needs to be cold in ice nearby. A metal ice bucket is easy to pick up and adds a gorgeous tone to an evening while also being extremely practical. If you choose to invest in one, you will have it for life. They also make the perfect housewarming gift, if you're ever stuck. Don't make the mistake of thinking that you just fill the bucket with ice, throw a bottle in and that is it. There is an art to this.

Take your empty bucket and fill a third with cold water (if you forgot to chill your wine you can use soda water for a faster chill). Pop the bottle/s into the water, then top up with ice. A mixture of water and ice allows you to slip the bottle back in with ease. It also keeps the temperature more consistent.

Fold a large white napkin (if you don't have one, a pristine dish cloth is also gorge; you just want to make sure a) it's absorbent, to prevent your hand from slipping, and b) won't leave fibres on the bottle) so the seams are facing in and hidden. Place this over the bucket, with the top of the bottle poking out. Each time you go to serve, this will remind you to give the bottle a wipe down to dry it first or it will drip all over the place. You can wrap the base of the bottle in the cloth as you pour to catch any further drips and for grip. After she's back in the bucket, place the cloth back over the bucket to air dry while you continue your conversation about what lip sync was best that season.

DRANKS

Serving drinks at a dinner party can become quite stressful. Here are the simple rules I stick to:

- Always have a non-alcoholic drink that takes as much effort and looks as stunning as the alcoholic options. Even if it's making sure that sparkling water has a glorious fruit curl or curating a virgin cocktail with some pizzazz. Remember, if someone isn't drinking alcohol, even just for one round, it doesn't mean they want to load up on sugary drinks or feel like they are missing out on fuss. Avoid soft drinks and opt for refreshing long drinks that will make others skip a wine or two at the sight of her and make those who are not drinking feel like they haven't got the short straw. A thirst-quenching alcohol-free drink at a good dinner party is vital. Gone are the days of loading your guests with drink to enhance an evening.
- If you are really into wine, this will be the best part of your planning and something you can really throw yourself into. However, wine pairing can be overwhelming, especially if you're just not that into it. Don't get too side-tracked – an online search will help you quickly choose a grape to pair well with your dishes, so avoid overcomplicating it. You can always also ask in store where someone will be happy to tell you what has been popular recently or what will go with what. Most experts advise a bottle of wine per guest. While this sounds excessive, it has to last the course of an evening and allows for spills, someone going through a break-up and, of course, for the night to go on longer. When guests inevitably ask if they can bring anything, send a picture of the wine you intend to serve and let them know that either that label or grape would be appreciated. This is pretty normal for a casual dinner party among friends. It removes the guessing for everyone and keeps

the night on the same track. Never send a pricey wine for guests to bring. If you choose to go big on the spend, then supply it for the entire night.

- Don't go in heavy. Starting everyone off on bubbles can feel traditional, but it can be a bit much if there is a night of alcohol ahead. Prosecco and champagne are there to add ceremony to an evening, so are great to create some buzz and drama, but don't always feel they are a must. You don't have to automatically go for something strong to start. You can still add a wow factor but in a different way. Most people will arrive and appreciate something hydrating.

- Temperature is something to keep in mind throughout the night. Ice buckets are a stunning way to keep whites tableside, and ice is a must. Dinner parties are a humid affair, so keep water topped up with ice. If you have your wine colder than your water, it rarely bodes well.

- Always have an after-dinner drink that is a break from the chosen drinks of the night. Pots of fresh mint tea always go down a treat. It will aid digestion and doesn't mess with your sleep that night.

ADDED EXTRAS

There will be occasions when you wish to go the extra mile:

Handwritten menus

A menu can add a gorgeous touch to the table. Just remember, it doesn't need to be a calligraphy masterpiece. A handwritten menu is charming and wonderful. If you are low on space, you can fold your menu and cutlery into your napkin.

Flowers

When it comes to foliage, you need to make sure they it is hampering eye contact or ease of serving. Instead, a sprig of something or a single flower on the napkin can work really well.

Place cards

I tend to keep these for larger groups. Name cards can be made from anything and are a good way to ensure someone you're hoping to match-make can sit where they should. The same goes for people who should avoid each other! Don't have them bigger than a business card and if you are low on space they can look great stood on a glass rim as you would a fruit slice. It will also create some height. You can also make them from paper and create napkin rings.

GRILLED LOI
HERB B

KOFT
ÇOBAN

BISH BREW

Ingredients

Tequila - 35ml per person
Cointreau - 10ml per person
Lime Juice - 25ml per person
Butterfly Pea Tea - brew a batch and let it cool, 50ml per person
Ginger Beer - this will be used to top up the glass
Cherry - for garnish

METHOD

1. Pour the tequila, cointreau, lime juice and pea tea into a shaker with ice

2. Shake to the beat of some great disco

3. Pour into coupes, top up with ginger beer and throw in a cherry for some colour

NOTE

Butterfly pea tea is made from the dried flowers of the Clitoria ternatea plant. She brews to a deep inky blue (divine) but changes colour when you alter her pH.

By adding something acidic like citrus she transforms into a light mauve before your eyes.

A stunning visual for guests.

THE PARTY'S OVER

You have wined, you have dined, what now? As the last guest wraps her bouclé overcoat around her and heads into the night, I am sure the last thing you wish to do is to clean.

Only do the 'musts' the night of and then tackle the rest the next day with fresh eyes and in daylight with a great disco playlist on. Here is what you shouldn't forget to do before slipping into your nightgown:

- Group similar items together on your counter tops first to make it easier. You'll automatically end up with the dirtiest dishes together, handwash only together, and so on.
- Load as much as you can into a dishwasher if you have one and turn it on. It's much easier to wash before food dries on. You won't be able to fit everything, so start with the dirtiest things and leave the rest for tomorrow's load or handwash.
- Scrape. Anything that will stay overnight needs to have all the food removed. This will make it easier tomorrow. Also, get a spoon and scrape any major food or wax off your linen.
- Soak your linen in plain cold water. Throw your ice bucket contents on top so it's extra cold. No detergent yet. These just need to be soaked to avoid stains setting. Next, soak your pans and roasting tins with washing-up liquid and hot water to loosen dried-on food and make tomorrow a breeze.
- Box or wrap up leftovers.
- Surfaces. Give counters and tables a wipe down first, then give the floor a once over. You just want to make sure all food is gone.

Once you have these bases covered, it is time for a well-deserved rest. Dinner parties are no mean feat and one must recognize the accomplishment once they are done.

While the tips in this chapter are mainly centred around a dinner party with guests, the essence should exist in our day to day. Every time we eat or drink, be it a glass of water or a bag of crisps, there is an opportunity to make it a meauxment. A chance to make the ordinary a little extraordinary. After all, it's what we deserve. The next time you crack open a bag of quinoa chips, grab a great bowl. Thinking of juice? Why not sip from a slim coupe. We learn so much about being a great host once we master how to host ourselves.

CHAPTER 9

IT'S CHRISTMAS

For me, Christmas is more of a feeling than something that can be bought. To truly feel Christmas I don't think you need to overspend or over-decorate; instead, it is as simple as considering the senses and letting that be your starting point. Usually we decorate with only the visual in mind but tying in smell and taste is what will really separate this time of year from any other. You'll see that this approach can be kinder to our pockets, the environment, our soul and our storage.

Let's talk about how we can visually create a Christmas vibe in the home first.

A FOCAL POINT

Christmas trees are, of course, the most popular focal points when it comes to festive décor. They add an instant Christmas feel and, if real, can add a gorgeous smell. Stunning. Marketing and movies have taught us that decorating a Christmas tree is a joy-filled, fun and glorious event, spent laughing with loved ones, delicately placing ornaments while wearing Fair Isle. The reality involves suppressed screams of frustration, blown bulbs and tension. So how do we make decorating the tree more like an ad for peat bricks and less like a murder documentary? Why, it's all in the prep and approach, of course.

First things first. Take out every single item you want on that tree in advance. There is no point going box by box: you'll never be able to create a lewk without being aware of what you need to use. Whether the style is kitsch, traditional, grey velvet (get out) or minimal, you will also need:

- Scissors (for snipping branches, opening boxes and helping with the below)
- Ribbon, thread, twine (decoration hangers fail, so you may need to fashion a new one)
- Glue (broken decorations)
- Wire (to reinforce a weak branch for a heavy bauble)
- Hoover/dustpan and brush (I hope you will only need it for branch trimmings)

Before you even think about buying anything new, look at what you have. If they are in perfect condition but you just fancy a change, swapping out the decoration hangers for new ribbon can create a whole new look for very little spend and very little waste. Red velvet can bring a more traditional vibe and tie in mismatched decorations really well. There is also the option of tszujing what you have completely. If you have a set of plain baubles you can glitter or metal dip, embellish, spray paint and so on. A box of decorations you hate can actually be the perfect blank canvas for creating the look that you really want. Plus, it's unique.

Faux trees need to be fluffed from the bottom up; it's much more difficult if you stack it all together and then start to work the branches out. Place your first stack, start from the back, and fluff it all right through, then do the same to the next bit and the next until you have them all in place. If you have individual branches, start at the back for each tier to ensure you are not creating a tree that is only full at the front. Give one last fluff when all is in place. Taking time to do this properly makes a huge difference, as you won't have uneven fullness. If the tree is real, make sure you have access to keep water in the base topped up. Trim any branches before the decorations go on.

Lights

Opt for solar or battery-powered where possible, as they are safer. If you choose plug-in lights, go for low-energy options, as these don't get as hot. Before decorating, turn on the lights to make sure they all work. You don't want to wait until they are all beautifully hung to realize they need to be repaired.

When it comes to using fairy lights well, you need to think of them less as decorations and more as gorgeous spotlights. Use them to light up the darker pockets of the tree rather than as an added decoration. This not only gives you more places to hang decorations, as they will get seen, it makes the tree look fuller. If you only focus light and decorations to the outer part of the tree you'll have less space and, to be honest, it can look a bit 'Tree In Box'. Instead, sit lights further back to light up branches in the middle and put decorations in front.

Don't hang lights horizontally along branches. This can waste a lot of yardage and a lot of bulbs can go unseen, as they literally sit on the branches. Instead, go vertical. That way you have bulbs in between branches as well as on them. If your tree is not seen from all angles, it will also give you double the coverage as you don't have to light up the back that is never seen.

Decorations

One thing I love about decorations is that everyone can do what they want. There are no rules. You can literally choose a look or colour you like and go for it. Some people have a style they absolutely adore and stick with it, perfecting it more and more each year. Others will look forward to creating a whole new theme.

If you are starting out, don't buy too many in year one. Just a simple box of plain baubles in a colour you love can be added to each subsequent year but is enough to get you through the first Christmas. On year one, you can add anything from bows to paper decorations to fill it out and get a feel for what you like. You can then also start to build a sentimental collection that you grow, without it all taking up a lot of space or spend while keeping the plain set to fill in between. Christmas decorations are so personal, you almost need a trial year to feel it out. Unless you are certain about what you like and know you'll want to use it all again. The main thing you want to avoid is having to buy and store a lot of stuff that is essentially for the bin.

While what we each want in a tree lewk can vary, one thing is for sure: there is an art to hanging. Before you hang anything, lay out your decorations in order of size. When we do this, it allows us to hang in a more balanced way. Within the size categories, divide into plains and specials. This allows you to prioritize special or sentimental decorations at the front, with the less ornate further back.

Begin by placing your largest plain baubles closer to the tree's spine. This will give a sense of fullness. As they are simpler, they don't need to be centre stage. Then place your largest specials. These should also sit a little further back on the branch. This means not only are your branches not overloaded at the weaker point but also your larger decorations won't be blocking smaller ones at the end. I would always place sentimental or the most special decorations at eye level. Pets are less likely to get at these girls here, but you are also able to see them better.

Next, go in with your mid-sized, and then your small baubles can hang from the branch tips. Keep standing back to see where you are getting too heavy or too light. Creating balance is not just good for practical reasons, it's also fabulous visually.

I personally think that you don't have to have a Christmas tree. GASP. Said it, won't regret it. They are absolutely glorious but not everyone has the space or will be spending enough time in their home around Christmas to make it worth it. This is where other focal points come in.

FIREPLACE

If you have a fireplace to decorate, stunning! A note here is if your fireplace is functioning, make sure you always decorate with fire safety in mind.

Garlands are perfect for a fireplace, as she can take a lot of decoration and you don't have to hang her from the fireplace itself. You can opt for a minimal look, where the garland sits on top; traditional, where it sits along the front in arches; or all swept to one side, for a modern approach. Play around with placement before you commit.

Something to consider with a fireplace is height. It doesn't have to be all flat. Tall candlesticks or eucalyptus can add some drama and height and make it look like you bought it as a pre-decorated garland. Hang baubles at different lengths on see-through string for a visual treat but don't forget to nestle baubles among the branches for balance. You can opt for whatever vibe you wish with a garland, but I personally love long silky ribbons to add volume.

SIDEBOARD

I say sideboard, but this can be a table top, counter top, chest of drawers . . . All you need is a flat surface. Make sure it is not too precious in case you get a water mark.

This is for anyone who isn't doing a tree but would love a Christmas feature. A truly gorgeous alternative is a floral and foliage arrangement. They are pretty easy to put together and care for when using jars. I've learned that oasis is a gal you do not want kicking about your gaff, as not only is she bad for the environment but she is not great for those fabulous eyes and lungs of yours. So let's scrap her and focus on water pots for hydration instead. This is the perfect way to have a long-lasting arrangement that is kinder to you and the world.

What you need:
- Jars, vases, pots or a mix
- Twine
- Wire
- Scissors
- Flowers and foliage – go to your local market for more choice and cheaper prices

SIDEBOARD SASS

1. GATHER JARS AND CONTAINERS. A MIX OF SIZES WORKS BEST, AS YOU WANT TO HAVE DIFFERENT HEIGHTS. FILL THEM 3/4 WITH WATER

2. WRAP CHICKEN WIRE OVER THE TOP OF EACH JAR, HOLD IN PLACE WITH TWINE. IF YOU HAVE NO CHICKEN WIRE, YOU CAN FORM A GRID WITH REGULAR LENGTHS OF WIRE

PLACE THE LARGEST TO THE BACK AND THE SMALLER JARS TO THE FRONT AND SIDES TO HELP YOU ACHIEVE A TIERED ARRANGEMENT. IF YOU HAVE A LOT OF FOLIAGE, YOU CAN ANCHOR JARS TOGETHER

3.

4. PLACE THE LARGEST STEMS FIRST TO CREATE YOUR SILHOUETTE. ONCE HAPPY, START TO PLACE FILLER AND FINISH WITH FLOWERS AND MORE EXPENSIVE OR SMALLER FOLIAGE

TIP

TO KEEP HER LOOKING STUNNING FOR LONGER:

CUT STEMS AT AN ANGLE (MORE SURFACE AREA FOR DRINKING) & TRIM OFF ANY LEAVES BELOW WATER LEVEL

SPRITZ HER DAILY AND CHANGE THE WATER EVERY THREE DAYS

What you use is totally up to you, but I always go for a bunch of eucalyptus and then ask what they have that could work as filler around it. There is so much foliage that works well with eucalyptus for around a third of the price, so use this for bulk and then place the eucalyptus in the more prominent parts and the top layer.

When I lived in Scotland I developed a love for thistles, so I like to have these around every Christmas, and I do always enjoy a red rose. As blood red as possible and with a long stem. You can go for whatever you want; think about what has meaning for you if you want to create a chic and sentimental arrangement.

Drawings and notes

If you really, really loved the set-up this year, take a photo of it or draw a quick sketch, so it's easy to recreate next year. If you went for foliage, keep a note on what you bought from the market and how much was used. You can also group decorations together for a quick set-up. If you store your decorations grouped by room, it will be a cinch.

WINDOWS

If you want to make windows your focus, a gorgeous touch is to make paper lanterns for solar-powered candles to sit inside. These can be made easily from A4 copy paper and hung from red velvet ribbon. It removes the worry of candles and the hassle of plugs, and adds a really chic point of interest. A lantern made by each person in the house can also be a gorgeous touch.

TASTE

When it comes to taste, you want to go for something that fills the house on Christmas Eve and lingers. What says Christmas more than mulled wine? This is also something you can make the evening you put up your decorations or when having people round for a pre-Christmas gathering. Basically, it roars Christmas. The joy of mulled wine is that it doesn't need to be a hard drink: you can make this using a non-alcoholic wine too and with little difference in taste. The other bonus is that you can make it look and taste absolutely stunning. Remove any notions you have of chunks of purple apples at the bottom of mugs and strap yourself in for a lesson on a chic mulled wine to please your taste, smell and sight.

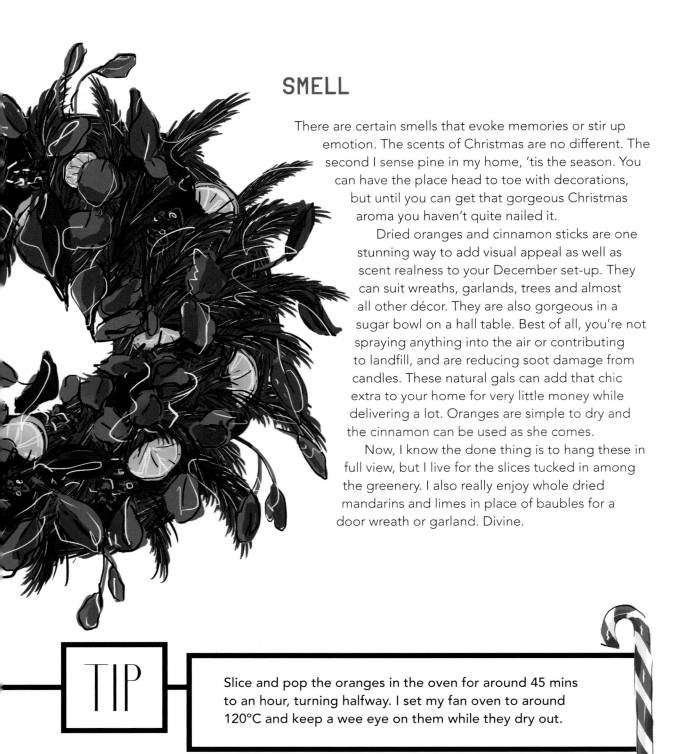

SMELL

There are certain smells that evoke memories or stir up emotion. The scents of Christmas are no different. The second I sense pine in my home, 'tis the season. You can have the place head to toe with decorations, but until you can get that gorgeous Christmas aroma you haven't quite nailed it.

Dried oranges and cinnamon sticks are one stunning way to add visual appeal as well as scent realness to your December set-up. They can suit wreaths, garlands, trees and almost all other décor. They are also gorgeous in a sugar bowl on a hall table. Best of all, you're not spraying anything into the air or contributing to landfill, and are reducing soot damage from candles. These natural gals can add that chic extra to your home for very little money while delivering a lot. Oranges are simple to dry and the cinnamon can be used as she comes.

Now, I know the done thing is to hang these in full view, but I live for the slices tucked in among the greenery. I also really enjoy whole dried mandarins and limes in place of baubles for a door wreath or garland. Divine.

TIP

Slice and pop the oranges in the oven for around 45 mins to an hour, turning halfway. I set my fan oven to around 120°C and keep a wee eye on them while they dry out.

MAGIC MEAUXMENT

Mulled wines have been kicking about for ever. During the Roman Empire it was believed to stave off sickness and keep people in great health, but it has had many a rebrand over the years. Now it is a Christmas drink that makes your house smell nice and keeps you warm at Christmas markets. *Bon.*

Full disclosure, I used to think mulled wine was awful until I realized I had just been drinking awful mulled wine. There are a few essential elements to creating a great one.

You want a deep wine, spices and fruit. A pre-made bottle will just not cut it here. Visually, the fruit should float as much as possible, so I like to cut it in thin slices. No one really wants the cubes of fruit that sink to the bottom, now, do they? Also the type of fruit is important. You don't have to use apples if you don't like apples, you can use cranberries, pomegranate, pear, oranges, whatever you love. You want something rich in both taste and visual appeal. The vessel is also important. I love a goblet that can take hot liquids, a wrap made from a Christmas napkin to protect your hands, and of course a wee dessert fork should you want to stir but also nibble on some fruit.

LdB CMW (Chic Mulled Wine)

Serves 4 large glasses or 6 lovely glasses

Ingredients:
- a bottle of red wine (a hearty Italian is best) or a bottle of alcohol-free red wine. Simply fabulous. *Don't go for the cheapest red wine, as it will overpower all the other ingredients, but don't waste an expensive one as you'll be adding so much to it. Something you'd have with a delicious bowl of pasta is ideal.*
- 2 oranges
- 1 lemon
- 1 small apple or pear (a pear's shape is also stunning. Oh, that curve!)
- ½ cup honey/caster or brown sugar
- 4 cloves (if you like a stronger flavour, use 8)
- a stick of cinnamon
- a couple of star anise and a pinch of nutmeg (optional, if you don't think you'll use it again)

Prep:
1. Zest one orange (avoid the pith, which can be a little tart – while I love a tart, here you'll want only the zest, as this is where the oils and a lot of flavour is). I use a peeler instead of a grater to avoid removing too much.
2. Do the same with a lemon. Large strips of both are ideal, as they don't fall into glasses when serving.
3. Chop the lemon and the orange you have just zested in half and squeeze out the juice. Set aside.
4. Cut the other orange into discs, peel still on. These are what you will see in the glass at the end, so bear this in mind.
5. Slice the pear and/or apple the same way. You want thin slices that float to the top of the glass. I use all of the fruit, as it will darken in different parts and give a lovely depth. Keep the cranberries whole.

Cooking:
1. Pour a large glass of wine into a pot – not the whole bottle. So many recipes will tell you to use it all, but it can actually burn off the alcohol. Also, you want flavour to infuse, so start small, like you're making a stock: you'll add the rest later. Oh, gorgeous.
2. Set to a medium heat. You don't want this to boil, so keep an eye on it; one or two bubbles is fine, don't panic.

3. Add your honey or sugar (if this is not sweet enough for you, add more later) and stir. Pop in the rest of the bottle after your sweetener has dissolved.

4. Add your star anise (1 for those who don't love her, 2 to 3 if you adore!), the stick of cinnamon, cloves and a wee pinch of nutmeg. Can you smell that? Divine.

5. Pick up your orange zests and squeeze them over the pan of wine to release a glorious spray into the mix. You'll see the oils on the surface that will add to the flavour and probably do something lovely to your hair. When they are fully spritzed, pop the strips of peel into the wine. Do the same with your lemon strips.

6. Give it a good stir. Pour in your orange and lemon juice and add your fruit.

7. Keep to a light simmer. Never let the mix boil or the fruit will turn to mulch and the taste will spoil.

You can drink this after 15 minutes, but I like to leave her for just under an hour to get more depth of flavour and to fill the room with that wonderful smell.

So there you are, waking up on Christmas morning, mulled wine spices and dried orange and cinnamon filling the air, your focal point thriving, as you push a Ferrero Rocher between your red lips to kick off breakfast.

POST–CHRISTMAS
Storing for next year

The Epiphany is not just the moment you realize you forgot to watch the 'Secrets Revealed' episode of a *Real Housewives* season, it's also the day the Magi (the three wise men, to you and me) popped in to visit baby Jesus. Aside from their presents and presence, this date is also significant for another reason; it's when your Christmas décor should come down.

When it comes to storing your Christmas décor, the temptation to just get it out of the way quickly will be strong. As will the urge to buy plastic boxes for storage. We are living in a world where we are told that lots of plastic boxes make an organized home. Shudder. Instead, let's pack up with next year and the environment in mind.

Preparation is key to storage success. If you have not held on to the original packaging for baubles and decorations, there are some really great solutions. Here are the things I keep in December to use when taking down decorations.

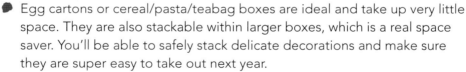

- Egg cartons or cereal/pasta/teabag boxes are ideal and take up very little space. They are also stackable within larger boxes, which is a real space saver. You'll be able to safely stack delicate decorations and make sure they are super easy to take out next year.
- Wrapping-paper or kitchen roll tubes taped together are perfect for wrapping lights around. You can then slide them into a postal tube or fashion one from the card. This means they are safe from harm during storage and you won't have to spend time unknotting next year. These tubes are also good for things like tinsel or string decorations.
- Hold on to wrapping paper and wrapping tissue on Christmas Day and use them to wrap baubles, line the bottom of boxes and, of course, the tissue paper will be able to absorb any moisture in the box during storage. Don't forget you will also need to wrap things like wreaths and garlands, so this is ideal.

- Wine delivery boxes come with inserts that are ideal for stacking baubles and decorations, so if you get one of these, keep it. If you want to make your own, just fashion from other delivery boxes. The flaps are super easy to slot together to make inserts. You can then place sheets of cardboard in between each layer to keep them super safe.
- Chocolate boxes and biscuit tins. Why do I love these so much? They are great for protecting anything delicate. Smaller tins are ideal for storing decoration hangers or command strips, tape, etc.

Storage in the home is usually bottom heavy, with the top part of storage cupboards frequently unused. As Christmas décor can be so light, tension poles are ideal here to keep the boxes up off the floor and out of harm's way. You also have the option of taping boxes together to stand in one tall, light column that can easily be moved as one when you need to get at something else or when you're ready for next year!

My takeaway with Christmas décor is to keep it simple but effective. Ensure you are using natural materials as much as possible, and appealing to more than one sense to get the most out of it. There is a lot of pressure around Christmas: let your décor be a part that you can really enjoy. Making a meauxment out of putting it all together, and even putting it away, can really add to the festive period rather than feel like another deadline or another chore.

Nollaig Shona Daoibh! (*Raises a mulled wine, rearranges an off-the-shoulder velvet gown.*)

CHAPTER 10

HAUSKEEPING

I AM THE CHAPTER THAT HAS YOUR BACK

There are so many (too many!) grey areas when it comes to home care and many of them are either hard to find wrapped up in a sales pitch or just downright boring. In the pages of this chapter you will find solace and guidance when it comes to some of the trickier moments in the home . . . including what on earth you do the day you move in, right through to topping up paint, cleaning your couch and when servicing needs to go down. (*Clicks finger.*) Let's go!

SHE'S IN!

When you move in to a new home, from rental to first buy, it's easy to forget to do the things that give us the best start. There's an easy method to follow that won't let you down.

First hour

- Check every key you have been given works where it should and tag clearly.
- Open all windows, turn on all extractors to breathe some fresh air into the space.
- Flush all toilets, run all taps (note if there is hot water!). This is to make sure that all is working as it should, as well as removing any sitting water.
- Turn on the fridge right away; it should never be off but is usually left so.
- Check fuse board looks good.
- Check all alarms work.
- Take meter readings.

TIP

Before you move, pack a Three Night Kit separately. This should have everything you'll need over three days, from your daily kitchen items to the clothes and cosmetics you'll use. This will make life a little easier for the last three days in the old place and the first three days in the new one.

First day

- Check that all locks and external doors are secure in daylight, so you have a perfect lock-up on your first night. Note that external lights are all in good order.
- A kettle of water down each drain with some washing-up liquid to get rid of anything that could cause a bad smell. Double check under kitchen sink is dry and has no leaks.
- Clean and hoover. It is always good to unpack in a clean space. This can be a wipe down of all door handles and surfaces, or if a deeper one is needed, now is the perfect time. Don't forget to check your appliances (guides on how to clean these in *Gaff Goddess*).

First week

- Register all utilities.
- Download a manual for every appliance.
- Note any missing lightbulbs, including appliances.

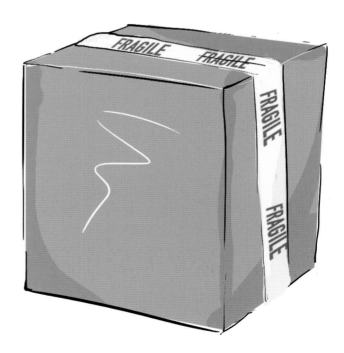

NEW ADDITIONS

To make sure that what you add will work well in your home, keep FRAME in mind:

Function

Ask yourself, is this piece fit for its intended purpose? Suss if it can cope with what you want and need it to do. Will it last? Make sure that the materials are suitable for the environment and the use. Multi-use? Most rooms can only fit the necessities, so any addition that can also store or display, for example, is stunning.

Routes

What is the main thoroughfare that needs to be kept free, or could it do with another pit stop? This could mean you can only have a double instead of a king bed.

Access

You need to make sure that nothing you add prevents access to something else. Can all doors open as they should? Can you enter the room easily without anything getting in your way? Don't just think about main doors – drawers, windows and sockets also count.

Measure

There are many elements people forget to consider when measuring a room for a large piece of furniture. Don't forget about skirting boards and measure the bottom, top and middle of the space you are considering. Walls can dip or have sockets or fixtures in place that can affect how wide it actually is.

Example

In dressmaking, one will always make a 'toile' of the garment in cheaper fabric before cutting into the good stuff. This allows you to see if you need to make any amendments to the pattern. This concept also works well for new additions to the home.

You can use many things to make your 'toile' – old painting sheets,

FRAME

tarpaulins, curtains, etc. Just cut or fold to size and you can then see how it looks and feels in the space. If you are worried about height – say, the arm of a couch, and how it might affect natural light – cut this out in card and tape it into place standing up. When the placement doesn't have options – like a TV or bed – use masking tape and stick it straight to the floor, marking out the dimensions.

Deliveries

Once you have decided on your furniture, you also need to make sure it can get into your home. You'll be able to get the dimensions for each box from the online store and assess how smooth its arrival will be.

Don't just measure your front door, measure any hallways, lifts (especially height) or stairs that need to be navigated. Many people will just measure one spot on the width of a hallway, but you need to be certain that it is indeed the narrowest width. Walk through the hall and note any fixtures, handrails, postboxes or switches that could lessen the space.

There is also usually a limit on how many stairs a delivery company will carry an item when there is no lift. The most common is three storeys. Always check ahead if you are buying something large or heavy and getting it delivered to anything above ground level.

Don't forget to check the fine print about deliveries. You need to see if you will have any potential long waits if a part goes out of stock before delivery.

BUYING FOR WALLS

Aside from frames, there will be other things you may want on the walls. Hanging lights, shelves and mirrors can all help add to your space, so it's good to know how to get it right.

Shelves

Once you know what dimensions your shelves are, make a masking tape outline where you want them to go. Live with this for a day or two to see if the contents going on the shelf will be affected by sunlight, if doors open OK with it there or if it restricts movement in the room at all. If the shelf is for display, you will also want to see how this placement feels as you use the room from different angles. It may be that the contents of the shelf are completely invisible when you sit and it would work better lower. If the shelf is for storing things you use, consider your position when reaching for them. If it's above a desk or next to a couch, be sure to make it a height that doesn't mean you have

to get up to get at it. As a whole, avoid shelving above beds. If it's for display, you're better having it on a wall that you can admire from your bed. If it's for storage, pop it somewhere easier to use. Also, sleeping under a shelf cannot be great for the ultimate switch-off.

Hanging lights

These have become so popular and are a great way to save space. If you are considering one that hangs from a ceiling or wall, make sure it doesn't cause any clearance issues. This is especially important at the bedside, for getting in and out, and opening curtains or doors.

Mirrors

Ever since reading that a mirror facing a front door will repel positive energy entering the home, I have always been pretty wary of this placement. However, a mirror near the front door is essential, a wee pit stop for one last look. There is also more to mirrors to keep in mind.

We like to naturally stand back from bigger mirrors, so make sure where it is placed allows you room to do so. As with shelves, it is always important to tape up a trial for a few days before you hang. Sunlight against the mirror could cause glare or you may need to readjust the height once you realize how you will be passing it or using it. As with frames, only larger mirrors will work as standalone pieces; keep smaller mirrors above units.

Picture frames

If you have ever shopped for frames, you'll have noticed the price can really vary. This will usually be due to the size of the frame and if there is a mount. You will most likely want your more expensive artwork to be in a suitable frame, whereas less expensive posters and prints won't need as much protection. Let's kick off with getting to know the different parts of a picture frame.

Frame

Frames come in a variety of materials and their construction will vary. Everyone has their own style preference, but here's my two cents. If you like a minimal vibe in your home, carry it right through to frames. Adding a moulded or carved frame into a space with industrial or clean lines will instantly give off a (*gulps*) steampunk vibe. If you have a room with trims that you don't love, like a rental with lots of '90s pine trim, use minimal slick metal frames to dull their presence. If you are into a more opulent setting that rivals Mariah, frames are a way to add an over-the-top tone. Go for glitz, with metallic tones with lots of moulding, carving and contours.

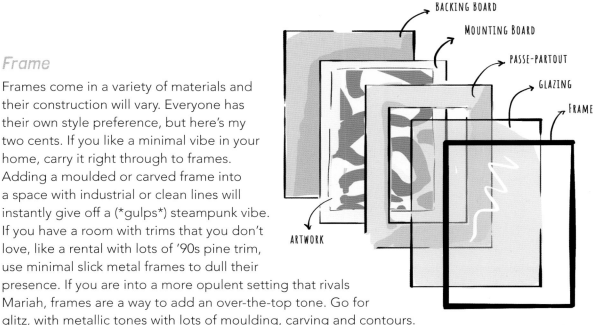

BACKING BOARD
MOUNTING BOARD
PASSE-PARTOUT
GLAZING
FRAME
ARTWORK

Glazing

This comes in many varieties. The regular clear glass found in most high-street frames will not be anti-glare, so these aren't great on walls opposite bright windows. You can get frames with UV protection or museum glass but avoiding direct sunlight is the best prevention if it is a treasured piece. Acrylic or plastic is good for safety concerns, like on a stairway, above a couch or in a kid's room. They are also great if you are renting, as their lighter weight means a smaller hole in the wall. I avoid glass mainly because I like large frames and the risk of them falling is lessened when it's lighter. Don't use plastic on charcoal or pastels, as it can cause them to lift. Anti-glare and UV protection are super common with acrylic, but remember that anti-glare can slightly blur the picture, so I prefer it for a portrait or pastels.

Mat boards

Also called mounts – or my favourite, *passe-partout* – mat boards are the white or cream trim that sits behind the glass, before the artwork itself. These serve two purposes: visual appeal and protection. They stop the artwork from touching the glass, preventing condensation damaging it and also keeping it from sticking to the glass. If it is an expensive or one-off piece, make sure that you choose an acid-free option, as acid-based mats can brown the artwork over time. More expensive frames will have a bevelled edge so that it doesn't create a shadow over the frame's contents; cheaper frames will have a straight edge. When sizing, you want to make sure you're not covering the signature or any of the content. You can buy custom mounts to pop into your frame, if needed. Any good framer will do this for you.

Mounting board

This sits behind the artwork. She will give a tighter fit and will make sure there is no warping or wrinkling. Again, she needs to be acid-free.

Backing board

This is what you'll see at the back of the frame.

Dust cover

This will often be a paper cover over the back of the frame for added protection. Again, it should be acid- or lignin-free.

Before you buy any frames, make sure you run a detector over the wall to make sure it's a suitable place to hang.

Digital printing

With digital prints you don't need to worry about paint or pencil rubbing, which is great, as I don't love a mount on a poster with a stunning graphic. I love these prints in thin, minimal black frames where the content does the talking. As they are usually quite large, I avoid a glass frame.

Canvas

Paintings on a canvas usually won't need glass, as they will be acrylic or oil, but will need some form of spray protector applied to prevent light damage.

Pencil

Pencil on paper is susceptible to wrinkling or moving within the frame. For this reason, make sure you have a mount board to give it a more rigid backing and to avoid it sitting against the glass or acrylic.

Placement of frames

Clever frame placement can really set off a room and can even create a seamless zone boundary.

When it comes to where to place your frame, size is a huge factor. My best advice is to hang anything less than A3 above something that is at least waist height. When we hang smaller frames on larger walls with a lot of negative space around it, we can make the walls feel shorter. If you have a piece that is dear, hang it above something you stand at often, like a dresser in your bedroom, where you can enjoy it more.

For large frames, they are a stunning way to add symmetry to a space, which always invites calm. Rather than having one centrally placed large frame, go for two if you can. They don't need to be a dead-on match, just keep the colour and frame similar to pull this off.

Frames above lamps can look fabulous by night, as it looks so curated. It's also a chance to add a sharp boundary that travels up the walls. A frame at the edge of a living area or above a bedside unit or reading zone can finish it off really well.

When it comes to canvases, these can gather dust, so avoid placing them near front doors or too close to windows. Instead, take advantage of their lightweight nature to place them above couches or in landings.

Any frame that could sit on a surface, like a photo size, should never be on a wall unless, at a push, you're doing some form of gallery wall – but even then it needs to be a gallery wall you can walk right up to, so you can view it properly. Turn the frame around: if there is an optional leg for standing the frame, find a spot for it to sit and save larger frames for your wall.

ACCESSORIES
Rugs

When it comes to rugs, you must first think about why the rug is going in the space. If it is in an area where you are mainly barefoot and it's going in for comfort, make the materials your priority. A sisal or jute rug may look great but feel too rough. If you are trying to cover old flooring underneath, make size your priority and go for flatweave to get the most bang for your buck. Having a rug big enough for its edges to be placed under furniture will work best. If you are trying to add another colour to a space, note the tones of what's around and stick to the same family. For example, if you have mainly cool tones in the couch and walls, a warm-toned rug could fight with it too much.

Bigger isn't always better. If you just want to add some warmth or pizzazz with a rug, note the main routes of the room and avoid having the rug run through them. A smaller feature rug will be more effective long-term, as it won't wear as badly.

Bulbs

It can seem logical to buy a multipack for all lamps in the home, but you are best to buy according to the use of the room. Too cool can affect relaxing in a space, too warm can hinder safe use. I am passionate about kelvins and have touched on these throughout the book, but here is a quick guide for you to come to when you buy your next bulb.

KELVINS

- 5,000K PLUS. SUPER ALERT

  SECURITY LIGHTING – INTENSE TASKS

- 4,500–5,000K. KEEPS YOU FOCUSED AND ALERT

  DESK LIGHT – HALLWAYS – TASKS

- 3,000–3,500K. PERFECT LIGHT FOR MORE RELAXED READING

  READING – LOUNGE TASKS – BIG LIGHT IN ROOMS WHERE YOU RELAX

- 3,000K AND UNDER. WARM, COSY, RELAXING. YOU CAN READ IN THIS TOO.

  BEDSIDE – AMBIENT LAMPS – DOWN TIME

SERVICING

So many items in your home need to be serviced at least every year to avoid any major breakdowns or costs due to replacement or avoidable repairs.

Boilers

These need an annual service, especially if they are gas boilers. You should always have a valid gas safety cert for your boiler and these run year to year. Most companies will offer you a discount if you get the cert and the service done at the same time. Try to get into the swing of having them done each summer or spring, where possible, as you will be sure that it is in full working order when you need it in the colder months.

Appliances

When it comes to your appliances, a lot of the 'servicing' is up to you. Often if the appliance didn't cost much more than a few service appointments, people will wait until something happens to get it serviced. However, if you have moved into a new property and appliances are in place, I would ring the manufacturer and see how old the machine is and if they would recommend a service. Your manual should also state what kind of maintenance is needed for the appliance.

There are 'Clean' or 'Service' modes on almost every appliance that uses water now and these need to be done as per the manual. This makes sure that the machine stays in good shape, but deep cleaning yourself is also essential. You can prevent any major issues by ensuring you are not using powdered detergents or tablets, as these can clog pipes and lead to costly repairs. Another thing you can do is run a hot wash at least once a month. This will help greatly if you are running eco washes most days.

Fuse box

Your fuse box will usually have a sticker on it with the last service and next needed service date.

PAT testing

Portable Appliance Testing is done to make sure that your appliance is working safely. There is no legal requirement on how often appliances need this done, but usually there will be something that will tell you visually if one is not working as it should. Check appliances to make sure there are no signs of wear, or loose or damaged cables. Approach portable-appliance safety sensibly, especially if you have bought something quite old or have moved into a property with very old appliances. The great thing about these is that the charges are usually for bulk checks. So you will have multiple appliances checked during one appointment.

When it comes to servicing, you'll need to make sure you are contacting the correct contractors for quotes. For a washing machine, you'll need an appliance engineer, as a plumber will be able to take a look at some parts but not others.

PAINTING AND TOP-UPS

Painting

Painting walls in our home ourselves is a great way to keep costs down. If it is done correctly and with the right gear, you can achieve a decent outcome. While the difficulty level is pretty low, I have never seen anyone achieve the same look as a seasoned painter, but it is something you can do well if you prepare well.

You may be able to paint onto what you have already, but some walls will need a base coat. Think of them like make-up primers: they create a better surface for the paint to sit on and some have added benefits.

Undercoat

Also called a base coat. This is for older walls or walls that are smoke- or water-stained. It will fill in fine lines and any small imperfections. If you want a fresh start and don't want to waste money on more layers of your expensive top coat, this is perfect. If you are bringing dark walls back to a lighter tone, an undercoat is a must, as it will mute the colour in a couple of coats, where a top coat would need many more. The same goes for painting a darker colour – you can get a dark undercoat to speed up the process.

Damp seal

This can be used on areas where there has been damp and mould previously to stop it coming back. You will still need to truly solve the reason behind the excess moisture or it will end up cropping up elsewhere.

Primer

If your walls are freshly plastered you will need a primer to prep the surface. This is usually heavily water-based and the plaster will drink this up instead of expensive paint. Once she is on and dry, you can paint on your top coat without worrying that it will be soaked up by the fresh plaster. You can get primer and top coats in one now.

Choosing paint

You'll hear about many different paint types when shopping for yours. It is always good to know what each type does, so you can find your ideal match.

Gloss

This is what is usually used on wood such as skirting, trims, doors and panelling and it gives a luxurious feel due to its high shine. It is traditionally used in these areas as it is durable and can be wiped clean. You will have hands, feet and furniture legs brushing against these areas, so it provides a tough layer.

Gloss has a bad rep, as it was quite toxic back in the day due to its oil-based nature. This all changed with new laws in 2010, which ruled that levels of harmful VOCs (volatile organic compounds) in paint had to be lowered. However, this new formulation caused an issue even among higher-end paint manufacturers. The most commonly used gloss colour, white, started to yellow quite quickly.

Anything you choose to paint in a white gloss will yellow over time, with some brands yellowing in just a couple of months. It can also yellow in patches. Have you ever noticed a yellow bit of skirting when you pull out furniture? This is because lack of natural light speeds up yellowing.

To avoid this, I go for a water-based white on all woodwork and doors. It doesn't give such a high shine, but there are other advantages that make it a better choice:

	Oil-based	Water-based
Eco-friendly	X	You can find eco-friendly options
Drying time	Has a longer drying time but, as the paint stays wetter for longer, it is easier to work with	Dries very quickly, meaning multiple coats can be achieved in one day. Over-working it can make it lumpy. Wait for it to dry, then recoat!
Thickness	Thick – fewer coats needed and brush strokes disappear.	More coats needed and you will get brush strokes.
Odour	Strong	No strong fumes
Whites	Always yellows over time	Doesn't yellow over time
Mess rating	You'll need a solvent cleaner for surfaces and brushes. Be careful of splashes and drops.	Easy to clean with domestic cleaners. Drops and splashes really easy to clean when wet.
Brush	Real hair can hold the oil base well	Synthetic needed, as real hair will absorb the water and warp
Shine	High shine	Lower shine
Kids' rooms	I wouldn't	Go for an eco-version
Cleaning	Wipeable and stain-resistant	Gentle cleaning recommended, as it can come off. Not as stain-resistant as gloss.
Coats	You'll need fewer	You'll need more
Imperfections	Will spotlight any bad bits	Will not show up as much

Painting over gloss

To check if a paint is water-based or oil-based, the shine and lack of brush strokes will usually give oil away. If you rub it with a wet cloth, water-based paint will usually come off a little, while gloss will stand firm. If it has yellowed, go over it with a water-based option instead of constantly topping up with another oil-based gloss. However, you cannot simply paint a water-based variety over an oil-based one. You will need to prep it to avoid chipping down the line. Here's a quick guide.

1. Clean down the surface with sugar soap.
2. Key the surface. This means roughing it up, usually through sanding, so whatever is going to go on next can stick better. I use a fine grade sanding paper. This can take a while: put on a podcast, and wear a mask and goggles, as what you'll sand off is not good for you.
3. Apply a primer. I usually use a 3-in-1, which does the best job. Two layers is ideal.
4. Apply the top coat in your chosen water-based gloss finish. Stunning.

Finishes

The main finishes for woodwork all come in oil- or water-based options.

High gloss	This is your standard gloss. I always think oil-based looks like a gorge PVC skirt while water-based will look more like a leather. This level of gloss will be hard-wearing.
Satinwood	This is a mid-sheen, like a satin.
Eggshell	Smooth sheen with a dry hand feel, like the shell of an egg. This is ideal for older woodwork, as the light won't bounce off dents and uneven areas.

Gloss on walls can add a glorious tone to any space. The darker the colour, the glossier the outcome. High-gloss ceilings or walls look fantastic in heritage spaces and add a lot of drama. It becomes almost glass-like. For the highest sheen, you need to use an oil-based paint, so there will be fumes. One other thing to note is that the surface has to be pristine – gloss will highlight any uneven parts or dents.

Emulsion

Emulsion is a word you will hear a lot. She is water-based but she will contain vinyl or acrylic to give her staying power. This is what will go on most walls and ceilings in the home. There are different finishes and compositions to achieve different looks as well as to suit different rooms.

Matte

Matte emulsion in brilliant white is what I use most often. It has a velvet feel, and because it doesn't have a shine – instead it diffuses light – it doesn't show off imperfections the way a glossier paint would. It holds more pigment, so one coat has a lot of coverage. I also find that top-ups don't stand out as much as they do in other paints. It's not as easy to wipe clean, so it can mark easier than other paints. Avoid using it in a hallway, kitchen or child's room. If you have a busy home, she'll be better in bedrooms and is ideal for ceilings.

Satin

This has a soft sheen which gives a lovely gloss to walls. It is more durable than a matte, so you will see 'wipeable' or 'washable' on the tin, as it has more staying power. If you have older walls and don't love matte, this is great, as she isn't going to highlight imperfections as much as a glossier option.

Silk

The light-reflecting qualities of a silk paint will help to make rooms feel bigger. However, they will show up every single imperfection, which is why many will not use it. That said, it is good for rooms with high humidity like a kitchen due to its staying power. The higher the shine, the more it will stay put and not absorb moisture.

Kitchen and bathroom emulsion

You can get specific bathroom and kitchen emulsions which contend with moisture and airborne grease really well. These contain ingredients to prevent surface condensation, so they're also ideal for older homes. It's not to say a regular emulsion wouldn't be OK in a kitchen or bathroom, but if humidity is an issue, look into these.

Chalk

This is now super popular, as the plaster look has started to trend. It is even more matte than matte and looks like chalk or raw plaster. It gives a modern feel to walls, but in my experience things like soot can show up quickly and it is not great in a kitchen.

Magic white emulsion

This is a white paint that goes on pink and dries white, so you can see where you have already painted. It's ideal for when you are painting white on white, as it stops you doubling up.

The kind of finish you go for is up to you. You will always hear so many rules about what can and cannot be used where but it is really down to how you use the room. They say no mattes in a hallway but that's assuming it's a busy family hallway. Satin is always advised in a living room, but if all you intend to do there is read magazines to Sade's greatest hits, you can do as you please. You get the picture. When it comes to paint finishes, you have options to manage wear and tear, but it doesn't mean you need to take them.

Buying paint

How much paint do I need? This could not be easier, as there are many online paint calculators which allow you to pop in the measurements of your room, answer a few questions to take in the number of coats needed, and they'll then tell you how much paint to buy.

Tools

When it comes to price, go for the best quality tools your budget can cover. They will make all the difference. You'll also be able to use them again and again. Here is what you need for the best finish:

- *Three-inch brush, angled, synthetic.* Remember I mentioned that real hair will only soak up a water-based paint? Synthetic is best if you are painting with emulsion. If you have a really tight space and you are not confident enough to use your three-inch, then go for a one-inch.
- *A roller*, which will consist of a cage and cover. For walls, I go for the widest roller I can manage – a twelve-inch is my favourite. This makes much lighter work of a large wall. But you'll notice there are many options when it comes to rollers, so let me break it down to show you which one you need:
  - 6–8mm – gloss/semi-gloss
  - 10–12mm – flatter paints
  - 30–32mm – texture
- *Extension pole*. I live for these. They make rolling much easier. They attach to regular roller handles and off you go. For me, they help apply the right pressure and you can do long, clean motions. I also hate to roll standing on a ladder step.

- *Scuttle or tray.* If your room is fairly big, a scuttle is great as it's like a large bucket with grooves on the inside for you to roll against to remove excess paint. Whichever one you go for, make sure the roller fits!
- *Paint kettle:* This is great if you are doing trims as well as walls, for example skirting. As paints for wood are thick and gravity does what she does, if you overload your trims, it can end up dripping and pooling at the bottom. To avoid this, you can fill just an inch or two at the bottom of a kettle so it's impossible to overload your brush and it's also easier to move with you as you work your way around the room.
- *Tape:* I like to use a two-inch tape, as it will be thick enough for the floor too. I don't use masking tape; instead, I go for a painter's tape. All DIY stores will have it. It is thinner, has a sharper edge and I find it doesn't bubble. Its adhesive is also not as strong, so it slips right off. This means no bleeding, easy application and easy removal.
- *Dust sheets.*
- *Sugar soap and sponge.* For cleaning.
- *Filler knife, filler and sanding block.* For holes.

Preparing to paint

Allowing three days to paint is ideal. You want to cut in and paint the walls in the one day. If you stop halfway through a wall, you will get uneven patches. The best way to paint a room is to allow enough time to prep and enough time to paint as much as you can in one go. People will often prep the day of painting and it will take them so long that they cut in in the evening and don't do the rest until the next day. Always aim to do all your prep one day, where possible, and start afresh the next day for painting.

Prepare with passion

A great paint job is all in the prep. Even the most expensive paints will look shoddy if you do not prepare well. Prep includes the room as well as the surfaces. Here is the best way to do it:

1. Empty the room of as much clutter and furniture as you can. For those items that have to stay, you'll want to push them all to the middle of the room. You need as much space as possible. How else can you take a step back to sway to Donna Summer mid paint? Remove the light shade – trust me, paint will get on it otherwise.
2. Hoover the room a few times before you start painting. I do this after I empty it. After I sand, after I wash the walls down and then on the morning of painting. This is to get rid of dust and dirt that could float its way onto the paint as it dries. A room that is not hoovered well will have gritty patches.

3. Go over the walls and see if there are any holes or cracks that need to be filled (a guide on how to do this is in *Gaff Goddess*). Next, remove any unused hooks or nails. Don't forget to hoover again after you sand.

4. Wash the walls, even if they don't look too dirty. There will be grease, dirt and dust on them. All of this will prevent the paint from adhering well to the surface. I use sugar soap and a sponge, then a final wipe clean after.

5. Protect any surfaces you are not painting. Especially the floor. I personally cover the entire floor just so it's really easy to move around and it's covered for any spills or knocks. I try to avoid plastic tarps, where possible. Obvious reasons aside, they are slippery and single use. Instead I will use poly-backed or laminated dust sheets. These look like regular dust sheets but are waterproof, so they are great at protecting floors, but you can also use them again and again. You will see dust sheets that have no backing. These are fine if you are wrapping up a piece of furniture, but I wouldn't use them for floors, as paint will seep through and you won't realize it until it's too late.

6. Tape off the skirts, trims, sills, etc. For switches, you can unscrew and leave them loose to paint behind or if that makes you a little nervous, you can also just tape.

7. Clean your roller sleeve the night before, even if the packaging says lint-free. Rinse her, squeeze her and leave her to dry out. You don't want to do this the day of painting. Lint from rollers is a total head wreck when painting, so this is a must for the best possible look.

Before you begin

First, plan your painting. Make sure you paint in the right sequence to avoid having to go over any areas again. A room should be painted ceiling first, so when you paint the walls afterwards you can hide any spray. Finish up with skirts and trims.

Next, mix your paint. All paints separate, so you want to give it a gorgeous mix together before you begin. If you are using many pots, mix them all together in a large container to make sure your colour is even.

PAINTING WALLS

Step 1

'Cut in' with a paintbrush around all skirts, switches etc. Your roller cannot roll right to the edges, so you need to paint these first by hand to get an even coat and great edges.

TO BEGIN, CUT IN AROUND ALL EDGES WITH A BRUSH

'V' OVERLAP FOR LARGE AREAS

'W' FOR SMALLER SECTIONS

Step 2:

Although it may seem logical, it is best to avoid painting in straight lines. For more even coverage, you want to work in V shapes (for smaller sections paint a W). This will ensure the paint is overlapping perfectly and you're not getting thick strips as you would with straight lines. Your roller will be loaded with paint initially so start a little further in to the wall to allow for less build-up. As you get to the end of a section and your roller needs a top-up of paint, go over the areas that meet where you have cut in. When the roller is a little drier, it can help you merge these better.

Step 3:

To finish a wall like a pro, you want to do something called 'laying off'. This is where you will go over the whole wall without loading up your roller. This is easiest done in straight lines, as you can keep track of what you have done. This will feather the paint to avoid any uneven patches. Gorgeous!

'LAY OFF' BY GOING BACK OVER THE WALL IN STRAIGHT LINES WITHOUT LOADING UP YOUR ROLLER

Step 4:

Remove the tape when the paint is touch dry. Paint dries first, then it cures or sets; removing your tape before this means the paint can seep where it shouldn't be. If you have used a high quality painter's tape, just pull it very gently and slowly away at a 45-degree angle. If you have used a tape that has peeled some of the paint, use a Stanley knife to slice along the edge of the tape and allow it to come away with no peeling.

Emulsion can be washed from the roller with warm water. If you need to paint the next day, wrap it in cling film instead of washing and she will be fine to pick back up. Just don't allow her to dry out.

TIP

When loading your roller, the key is to make sure it can spin evenly. If it can't, you need less paint.

Topping-up paint

Sometimes you'll need to just top up patches of the wall instead of the whole room. Perhaps a mark from a chair, or someone has left behind a work of art. Top-ups can be hard to get right, so consider wall erasers first. They can be bought at most large supermarkets and can make light work of removing the marks without removing the paint.

If you do feel paint is the only answer, there are times a top-up won't cut it and a full wall repaint is best:

- Glossy paint: A paint's shine will dull over time, meaning a fresh patch will never be a perfect match. It will literally outshine the rest of the wall. Make sure top-ups of shinier paint are in inconspicuous areas.
- Bad location: Avoid top-ups on parts of walls that the main light source hits for most of the day or near a focal point of the room. A patch here will be far more noticeable and a full wall paint could be a better move.
- Timing: How long ago was the wall painted? If it was years, there will be many factors that could have altered its colour, appearance and finish, meaning you won't be able to match it perfectly, even if it is the same tin of paint. This is why touch-ups are mainly used on recently painted walls, as it's so easy to get right.

If the patch has passed this assessment, there is a method to achieving a seamless top-up.

- Prep the wall. If you need to do any filling and sanding, do it first. Wash the area with something like sugar soap and let it dry fully.
- Keep your top-up as small as possible, particularly on a glossy surface. Mattes will fade in much better.
- Texture. You need to match the texture of the original paint. If it was done with a roller, top-up with a brush, then tap with a roller or dab with a kitchen towel to achieve the same texture.
- Coats. Two coats should see you right, but make sure you feather each one out at the edges to make it disappear into the original paint seamlessly.
- Finished? Stunning! Time to bask in the glory of your handiwork.

DEEP CLEANS
Couch cleaning

So overlooked, yet so vital. How your couch needs to be cleaned should be taken into consideration before purchase or at the start of a lease. Knowing what she can and can't handle will take the stress out of spills, help you buy the right cleaners and mean you never have to deal with a watermark again.

To assess the correct method for cleaning a couch, consult the fabric description, or if she is already *in situ* her label will usually be under the seat cushion. What you are looking for is an upholstery cleaning code. It is as follows:

W: I can take water! You can spot clean with water and a tiny bit of washing-up liquid or with a water-based foam. Some couches will also have removable covers that can be popped in the wash. It gives the go-ahead for cleaning such as:

Hot Water Extraction (HWE): A device that cleans the fabric by applying hot water and detergent at force to loosen and wash out the stains. You may see a little steam, as the water is hot, but don't confuse it with steam cleaning; the water and detergent are the cleaning forces here. HWE can be fab if you have allergies, pets or kids, as it doesn't leave behind detergent in the way other cleaners do. It also uses enough water to wash the fabric, so it can take care of stains, oil, etc. Her water is not absolutely roasting, so the chance of shrinkage is pretty low.

Steam Cleaning: This also uses hot water, but it has to be boiling hot to generate steam. The steam then flows through the fibres and helps remove odours, light staining, bacteria and other nasties such as mould spores and fungi. Girl, but what about these stains? While she'll remove odours and freshen up a couch, she can't remove stains as well as HWE. Extreme heat can set some stains, so always discuss the stain type before booking your professional clean.

S: Solvents. This gal is truly allergic to water and it will either shrink her, stain her, or change her appearance or texture. S is also classed as 'Dry Clean Only'. Solvent breaks down a stain and dries faster than water, avoiding the risk of a watermark. You can get out an old watermark with a solvent cleaner, as it re-wets the fibres, takes the water stain out and dries super quickly.

WS: This means both water and solvents are fine.

X: Forget about it. Nothing can be used to clean up oily or liquid-based stains on this bish. At most you can hoover her and remove any dried-on stains with a spoon, but nothing else will cut it. Get professional help and let them know the cleaning code is X.

Daily

When it comes to spills on your couch, don't leave it for one big clean. Heavily soiled, layered stains are almost impossible to remove later. Clean as you spill.

Once a week

To keep a couch looking her best, you should give her a once-over each week.

First up is a hoover with the upholstery attachment. If you are thinking WTF is that, it's usually the one that has a red velvet strip. This is what rubs against the fabric, drawing out the lint without causing damage or wear. Hoover all over, not just down the sides. I hate to break it to you, but your skin particles as well as crumbs, dust and dirt will be on it, so you need to remove them often to prevent odours and other issues. A good hoover will also prevent pilling, as it helps reset the fabric in its natural direction.

Shake and shape the cushions to prevent your filling clumping or sitting incorrectly in its cover. If possible, flip cushions so you're levelling out the wear on the fabric. Don't forget to make sure the fabric under the seat cushions is in the right place to avoid dragging and stretching.

Every six months

Deodorize her every six months, more if she's in heavy use. All you need is bicarbonate of soda and a hoover (with upholstery attachment). Simply sprinkle it over the couch and leave as long as you can – overnight, if possible. The bicarb absorbs odours and when hoovered she'll take smells with her. It's a great treatment if you have pets or spend a lot of time on your couch.

Bathroom deep clean

Most people abhor cleaning the bathroom and want it to be as swift as possible. To ensure you are never landed with a bathroom 'big clean', little and often is what you are after. Natural cleaners are also your best friends. Here are my top tips on how to care for your shower.

Daily

To keep soap scum at bay, rinse down the shower after use. To prevent limescale build-up on doors, always squeegee after each use. This will mean almost zero door maintenance in future. Don't leave bottles on the silicone, as pools of water gathering behind plastic bottles is the mould equivalent of blasting 'Mi Chico Latino' from a party boat with a sign saying free margaritas. Everyone is going to show up. If you have no shelving, buy suction cup holders but hang them down low so there is no risk of injury should they come away from the tiles.

Weekly

As your hair mask sets on a Saturday morning, it's a great time to give the shower a scrub. Everything will be loosened by the steam, so all you need is a microfibre cloth and a cleaner. I go for a mix of lemon, vinegar, bicarb and water. This will have enough cleaning power to lift grease and grime, as well as most bacteria. Wipe down the tray, silicone, tiles, door seals and shower fittings. You can't use this mix on plated fittings or natural stone, as it will erode them. Remember to clean the drain. Most shower drains come apart in pieces that allow you to empty the strainer-like piece inside. This will save you getting blockages down the line. Finally wipe inside the drain to remove any soap scum.

Deep clean

If your shower or bath is in need of an overhaul, fear not, it will only take a few steps to get her gleaming.

Shower screen

If you have hard water and have not been squeegeeing, your shower door or screen will probably look like a frosted pane. You may have found that cleaning will make her go transparent, but once she dries those white marks are back. This is due to build-up of limescale deposits.

Next time you are making a margarita, save half a lime for your shower (a lemon will also do). Rub the flesh of the fruit into the glass, working in circular motions, focusing on the side of the door that gets exposed to the spray of the shower. The acidity of the juice will break down the deposits, while the flesh will work like little arms, wiping it away. Divine. Once you've treated the whole screen, rinse the juice and buff dry with a microfibre cloth. No nails, skin, eyes or lungs are harmed in this transformation, which cannot be said for harsh cleaners.

Shower head

If this girl is not performing as she should, limescale may be building up inside her. Pour a 50/50 mix of water and vinegar into a sandwich bag, place over the shower head and tie or tape it into place. Allow this to stay on overnight to eat into the limescale within the shower head, breaking down anything that's clogging her up. If your entire hose is looking worse for wear, you can submerge the whole thing in a large bowl or bucket of the mix. Hoses get limescale build-up because of leaks, so tighten or replace the washer where the hose connects to the head to avoid water seeping out. Once the soak is over, just like any good pedicure, pat off the excess water. Once she is back in place, blast some hot water for a few minutes, then wipe it all down with a damp cloth and buff dry. Beautiful.

Shower tray

Common issues with shower trays are rust rings from foam cans, build-up of limescale and soap scum. Again, you don't need harsh cleaners to fix these.

Soap scum

This staining happens in showers and baths if they are not cleaned enough or if you have slow-draining water that sits in the tray longer than it should. It's totally normal in a busy home where the shower is used often.

Grab a spray bottle and mix 50/50 warm water and vinegar and a good squirt of washing-up liquid. Shake that bish up. Now spray liberally all over the staining and leave for half an hour. The washing-up liquid will work its magic on the product and protein elements, and the vinegar will tackle the minerals from the water. Wipe with a non-scratch sponge, then rinse and buff with a microfibre cloth. To keep this from coming back as badly, why not give the tray a wipe down mid-week as well as at weekends? Soap scum can be really intense in places with hard water so having a squeegee as well as a microfibre cloth that can dry out on a radiator after can be a godsend.

Limescale

Hard water leaves behind a chalky deposit of minerals on shower trays, as well as screens. Again, just rub a lemon or lime, flesh side down, in circular motions to break down the deposits. You can also soak cloths in an 80/20 vinegar to water mix and lay them over the stain for thirty minutes. After either treatment, scrub down with a non-scratch sponge and some warm soapy water, and then rinse and buff dry.

Pink stains

A peachy stain on the tray, grout or shower curtain can look like mildew or a dusky sunset strewn across your shower. Some say it's from copper pipes or products, others call it pink mould. I won't get into the fact that it is more like coral peach and not a gal I would pop in a pink category. It is, in fact, caused by a bacteria: *Serratia marcescens*. While she sounds like a great knife brand, she is a waterborne bacteria that is obsessed with your bathroom. OBSESSED. She lives for damp conditions, and soap scum calls to her like one large bag of crisps over a *Housewives* episode. She is also that bish behind religious statues crying bloody tears and a sinister breakout of 'bloody polenta' in Italy in 1819, both of which the devil was blamed for. The more you know . . . (*sips martini*).

Although she cannot be gotten rid of entirely, she can be managed. You need to tackle her with a 50/50 mix of vinegar and water. Leave that in place for thirty minutes and the vinegar will chomp through the bacteria. Then mix some bicarbonate of soda with washing-up liquid to form a paste and rub all over the stain. If you have this staining on grout, just rub it in with an old toothbrush.

To keep her at bay, keep your bathroom ventilated and don't encourage standing water. This may mean unclogging the drain, squeegeeing doors and tiles, etc.

Rust

Look, it happens. There can be rust coming from pipes, a ring from a can, razors and of course . . . bobby pins. All you need here is bicarb and vinegar. Mix into a paste (it'll fizz), tap onto the stain and leave for as long as you can. Scrub off with a non-scratch sponge. If she is particularly strong, she may need a second treatment.

ADIEU

I hope you have enjoyed our tour around the haus of Décor Galore. It has been simply stunning having you here! You can come back any time you like. Our needs and wants around our décor forever change and she is always here for you when you need her.

Now, before you go, I have a small gift.

Something that I love about cookbooks are the page or two at the back, given to us to add our own recipes from friends or family. Or to jot down something we may come across in conversation or while reading a magazine. Other times it's an area to make conversion notes or work out measurements as we work. I really love to look at these pages in my mother's and grandmother's cookbooks. They are priceless pages that speak a thousand words. They reflect what was the 'must cook' recipe at the time or what they were challenging themselves to create. Such a gorgeous snapshot.

I have left a page here for you to use in this way when it comes to your She-IY or décor meauxments. As well as keeping your information safe and easy to find when you need it, it will make this book truly unique. As this page fills, this book becomes more special and one of a kind, something that cannot be replicated, and can be wonderful to look back on.

I hope you enjoy . . . be sure to use a nice pen (*winks and click-clacks back inside*).

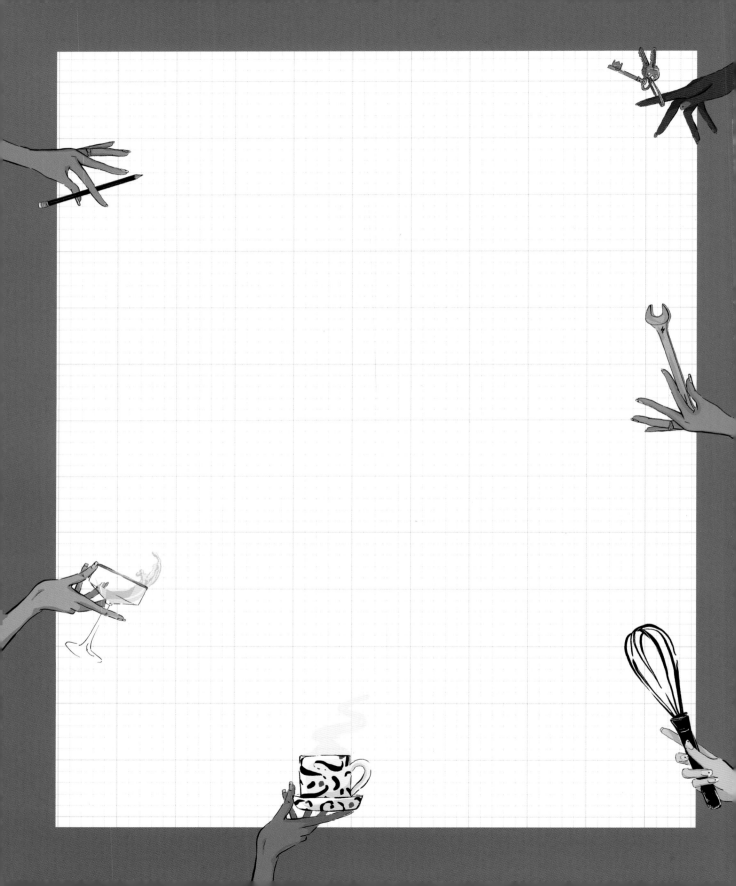

ACKNOWLEDGEMENTS

Thank you to my family, who I missed so much during this. Thank you for all your support and love through another book journey. We will be together again, and it will be glorious. Shane, this could never have gone as smoothly if it wasn't for you. Thank you for everything you did that got me through, from the meals made with such thought and love appearing at the door, to the never-fading belief that I could do it and it would be fucking fabulous. I love you.

Fiona, thank you so much for all your hard work and dedication. For helping me to bring DG to life as only you could. A massive thank you to all the Transworld team, Debs, Bobby, Katrina, Josh, Phil, Beci, Aimee, Laura and Sorcha.

Joe, Louise, Mary-Kate, Richard: 'mere t'me, how did a girl get so lucky? Every call, text and even song-note (you know who you are) brightened some very long days in a way I could never thank you enough for . . . but I will try, starting with margaritas.

Jerry, thank you for always giving me such sound and honest advice in the early drafts and, of course, for always making me laugh. You're a gem.

INDEX

Laura de Barra is a Cork-born property portfolio developer and illustrator working in the competitive London market. She is the author and illustrator of No.1 bestseller *Gaff Goddess* and has a regular She-IY column in the *Irish Times*. Her Instagram account @lauradebarra is a gold mine of clever repair, décor and She-IY inspiration, and her joyful passion for her work will inspire even the most hesitant tenant or homeowner to discover they really can do it for themselves. *Décor Galore* is her second book.